VIVEKANANDA INTERNATIONAL FOUNDATION

10th Anniversary Book

A Decade of Discourse on Defence Matters

VIVEKANANDA INTERNATIONAL FOUNDATION

10th Anniversary Book

A Decade of Discourse on Defence Matters

Edited by

Lieutenant General Gautam Banerjee, PVSM, AVSM, YSM (Retd)

Foreword by

General N C Vij, PVSM, UYSM, AVSM

Former Chief of the Army Staff

Vivekananda International Foundation
New Delhi

PENTAGON PRESS LLP

A Decade of Discourse on Defence Matters
Edited by Lt Gen Gautam Banerjee, PVSM, AVSM, YSM (Retd)

ISBN 978-81-944659-5-9

First Published in 2020

Published by
PENTAGON PRESS LLP
206, Peacock Lane, Shahpur Jat,
New Delhi-110049
Phones: 011-64706243, 26491568
Telefax: 011-26490600
email: rajan@pentagonpress.in
website: www.pentagonpress.in

Printed at Aegean Offset Printers, Greater Noida, U.P.

CONTENTS

*

FOREWORD

The 10th Anniversary of founding of the Vivekananda International Foundation (VIF) is a significant land mark for all those, who selflessly undertook to dedicate their strategic intellect to the empowerment of the Indian nationhood. The aim and purpose of founding the VIF was to bring about a paradigm shift in the national and global discourse in India. It was also aimed at aligning our vision and concepts with the realities of time and India's rising potential. VIF has assiduously stuck to this goal right through. It is therefore an occasion for all of us to redouble our efforts in this direction.

National strategic concerns, defence and preparedness have been amongst the prominent fields in which the VIF has strived to excel. Thus, there was always an idea of publishing a collection of selected papers, authored by eminent strategic thinkers, to analyze India's concerns as related to our national security paradigm. 30 of these papers, published/uploaded by the Foundation over the past decade, would provide to the readers a panorama of the challenges India has been confronted with along the path.

Notably the contributions have been selected from amongst the young, middle piece and senior level strategic thinkers. This brings in a vast and varied set of ideas together, with regard to developing our national potential.

I am sanguine that this book would find a notable place in the world of politico-military thoughts and debates, and play a singular role in spreading awareness about the sanctity of our national preparedness.

New Delhi
10 December, 2019

General N C Vij, PVSM, UYSM, AVSM
Former Chief of Army Staff &
Former Director VIF

*

EDITOR'S NOTE

For a think tank of international repute, the Vivekananda International Foundation (VIF) distinguishes itself in a unique manner. This distinction manifests in the range and depth the Foundation delves into in analysing the difficulties, dilemmas and challenges that India's national defence and its military institution is confronted with.

This indeed is a break from most strategic think tanks who prefer to confine to just the broader politico-military considerations of India's national defence, leaving its deeper aspects for the incumbent hierarchies to deal with. Arguably, that leaves the serious matter of the nation's management of military security entirely to the devices of the incumbent policy makers, thus sequestering them from independent professional analyses and articulation of alternate possibilities, propositions and options on matters of the nation's strategic concerns. In its own way, the VIF has been intent on bridging that gap.

Over the past decade or so, the geo-political situation has pushed India's national defence challenges onto an upward curve. It was so that from the early stages itself, the Foundation has been engaged in deeper analyses of the nation's defence encumbrances and its military dilemmas.

On the 10th Anniversary of its foundation, the VIF fraternity has undertaken to present to its wide readership a compilation of pioneering papers published by it over the past decade. Thus, there are 30 papers selected to cover a wide range of aspects for the readers to appreciate the finer nuances and trends that determine the course of national defence. Significantly, the papers also indicate an evolution of strategic thinking that influences defence decision making to this day.

The book aims at invoking national strategic conscience among the thinking fraternity. The VIF is sanguine that the book will find that noble objective.

New Delhi
December, 2019

Lieutenant General Gautam Banerjee
PVSM, AVSM, YSM
Editor

ABOUT THE CONTRIBUTORS

Brigadier Vinod Anand is a Senior Fellow at the Vivekananda International Foundation (VIF), New Delhi. Earlier he was a Senior Fellow at the United Service Institution and the Institute for Defence Studies and Analyses, New Delhi. His publications include *Joint Vision for Indian Armed Forces, Defence Planning in India: Problems and Prospects, Pak-Af Equation and Future of Afghanistan, Multi-Vector Politics of Central Asian Republics and India* and *Strategic Environment in Central Asia and India.* Recently, he has presented several papers and written on China's Belt and Road Initiative, India's Act East Policy, Situation in Asia Pacific and Developments in SE Asia.

Mr. Radhakrishna Rao has worked in the documentation and publications division of ISRO for about 20 years after obtaining a degree in science from Calicut University in Kerala. For nearly two decades, he has been writing extensively on issues concerning outer space, defence, aerospace, computers and communications. He has contributed to a number of national newspapers and international media including the *Tribune, DNA, International Aerospace, Flight International, Air and Cosmos* and *Military Technology.*

Ambassador Kanwal Sibal has been India's Foreign Secretary from July 2002 to November 2003. He has also been India's Ambassador to Turkey, Egypt and France. Dr Sibal is the First Grand Doctor of Philosophy in India. He received the title of Full Professor from the European Academy of Informatisation, the World Information Distributed University (WIDU).

Ambassador Prabhat Prakash Shukla is an alumnus of Delhi School of Economics, and is a former Indian Foreign Service officer. During a career spanning 37 years, he served in Moscow, Brussels, London and Kathmandu, among other places. He has also been the Diplomatic Adviser to the Prime Minister from 1996 to 2000 before retiring in 2011 as Ambassador of India to Moscow. He is a Distinguished Fellow at the Vivekananda International Foundation, New Delhi.

Ambassador Satish Chandra is a much regarded career diplomat who has served as India's Permanent Representative to the UN Offices in Geneva and later as High Commissioner to Pakistan. He subsequently went on to head the National

Security Council Secretariat and was India's Deputy National Security Advisor. Presently, he is the Vice Chairman of the Vivekananda International Foundation, New Delhi.

Lieutenant General Gautam Banerjee, PVSM, AVSM, YSM, is a former Chief of Staff, Central Command, and former Commandant of the Officers Training Academy, Chennai. A prolific writer on military strategy, he has so far authored seven books on *defence modernisation, Maoist insurgency, China's military power* and *Kashmir militancy*, besides editing and contributing to five more. He also regularly writes on military matters for various defence journals. He is a Senior Fellow & Editor at the Vivekananda International Foundation, New Delhi.

Air Commodore L M Joshi is a 1985 commissioned, serving Indian Air Force Officer who had been on a study assignment with the Vivekananda International Foundation in 2015-16.

Brigadier Narender Kumar, SM, VSM, is a regular author on defence matters. He has been a Senior Fellow at the Centre for Land Warfare Studies, and is presently with the Institute of Defence Studies and Analysis, New Delhi,

Shri G. Mohan Kumar is a former Secretary Defence Production and India's Defence Secretary. An Indian Administrative Service officer who retired in 2017, he has extensive experience, besides defence administration, in areas like Fisheries and Water Resources. He is a Distinguished Fellow at the Vivekananda International Foundation, New Delhi.

Dr. Arvind Gupta is a former Indian Foreign Service officer who has been intimately associated with the matters of national strategy. He has served in Indian diplomatic missions in Moscow, London, and Ankara, and dealt with Afghanistan, Kashmir, Soviet Union, Russia, and Central Asia. A former Director General of the Institute for Defence Studies and Analysis (IDSA), New Delhi, and a former Deputy National Security Adviser and Secretary, National Security Council Secretariat (NSCS), he has dealt with a wide range of national security issues within the NSC structures. With his wide-ranging interactions with national and international delegations and think tanks, he is a known figure in Track 2–level strategic confabulations. Author of four books, his latest publication, *How India Manages Its National Security*, was published by Penguin Random House in 2018. Presently, Dr Gupta is the Director, Vivekananda International Foundation, New Delhi.

General NC Vij, PVSM, UYSM, AVSM is a former Chief of the Army Staff. His tenure as the Army Chief is remembered for many notable improvements in operational and administrative postures of the Army. Before that, he was the Director General of Military Operations (DGMO) during the Kargil War in 1999. After superannuation, he was appointed Founder Vice Chairman of National Disaster Management Authority, in the rank of Cabinet Minister. He has been a Director at the VIF and presently a member of its Executive Committee.

Colonel Karan Kharb is a military veteran, who as an acclaimed writer and analyst on defence matters is also a well-regarded social activist. A committed nationalist, he is a pioneer on training the youth on leadership and management, besides being associated with many social service NGOs.

Jayadeva Ranade is a former Additional Secretary, Cabinet Secretariat, Government of India. A well-regarded China expert, he is presently President of the Centre for China Analysis and Strategy.

Brigadier Rahul K. Bhonsle is a reputed thinker-author on strategic matters. He manages a 'strategic risk and knowledge management' consultancy, *security-risks.com* – which focuses on strategic culture and security trends in South Asia, future warfare and human security. His incisive inputs are highly valued in the academia, think tanks and the wider strategic circles.

Lieutenant General S A Hasnain, PVSM, UYSM, AVSM, SM (Bar), VSM (Bar), is a military veteran whose expertise on Kashmir affairs is valued at the top opinion-making level in India and abroad. As a strategic analyst, author and military intellectual, he enjoys an international standing. He is also a Distinguished Fellow at the Vivekananda International Foundation, New Delhi.

Rana Banerji, a former IAS officer, is a top expert on security issues, and an authority on Pakistan affairs. He retired as Special Secretary, Cabinet Secretariat. He is a regular member of security related confabulations at the highest levels.

Air Vice Marshal Rajesh Isser is an experienced aviator of the Indian Air Force having extensive operational and combat record. He has been Humanitarian Assistance and Disaster Relief Task Force Commander in many national and international rescue and relief ops, including Nepal, Bhutan, Bangladesh, Sri Lanka, Congo, Rwanda, Burundi and Uganda. He is currently pursuing doctoral studies on leadership challenges in disaster response.

Major General G. D. Bakshi, SM, VSM, is a former general officer commanding of a Counter-Insurgency Force and a Senior Directing Staff at the National Defence College, New Delhi. He is a prolific writer and a well-known commentator at the national media.

Vice Admiral Pradeep Chauhan, AVSM and Bar, VSM, is a former Chief of Staff, Western Naval Command, and Commandant, Indian Naval Academy, Ezhimala. One of the top thinkers on naval strategy and India's leading analyst on maritime affairs, he is presently the Director at the National Maritime Foundation.

Lieutenant General Davinder Kumar, PVSM, VSM Bar, ADC, is a former Signal Officer-in-Chief of the Indian Army. After superannuation, he was the CEO and Managing Director of Tata Advanced Systems Ltd. An expert in the network-centric, information and cyber warfare, and strategic communication, he has published more than 400 papers and spoken at various fora in India and abroad, besides being instrumental in higher level policy making with the Government.

Lieutenant General (Dr) V K Saxena, PVSM, AVSM, VSM, is a former Director General of Army Air Defence Corps of the Indian Army. An experienced defence analyst, he is presently a Distinguished Fellow at the Vivekananda International Foundation, New Delhi.

Ajit Kumar is a former Ambassador and a Permanent Representative of India at the United Nations, Geneva. He has also represented India in various other International Organisations.

Major General P K Mallick, VSM, is one of the country's top experts on automated data processing, cyber security and information warfare. A prolific writer, he regularly contributes to defence-related journals, is a regular speaker and participant at high-level panel discussions, besides authoring and publishing a large number of decision support papers. Presently, he is a Consultant with the Vivekananda International Foundation, New Delhi.

*

Part 1

Management of National Defence

March, 2011

1

Defence Capability vs Defence Expenditure

Brig. Vinod Anand and Brig. Arun Sahgal

One of the most keenly watched part of the Union Budget is the allocations of funds for defence expenditure. Given the prevailing security environment, modernisation of the armed forces and keeping them militarily prepared is a major challenge faced by both the political and military establishments, particularly so given the fact that our relations with two important neighbours – Pakistan and China – can at best be said to be in cold storage, with little sign of any early thaw.

Adding to above challenge is the two-front threat that Army believes it faces requiring a much higher degree of defence preparedness and above all military readiness. The latter is more relevant, whose components are not mere force structures and modernisation but includes preparedness and sustainability as well. This was alluded to by the Prime Minister in his address to Combined Commanders Conference in 2009, when he said that the armed forces have to be ready to fight anywhere, anytime and under any conditions. That basically implies that defence policies, doctrines and strategy, funding and structures, together with capabilities, capacities and logistical sustainability must be of the order that allows India to use its military power to support its national interests in concert with the vision set forth by the Prime Minister.

The Union Budget 2011-12 bears analysis from the above perspective of defence preparedness and readiness. This year, the Finance Minister has allocated Rs 164,415 crore for defence. The allocation signifies an 11.6 percent increase from Rs. 1,47,344 crore allocated last year. This increase was backed by the usual announcement that "funds will never be a constraint for meeting the genuine needs of the armed forces". However, such a caveat is of no practical significance; what it hides is the absence of long-term commitment of funds by the Finance Ministry to Five Year Defence Plans. Apart from some exceptions made in the wake of events like Kargil War or Mumbai terror attacks, the increase in defence expenditure has generally followed the trend line of 10 percent increase every year. Thus, for the financial babudom, the defence budget is merely an exercise in accountancy. It cannot be said that there is some long-term vision attached to this annual exercise in defence budgeting.

While the Ministry of Defence and the Headquarters Integrated Defence Staff have been involved in making Five Year Defence Plans (FYDP) and Long-Term Integrated Perspective Plans (LTIPP), it is very rare that these are approved by the government on time. For instance, the FYDP 2007-12, which should have been approved before 2007, has not been approved so far. In fact, it is in the danger of not being approved in the plan period despite many remonstrations by Parliament's Standing Committee on Defence (SCD).

Further, the MOD had promised to the SCD of the 14th Lok Sabha that LTIPP consisting of three plan periods would be based on articulation of National Military Strategy (NMS) that in turn will be based on formulation of National Security Strategy (NSS). This was to be done by 2009; however, the new SCD of 15th Lok Sabha composed of new members seems to have forgotten about the imperative. In all their reports since 2009, the SCD has not raised any observations on the non-articulation of NSS and NMS. While the defence forces are talking about transformation and revolution in military affairs, there is a considerable degree of skepticism on the conceptual philosophy about modernisation of the armed forces. Some analysts have rightly worded such an approach to military modernisation as 'arming without aiming'.

Reverting to the current year's budget, the sub-allocation thereof – Rs 99387.85 crore – is planned to be expended towards revenue expenditure and balance Rs 69,199 crore is earmarked for capital expenditure. In terms of percentage, it is mere 1.83 percent of GDP and nowhere near the oft-cited figure of 3 percent sought by the Services for filling the essential strategic voids. Addressing the Combined Commanders Conference in 2005, Prime Minister Manmohan Singh had indicated the possibility of earmarking 3 percent of the GDP if the economy continues to grow at 8 percent of the GDP. Looking at the worsening asymmetries against our likely adversaries, time has come to convert that possibility into reality. Evidently, rise in defence expenditure would have to be spread over at least one plan period.

A close look at the Capital Expenditure, which is essentially meant for meeting our modernisation needs, would reveal that complete Capital allocation is not for new acquisitions. It is important to note that as a rough yardstick, only three-fourths of the capital expenditure budget goes towards capital acquisition, balance being allocated for creation of capital assets etc. Out of that balance acquisition budget, approximately 60 percent is already earmarked for payment toward committed liabilities, i.e. purchases already made with deliveries in the pipeline. That leaves around 30 percent of the capital budget available for new defence purchases. As a rough estimate, about Rs. 20,000 crore is available for new acquisitions, but in real terms is close to 60 crore, given the long gestation period for defence contracts to be executed. The SCD, in end 2009, while reviewing the projections for the remaining two years of the Eleventh Plan had observed that capital budget requires growth of 35.96 percent and 17.13 percent, respectively, for the years 2010-11 and 2011-12 over the Budget Estimates of 2009-10. Thus, the growth of capital segment of the budget is inadequate.

As per estimates based on the current (2007-12) and next (2012-17) Five Year Defence Plans, armed forces are slated to spend nearly $100 billion and $120 billion on military hardware in these two plan periods, respectively. In addition, the LTIPP (2012-27) envisages substantial procurement of land, air and naval systems with a view to field lethal, mobile and networked defence forces in the future. Thus, huge sums are being spent upon procurement and capability building, but the question is do we get the desired payoffs?

The basic issue that needs to be addressed is asking "is above allocation together with the committed liabilities enough to meet the modernisation requirements of the Services to meet security challenges faced by the country"? Two issues are important in answer to the above question. One is, what are we modernising for? Does our military modernisation in optimum terms help in threat mitigation? Two, and that underlines an even more fundamental question, what is the nature of conflict envisaged and likely conflict scenarios that the country must prepare for and invest?

The scenario in terms of current threat perspective is that Pakistan has been raging a proxy war against India with near impunity for which we have at best a defensive answer in terms of effective Low-Intensity Conflict Operations (LICO) strategy. On the other hand, our conventional edge is getting slowly eroded owing to delay in the Services' modernisation plans and infusion of modern military hardware into Pakistani armed forces from both China and elsewhere. That has substantially neutralised India's capacity at conventional deterrence in the backdrop of nuclear overhang where too Pakistan, according to published reports, has forged ahead both in terms of fissile materials and vectors. That means that our ability to execute any punitive proactive strategy and manage escalation is incrementally getting restrained – if anything, our response to 26/11 is an example.

In so far as China is concerned, it is marching ahead in its military modernisation with the focus primarily on indigenous defence industrial base and development of new capabilities in terms of cyber, information, missile and space warfare. China has been increasing its defence budget in double-digit percentages since 1989. This year's increase has been to the tune of 12.7 percent; it is also well known that there is a great degree of opacity about China's defence spending – the actual figure could be twice of the claimed figure. However, what is to be noted is that China is creating a potential to project power anywhere around its near abroad. In short, asymmetry between India and China in military terms is on the rise. What is important that China intends to employ these stand-off capabilities to execute what it calls 'No Contact War' aimed at the adversary's strategic dislocation.

In the face of above challenges, our focus remains on attritional force-on-force kind of warfare mindset, as underlined by our desire for platform-centric procurement, in effect justifying the observation of 'arming without any strategy'. As a result, not enough attention is being paid toward developing adequate offensive-defence capabilities based on development of operational systems within the overall 'system of systems' approach or creating truly synergised force capabilities. This demands, among others, capacities of fielding an Integrated Command, Control, Communications, Computers, Intelligence, Surveillance and Reconnaissance (C4ISR) system that integrates sensors, decision makers and platforms. Here, sensors are as important as the platforms. Thus, we need to enhance electronic intelligence (ELINT) and Space capabilities, and develop capacities for constant ISR cover over areas of interest and those we would like to influence. Similarly, more attention needs to be given to not only defensive but also offensive information and cyber war capabilities, and development of anti-ship ballistic missiles and anti-satellite capabilities.

True defence capability must ensure dissuasive deterrence and maximisation of India's strategic space to ward off future challengers and create an environment for India's peaceful economic growth. Using national resources to raise military formations, or mere platforms would not suffice. India needs a system-centric approach to its defence capability development. Till that happens, we would be using buzz words like 'defence transformation', 'net-centric warfare' and 'revolution in military affairs' (RMA), while merely attempting to address the obsolescence factor without any real capability enhancement.

*

February, 2012

2

A Vibrant Indian Military Industrial Complex Needed for Self-Reliance

Radhakrishna Rao

According to Stockholm International Peace Research Institute (SIPRI), today India is world's largest arms importer with country's spending on defence hovering between 2.3 percent and 3 percent of GDP. While India's massive spending on import of weapons and defence hardware reflects the keenness to modernise its armed forces and equip them with the capability to take care of the Indian interests beyond the subcontinent, there is a concern that the country, which has demonstrated its prowess in space exploration and positioned itself as a software hub of global standing, has failed to acquire self-reliance in the vital sector of defence production.

Self-Reliance: Need of the Hour

Indeed, the fact that today India imports bout 70 percent of its defence equipment makes for a very weak case in the quest to transform the country into a global military power. As observed by Dr. Amer Latif, Visiting Fellow at Wadhwani Chair for US-India policy at Centre for Strategic and International Studies (CSIS), "India believes strongly that providing for its own requirements is indicative of being a global power." Of course, the policy of India's Ministry of Defence (MoD) is to equip India with the capability to produce 70 percent of its required military equipment domestically by the end of this decade. But as things stand now, the prospects of realising this goal within the set timeframe appears bleak. Over the next one decade, India is planning to buy defence equipment worth US $100 billion and if the country fails to progress sufficiently enough to develop the required military hardware domestically, a large chunk of this amount would go towards import. "Unless some drastic action is taken quickly and the private sector is incentivised to come into the defence production, the situation is not going to work", says Kutub Hai, Head, Mahindra Defence Systems.

Indeed, for quite some time now, there has been an animated debate in the country over the viability of building a robust domestic military industrial complex to help India usher in an era of self-reliance in defence production. India's proactive Defence Minister A.K. Antony has all along been making a strong pitch for the Indian defence self-reliance. "A country like India cannot indefinitely depend upon foreign weapons", says Antony. Antony has spiritedly urged the Defence Research and Development Organisation (DRDO) to strengthen its core competence and augment its research and development base to minimise Indian dependence on imported hardware. He has also driven home the point that "India's image as a global leader in Information Technology (IT) should be reflected in the national defence domain." Going a step further, he has urged DRDO to do to the Indian defence sector what ISRO has done to the Indian space exploration. In the similar vein, the veteran BJP leader L.K. Advani has stated that a country as large and populous as India with such a vast pool of scientific and technological talent must not remain exclusively dependent on imports for meeting its defence needs.

Import: A Solution with Hundreds of Problems

Even if India had invested a fraction of the mind-boggling amount it had spent on arms imports since 1950 on expanding the scope of its indigenous defence research and development, boosting its engineering and manufacturing skill and enhancing the infrastructure and expertise of its academic centres of excellence like IITs (Indian Institute of Technology), the country would have by now not only become self-reliant in meeting the requirements of its defence forces but would also have positioned itself as a major exporter of arms and ammunitions. But then, the sad part of the story, as stated by Air Marshal P.K. Barbora, former Vice Chief of Indian Air Force (IAF) in terms of exports, is the defence industry of Pakistan is ahead of its Indian counterpart. According to Barbora, India should go for reverse engineering – an area where China has proved its excellence – to boost its self-reliance in defence production. Perhaps one of the least noticed offshoots of defence self-reliance is that technologies developed for defence hardware have a variety of civilian applications. Both Indian Space Research Organisation (ISRO) and DRDO have a programme to exploit the spin-offs by transferring the technologies to industrial enterprises for commercialisation. Here the recipient industries should be asked to improve the scope and performance of the products through constant research and feedback.

The figures made available by SIPRI reveal that between 1950 and 2010, India imported arms worth US $64.84 billion from USSR/Russia. During the same period, India imported US $15.3 billion worth of arms from Britain against US $4 billion from France and US $1.9 billion from Germany. Not to be left behind, while Netherlands exported arms worth US $1.5 billion to India between 1950 to 2010, Israel exported arms worth a little over US $1 billion during the period.

USA, which happens to be a late entrant to the Indian defence market, is looking at emerging as a major arms supplier to India once New Delhi starts paying for a series of recent acquisition contracts. These include US $1.1 billion for six C 130 J Super Hercules Transport Aircraft, US $4.1 billion for 10 C-17 Globemaster heavy transport aircraft and US $2.2 billion for eight P-81 long-range maritime patrol aircraft. Not surprisingly then as revealed in a recent Frost and Sullivan Report between 2011 and 2015, Indian defence budget is expected to grow at more than 8 percent year-on-year.

The defence budget for 2012-13 to be presented in the Indian Parliament in March is likely to touch Rs. 2,00,000 crore to support the modernisation process of the Indian defence forces. Indeed, for the European, Russian and American defence and aerospace enterprises facing bleak prospects of marketing their wares in their home turfs, India's swelling defence budget with a large allocation for import seems to be a veritable manna from the heavens. But for India, the continuing dependence on imports would also mean a certain vulnerability to the technology denial regimes and a variety of coercion that would render the imported hardware unserviceable. And on the top of these, the murky role of shadowy middlemen in getting the defence deals clinched through kickbacks and influence peddling continues to dominate the Indian defence import.

Turning Technology to Advantage

In a way, the technology denial could act as a spur for the indigenous development of defence systems and hardware. As pointed out by V.K. Saraswat, Chief of the DRDO, the technology embargo has helped the country develop many critical products hitherto imported. In particular, Saraswat said the indigenous development of many high-performance systems for longer range Agni missiles has made "mincemeat of the US sponsored technology embargo and trade sanctions." There are now around 300-400 industries working with strategic sectors – defence, nuclear and space. For DRDO, they have succeeded in building ground systems, components and sub-systems. They are now graduating into integrating missiles. It is heartening to note that 60-70 percent of missiles components are made by Indian industries. However, "we need to concentrate on the research aspect especially since the technology denial regimes have not been relaxed", observes Saraswat.

The DRDO, which was earlier blamed for delays and far from satisfactory quality of its products, is now sprucing up its act to meet the needs of the armed forces in a timely and cost-effective manner. Of course, Saraswat did admit that there was a mismatch between technology maturity, industrial capability and project goals during 1980s and 1990s which did affect projects like Arjun Main Battle Tank (MBT) and Light Combat Aircraft Tejas. Marking a break from the past, the 120-mm tank guns developed for Arjun by the Armament Research and Development Establishment (ARDE) of DRDO has proved to be a distinct improvement over the Russian guns.

Meanwhile, DRDO has initiated work on Future Main Battle Tank (FMBT) to insulate against delays that plagued Arjun programme. The Combat Vehicle Research Development Establishment (CVRDE) of DRDO, which is spearheading FMBT project, has adopted public-private sector cooperation route to realise the tank that will be the backbone of Indian army's armoured column into mid-21st century. This high-profile project of national importance will largely co-opt domestic companies like Kirloskar Oil Engine, Bharat Earth Movers Limited (BEML), Mahindra and Mahindra, academic institutions like IIT and Pune-based Automotive Research Association. An Indian 'prime contractor' would assemble FMBT engine with the engine components supplied by a network of contractors. "Our approach is not engine specific; we are looking at developing the complete range of technologies needed to build engines. Not only design but also manufacturing, testing and evaluation," says CVRDE Director P. Sivakumar. Perhaps Indian defence production sector can adopt this innovative route to realise the systems and equipment posing technological challenges.

Rightly, the decision of the Indian Defence Ministry to bring the US $12 billion Future Infantry Combat Vehicle (FICV) project under 'Make India' procedure is a welcome step towards helping the Indian defence industry take up technologically complex, high-profile projects. The finally selected Indian company for FIVC is free to choose its technology partners. But the intellectual property will be Indian and Government will fund the technology development up to 80 percent. The successful culmination of FIVC project is expected to radically transform the landscape of defence production in India.

End Fascination for Imported Hardware

But all said and done, government agencies concerned with defence, DRDO and other stakeholders in the Indian defence sector are not the only ones responsible for the current state of Indian defence production. Defence forces too should take the blame for India's poor track record in defence self-reliance, for they not only want the products that meet all their stringent requirements in one go but also have developed the tendency to change the product specifications midway through the course of development. For instance, the IAF wanted the Tejas to be equipped with a higher performance engine many years after the development of aircraft was initiated. Going in for a higher thrust engine midway would mean bringing about many modifications in the aircraft structure, implying an investment in terms of expertise, time and money. This glaring lack of harmony and proper interface between DRDO and defence forces has gone to slow down the pace of indigenisation. Moreover, defence forces should help the producer improve the performance quality by providing feedback on a regular basis. As such, it is quite essential that the defence forces are made a stakeholder in any project involving the development of the military equipment. Further, the mindset that only imported hardware makes for excellence should be given a goodbye if India has to attain self-reliance in defence production sector.

How indigenous development and production not only saves a massive outgo of funds on imports but also makes for self-reliance in addition to contributing to the skill enhancement of local industry and the flow of spin off technologies to the civilian sector is demonstrated by the successful culmination of the Tejas fighter aircraft project. Compared to the phenomenal Rs. 75,000 crore that India would need to shell out for 126 French Rafale fighters which has emerged winner in the keenly contested Medium, Multi-Role Combat Aircraft (MMRCA) tender, the money invested on Tejas appears a peanut.

The facilities set up, skill levels acquired and quality control measures fine-tuned for Tejas are no doubt a precious national asset that could be scaled up as and when required with a very little investment to build better and more lethal fighter aircraft. India's investment since 1983 on creating a range of infrastructure for Tejas including a manufacturing base and flight testing of 20 Tejas prototypes is less than Rs. 10,000 crore. And development of a Tejas naval variant which is now getting ready for maiden flight is considered a tribute to the maturing defence industrial base in the country. The LEVCON test rig set up at the Hindustan Aeronautics Limited (HAL) for Tejas naval is considered a technological leap for the Indian defence industry. Only a handful of countries boast of such an advanced test facility.

Indeed, the success ofTejas has nudged the DRDO to take up the development of Medium Combat Aircraft (MCH) with stealth features and formidable strike capability. However, to sharpen the edge of aerospace technology in the country, the Indian Defence Ministry should ensure that vital technologies being transferred by Dassault Aviation, the producer of Rafale, and armament integrator Thales as part of the MMRCA contract are absorbed by the Indian industry fully well. It is high time India stopped accepting technology as a 'black box'.

Make India's Aerospace and Defence Production Base Vibrant

Nothing else demonstrates India's poor track record in defence production more stunningly than India's plan to acquire 75 Swiss origin Pilatus basic trainer aircraft. In sharp contrast, Pakistan's aeronautical complex at Kamra has managed to build 327 Mushshak three-seater light aircraft for training, communications and observation. Although initially license produced version of Sweden's Saab MF1-17, Pakistan has modified and adopted it to meet its specific training needs. Moreover, Pakistan Air Force (PAF) has managed to train its pilots on home-grown aircraft. Unfortunately to a large extent, IAF's training programme has been dependent on foreign trainer aircraft that were available in limited numbers. By all means, this begs the question why India a technological power does not manufacture even a basic trainer for the fourth largest air force of the world. With its expertise and infrastructure, HAL would have easily designed and developed a range of fighters required by IAF.

Clearly and apparently, India's indigenous aeronautical scene was quite encouraging till 1970s. India's state-owned aerospace enterprise HAL, which owes its origin to the vision and entrepreneurial spirit of Seth Lalchand Hirachand, was active in the development and upgrade of Marut HF-24, a single-seat ground attack fighter and two-seater basic trainer jet HJT-16 Mark 1 Kiran. In comparison to 1970s, things are now far from salutatory for the Indian aeronautical sector. On its part, China is not only self-sufficient in terms of trainer aircraft but also has exported a large number of them to a number of third-world countries.

HAL's current plight reflects a depressing saga of monumental failure to build the foundation of a resurgent aeronautical industry. Indeed, HAL had lost the golden opportunity of turning itself into an Indian Embraer. As ruefully recalled by one of the former chiefs of HAL (during the interaction with this writer), HAL's plan to develop civilian aircraft was consistently sabotaged by "vested interests". Moreover, there were occasional reports of a strong "import lobby" in the country supported by foreign aerospace and defence outfits working overtime to sap the vitality of HAL and make India dependent on imports.

Even after two successful instances of aircraft development – HF-24 Marut in 1960s and now Light Combat Aircraft (LCA) Tejas which is now winging its way towards final operational clearance along with a joint development project with Russia for the fifth-generation fighter on the drawing board – has India not learnt enough to be able to create a fighter liker Rafale aircraft from concept to operation? The time lag between the completion of Marut project to the commencement of the LCA was about 24 years by which time HAL had lost the expertise and talent it had acquired over the years. Whatever technical manpower was created in the design department of HAL withered under frequent doses of licences production of foreign aircraft.

Meanwhile, there are talks of transforming HAL into a world-class aerospace enterprise with a forward looking vision. HAL along with seven other defence Public Sector Undertakings (PSUs), 40 units of Ordnance Factory Board (OFB) and 50 laboratories under Defence Research and Development constitutes the mainstay of defence production scenario in India. Of course, HAL had all the potentials to make India self-reliant in all aspects of aeronautical engineering. Bureaucratic and political interference along with the defence personnel's thrust on meeting the criteria of the forces rather than self-reliance in defence production is at the root of the present plight of HAL. Moreover, the excessive thrust on licenced production went to kill the creative spirit essential to design, develop, and manufacture innovative products. Added to that, HAL was not exposed to the competitive environment since it was complacent with the captive orders from the Defence Ministry. Because the work culture of HAL was far from competitive and innovative, many of the experienced and talented engineers left this premier Indian aeronautical and defence outfit.

Around 85 percent orders of HAL are government driven and often the armed forces have complained about the poor quality of products. Although HAL has closely worked with front-ranking aerospace enterprise including Boeing, Honeywell, Airbus, Pratt & Whitney, Rolls Royce and Israel Aerospace Industries (IAI), it has failed to master many of the cutting edge technologies going into aerospace products. On the plus side, HAL has brought about qualitative improvement in its flagship product Advanced Light Helicopter (ALH) Dhruv which is not only in service with the Indian defence forces and coast guard but has also been exported to a few third-world countries. Currently, the two high-profile projects on hand of HAL are Intermediate Jet Trainer Sitara and Light Combat Helicopter (LCH). HAL has also a plan to build Light Utility Helicopter (LUH) for use of the Indian defence forces.

Turning HAL into a World-Class Aerospace Hub

Of course, over the years the defence delegations and teams from aerospace companies which visited HAL have been quite impressed with the facilities and expertise it has built up over the years. But their observation is that engineers here, though talented, lack exposure to modern management practices. "I have spent thirty years in aerospace industry and worked with global companies like Boeing, Airbus and Northrop Grumman, but I can say that HAL is superbly equipped with infrastructure, but one needs to use these to bring out a product. Most of the talent are just a waste as the higher management lacks the vision," says an American aerospace professional.

According to K. Tamilmani, Chief Executive Officer (CEO) of Bangalore-based Centre for Military Air-worthiness Certification (CEMILAC) facility under DRDO, creation of an autonomous body for design, development, testing and production of aero engines can help India attain self-reliance in aerospace sector. Tamilmani states that amalgamation of expertise and competence available in both the public and private sectors should be fused to create a high-tech platform. HAL and Gas Turbine Research Establishment (GTRE) have already built up a sound infrastructure and sufficient level of expertise in the area of aero-engines. Moreover, resources available in private enterprise including Kirloskar, Larsen and Toubro (L&T) and Godrej could be harnessed for giving a quickening impetus to the process or realising aero-engines of varying thrust ranges.

On another front, emphasis would need to be laid on state-of-the-art manufacturing facilities, quality assurance and quality production of international standards. "India has the capacity, teams, technology, demand and industry. We need to integrate them to be in the race", observes Tamilmani. For this to happen, the Government should need to set aside a large amount of money to fund research and development in research organisations and academic institutions. That is how the USA had made it to the top of the world defence production scenario. No wonder then that US Government continues to fund leading defence contractors like Boeing and Lockheed and Martin for research and development of newer and better performing systems.

Indeed, to be able to move out of the syndrome of 'dependence and import', India should demonstrate it technological excellence by producing at least one engine with enough parameters of thrust-to-weight capabilities. Around this engine, India can create a platform that will meet all the requirements of IAF. In this context, ground covered by India's home-grown Kaveri engine designed and developed by GTRE to power Tejas holds the hope of making India self-reliant in power plants required for a variety of applications. Against the original objective of generating 80-kN thrust, Kaveri is now able to generate 70-kN thrust. With little fine-tuning, Kaveri engine can be made capable of generating 80-kN thrust. However, with the IAF projecting need for a higher thrust engine for the Mark II version of Tejas, GTRE is planning to join hands with the French engine major Snecma to take forward Kaveri technology to realise an engine generating 90-kN thrust. This engine will feature the state-of-the-art single crystal technology.

Mastering complex technologies involved in a high-performance aero-engine will provide India a solid spring board to develop a variety of engines of different thrust ranges meant for use in ships, missiles, UAVs, armoured vehicles, aircraft and helicopters. China is yet to fully master the technology of aero-engine. Moreover, the engine technology has a massive application in civilian area and the technology developed by DRDO can be transferred to the Indian industries active in the area of engines. This would give a massive boost to the power plant industry in the country.

Strengthen Public-Private Partnership

All said and done, an enormous human resources initiative and financial investments are required to build teams and attract and nurture talent to sustain the growth of Indian defence and aerospace sector. Perhaps India's defence and aerospace sector can take a leaf out of ISRO's experience of handholding small- and medium-level industries contributing to the Indian space programme. Thanks to this innovative approach, today Tanuku-based Andhra Sugars is capable of producing a range of liquid propellants including liquid hydrogen for the launch vehicles of ISRO. Similarly, ISRO has been encouraging – through funds and technology – academic institutions like IITs and Universities to build mini and micro satellites. The idea is to help the students master the basics of satellite technology. Perhaps HAL and DRDO can take up similar initiatives to involve Indian private industries and academic institutions in the quest to achieve self-reliance in defence sector.

The recent decision of the Indian Government to allow defence PSUs float joint ventures with private companies in the country could go a long way towards bolstering domestic defence industrial base. This could in a way increase the opportunities for obtaining advanced technologies from foreign sources. The eight defence PSUs are now in need of massive transformation. Significantly, many small and medium-level industrial units in India have a good amount of resources and skill level to produce hardware meeting the stringent international standards.

Meanwhile, the micro, small and medium enterprise (MSME) sector says it is banking on the forthcoming revision of the Defence Procurement Policy which may reserve 20 percent minimum sourcing from the defence supplies contract to MSMEs which already supply a large volume of components, special alloys and metal parts for military hardware. "Successful SMEs (Small and Medium Enterprises) will be the ones which can innovate, adopt technologies, deliver customised solutions, develop and maintain a global standard in manufacturing quality and specifications while retaining their cost advantage", says Dhiraj Mathur, the executive director of Price Waterhouse Cooper.

For Private Sector Industry: A Bigger Pie of the Defence Production

Samtel Display Systems is now in a position to supply all types of Multi-Function Displays (MFDs) for all the Indian fighter aircraft including the Tejas. Until recently, India relied on imported MFDs for its combat aircraft. Buoyed up by the success in developing MFDs, Samtel is now looking at manufacturing infra-red search and track (IRST) sensors capable of spotting an enemy aircraft passively without alarming them to the presence of another aircraft. Visakapatnam-based Flash Forge is fabricating critical valves and pipes for the Indian Navy's underconstruction fleet of six French origin Scorpene submarines. They are a part of the expanding breed of small and medium enterprises that are making a mark on Indian Government–controlled defence sector. They are niche players who have cornered a key role in indigenising the defence industry by developing the cutting edge technologies. Indeed, their potentials need to be harnessed at a faster pace to speed up the process of defence indigenisation. They can very well become an important part of India's military industrial complex. "Indian companies should tie up with MNCs, utilise offset opportunities and leverage the expertise that arise from such synergies", says Karthikeyan Natarajan, Senior Vice President and Global Head (integrated engineering) of Mahindra Satyam.

In a development of significance to the Indian aerospace sector, the Bangalore-based QuEST Global has become the first Indian private company to become the direct supplier of sub-systems to the European Airbus industries. The company has an aerospace supply chain ecosystem in its Special Economic Zone (SEZ) in Belgaum in North Karnataka. QuEST Global, which has acquired engineering services division of UK-based GKN Aerospace, has been a supplier of aero-structures and actuator systems to the international aerospace players. Indeed, overseas acquisition by Indian defence, engineering and aerospace companies could help bring in expertise and technologies not available within the country.

India should also exploit the potentials that vehicles major Mahindra & Mahindra has built up in the area of aerospace. The acquisition by Mahindra of the Australia-based Gipps Aero has invested Mahindra Aerospace with the capability to produce small aircraft. In 2007, Mahindra had bought Bangalore-based engineering firm Plexion which had human resources in the area of aerospace. This led to a 2008 tie-up between Mahindra Aerospace and National Aerospace Laboratories (NAL) to build a five-seater aircraft named NM-5. The prototype of the aircraft was developed and tested at Gipps Aero facilities in Australia. Meanwhile, Mahindra Aerospace is looking at setting up a facility near Bangalore to produce aerospace sub-systems and hardware for the global aerospace firms.

On the other hand, Bangalore-based Dynamatic Aerospace, in tie-up with Spirit Aero Systems, is assembling the flap track beam for A320 family of Airbus aircraft. In 2008, Dynamatic Aerospace acquired Oldland CNC, a high-end engineering enterprise in Bristol with a strong focus on the production of aerospace components. This acquisition has provided Dynamatic Aerospace with unique state-of-the-art aeronautical manufacturing facility possessing complex five-axis machining system. Dynamatic Aerospace as part of its quest to enhance its capabilities in large aero structures, composites and complex engineering is building a new manufacturing facility in Bangalore. "It will enable Dynamatic to emerge as preferred strategic supplier to global tier ones and aerospace companies", says Udayant Malhotra, CEO of Dynamatic Aerospace.

In what has been perceived as a shot in the arm for Indian defence and aerospace sector, Tata Advanced Systems (TAS) has entered into tie-up arrangement with several international enterprises including the ones to manufacture components for aerospace and defence giant Boeing. Further, it has taken a one-third stake in Italy's Piaggio Aero while it has signed a Memorandum of Understanding (MOU) with Israel Aerospace Industries (IAI) for a joint venture that would develop, manufacture and support a wide range of defence and aerospace products including missiles, UAVs, radars, electronic warfare system and homeland security systems. On another front, TAS is already manufacturing Sikorsky helicopter cabin from its facility in Andhra Pradesh. TAS has also joined hands with US aerospace and defence giant Lockheed Martin to manufacture structural assemblies for C-130 aircraft. India's heavy engineering giant L&T has formed a joint venture with European Aerospace and Defence Consortium EADS to develop electronics warfare devices.

Harness Force Multipliers for Self Reliance

All these joint ventures should serve as platforms to acquire the latest genre technologies and help India move faster on the road of defence self-reliance. On another front, setting up of exclusive economic zones catering to defence, aeronautics and IT could go a long way towards sharpening the entrepreneurial skill for the design, development and production of components, hardware, sub-systems and even the entire systems under one roof. An aerospace SEZ, spread over an area of 2,500 acres in South Gujarat close to the Delhi-Mumbai industrial corridor, will have manufacturing, testing and MRO facilities. In parallel, there is an immediate need to considerably enhance the domain skill of the Indian IT companies active in the area of aerospace and defence. Both Gujarat and Karnataka are pushing for the setting up of full-fledged aerospace universities with a view to create a talented manpower pool for expanding the frontiers of Indian aerospace sector.

Perhaps the Indian aerospace sector could follow the path of auto sector which started its forays into the international auto market almost two decades ago as spare parts and components supplier to the global auto giants. The immediate thrust of the Indian aerospace sector should be on mastering fifth-generation technologies including stealth, super-cruise and high-performance composites.

Analysts believe the offsets that would flow to the Indian industry after the country enters into a final contract with Dasault aviation for the acquisition of Rafale fighter aircraft will have the potential to revitalise the Indian aerospace and defence space. The offset obligation forming part of India's defence acquisition programme has as its objective boosting the skill and production level of Indian defence and aerospace industry by binding a foreign vendor winning an order worth more than Rs. 300 crore to invest at least 30 percent of the contract value by way of sourcing services, hardware, manufacturing and technology transfer – for the MMRCA contract the offset obligation has been laid down at 50 percent of the contract value.

But then the task of monitoring the discharge of offset obligations by overseas vendors is easier said than done. Despite the tall claims on offsets by the Indian Defence Ministry, the details are rather sketchy. The Ministry claims that it has managed to sign offset contracts worth as much as US $2.1 billion and another US $8.5 billion are at various stages of negotiations. However, the recent decision to include civil aviation and homeland security sectors for offsets discharge would pave for the transfer of technologies that are really not the 'cutting edge'. This dilution of the scope of defence offset is by no means a welcome development.

Meanwhile, there is a concern that Indian artillery has not added a single piece since Bofors deal created a storm of controversy in the country in 1980s over the alleged kickbacks. The forces are now short of modern guns and howitzers of various categories. And Indian defence ministry's efforts to import artillery systems have been bogged down in uncertainty over the allegations of 'wrong doings and kickbacks'. This is a challenge and opportunity for India to initiate the development of artillery systems by diverting a part of the US $4 billion outlay meant for artillery modernisation for research aimed at developing artillery guns of varying specifications within the country. Clearly and apparently, developing artillery guns is not a challenging task for India, for by harnessing expertise available in the country, it would not be difficult for India to produce all types of artillery systems it requires. As it is India's excellent research and industrial base in the area of metallurgy can be harnessed to speed up the development of artillery systems. Moreover, the recent discovery of blueprint for manufacturing of the Bofors Guns that was in possession of OFB for more than two-and-a-half decades, while making for a shocking state of affairs could be used as a major input for developing Indian artillery guns.

In 2009, the consultancy firm KPMG in a report revealed that only 20 percent of Indian army's equipment is state-of-the-art, 30 percent are maturing fast and a staggering 50 percent are totally obsolete. Against this backdrop, S.D. Dimri, Director General (DG) of OFB has stated that modernisation plan for manufacturing and support infrastructure of all OFB units is essential to bring them to the level where they will be able to meet the needs of the defence forces in a fast track mode and with an eye on performance standard. OFB units have a core competence in manufacturing highly sensitive chemical compositions, propellant, explosives, missile fuses, and rifles, machine guns, under barrel grenades launcher, fire control system, and active and passive night vision devices. OFB also makes available advanced aluminium alloy used in the Indian space programme.

Need to Avoid Duplicity of Efforts

There are cases of scientific and research organisations in the country working on the same area, resulting in an enormous waste of precious resources including human talent. For instance, both ISRO and DRDO are into the development of Synthetic Aperture Radar (SAR), which is immune to cloud, darkness and haze. Of course, many of the technical specifications that DRDO is looking for its SAR may be different from the SAR that ISRO is developing. But at the fundamental level, many technologies – such as materials and electronic components – that are common to SAR can be shared by the two organisations. Similarly, there are many elements such as electronics, propellants, navigation and guidance which are common to both the launch vehicle and the missile. ISRO and DRDO, pooling their resources, expertise and infrastructure, could make for a win-win combination to turn India into a technological super-power and transform the Indian defence production scenario.

But for this to happen, Government of India would need to introduce a lot of policy changes whereby ISRO, a civilian organisation committed to the peaceful use of outer space, is allowed to work with DRDO in areas of mutual interest. Moreover, there is a need for a full-fledged national agency to assess the resources in terms of human talent, infrastructure, status of research and technology development in various scientific organisations as well as industrial enterprises to synergistically harness the available resources for a speedier self-reliance. Also, the Indian industry in private sector, whose track record in investing in research and development is quite dismal, should not only be incentivised to invest in original research but should also be enlightened on the long-term multiple benefits accruing from investment on fundamental research and technology development.

The strategy to put in place a robust Indian military industrial complex geared to make India self-reliant in defence production should harness the resources, expertise and infrastructure available in the country with a thrust on developing innovative, cutting edge technologies to help in the constant upgradation of military equipment and combat systems. Public-private partnership, floating joint ventures with foreign partner willing to offer the latest in technology and manufacturing process, nurturing talent in academic and research institutions, acquisition of overseas companies focussing on aerospace and defence, enhancing the domain skill of Indian IT companies, setting up aerospace and defence parks in exclusive economic zones, proactive government policy oriented to support defence research and development and private sector enterprises taking up the development of technologically challenging defence systems could pave way for the long cherished Indian self-reliance in defence production.

In the ultimate analysis, the focus should be on turning Indian from being an importer to the exporter of the defence hardware. And that alone could qualify India to lay claim to being a global military power.

*

July, 2012

3

ARMS AND THE COUNTRY

Ambassador Kanwal Sibal

European Nations Compete for Defence Ties with India

When listing India's defence partners Europe is mentioned, it would be more accurate to speak of individual European countries as partners. Europe is unified economically but not in the defence domain. Unlike on economic issues, on defence issues India deals with individual capitals and not with the Brussels. In this context, some points are pertinent to our defence ties with European countries.

One, these countries compete even more intensely with one another for defence contracts abroad than they do for commercial ones, as the former are fewer in number, the margins are bigger and the supply of spare parts and periodic upgrades provide large long-term returns. European countries compete with one another as zealously in India as they do with Russia, Israel or the United States of America, our other major defence partners.

Two, defence ties have a much more pronounced political element than commercial exchanges. Countries with serious political differences can have extensive economic ties, as is the case of the US and Japan with China. However, for defence ties, some geo-political understanding has to exist. The country supplying arms acquires a degree of political leverage over the recipient country. At critical moments, spare parts or ordnance could be denied because of sanctions. These considerations are important for India because of our past experience and potential concerns for the future. In this respect, France is considered more reliable than other European countries because it has eschewed sanctions on India, even for our 1998 decision to go nuclear. The United Kingdom's record is tainted while Germany has been squeamish about defence trade for humanitarian or conflict-prevention reasons. The sanctions issue has, however, lost its previous edge because of the lifting of nuclear sanctions on India by the US and the Nuclear Suppliers Group, the deterioration of US/NATO-Pakistan relations and the receding of the Kashmir issue from the forefront of Western concerns.

Bargaining: Ultra-Light Howitzers

Three, defence manufacturing is a high-cost industry as very advanced technologies and huge outlays on research and development are required. Exports help to achieve economies of scale and amortise development costs. European countries are maintaining large defence industries in spite of the absence of any real external military threat and dwindling domestic orders because of reduced defence budgets. Exports therefore become vital. We have so far failed to extract the maximum advantage for ourselves from this compulsion of theirs by way of obtaining genuine transfers of technology. This is in large part because all European countries adhere rather strictly to technology denial regimes individually, and some intra-European coordination exists on this score. In general, on issues of technology transfer, all of them are restrictive, with the latest generation technologies made almost impossible of access. We have also not used our bargaining power effectively enough because of systemic deficiencies which prevent us from integrating the opportunities we provide to European countries in diverse domains with a view to wresting concessions through cross-bargaining.

Four, the bigger European entities are habituated to wielding power internationally – such has been their domination of world affairs in previous centuries. Their big power status is intimately linked to the possession of a large defence industry. Its existence enables them to discharge their dominant role in maintaining international peace and security, whether through the Security Council, the North Atlantic Treaty Organisation (NATO) or a "coalition of the willing". In the race for technological innovation, the civilian off-shoots of defence technologies too are important factors for retaining a large defence manufacturing base. This may not be a material factor in bilateral defence ties, but is relevant in the larger context of global power equations.

Five, rivalry with the US, which is both an ally and a competitor, is a powerful reason for major European countries to maintain a sizable, independent defence manufacturing base. This allows for a degree of independence in foreign policy making and avoids complete subservience to the US. This rivalry with the US is being sharpened in relation to India because of improving India-US defence ties and the US success in bagging major defence contracts. In fact, the foreign military sales route is giving the US an edge as it excludes middlemen, and consequently, the problem of allegations of corruption that hobble acquisition decisions is avoided.

Six, it is important to note the increasingly 'multinational' nature of the European defence industry resulting from its consolidation through mergers and acquisitions on account of high costs of production, reduced domestic orders, the need for economies of scale and international competition. Various European countries have been forced to pool defence requirements and jointly funded production programmes. It is not only that complex defence products are now seldom purely 'national', but also that European products are likely to contain even US-made components.

Of European companies active in India, the European Aeronautics, Defence and Space Company, for instance, combines some leading French, German and Spanish companies. Its missile branch was merged with the UK's BAE systems and Italy's Finmeccanica to form the Minority Business Development Agency (MBDA). The Eurofighter is jointly produced by Germany, Britain, Italy and Spain. Dassault, whose Rafale has been selected in preference to the Eurofighter, is owned by the Dassault Group (50.55 percent) and the Engineering Analysis and Data System (EADS) (46.33 percent), the manufacturer of the Eurofighter. Thales, another French company involved in major Indian defence programmes, is tied up with the US's Raytheon and the UK's BAE which, in turn, is the manufacturer of the Hawk trainer aircraft sold to India and will supply Ultra-Light Howitzers to India through the FMS route on account of its several American acquisitions. In view of these links between European defence companies – and this sector has been largely privatised – the reality of dealing with 'individual' European countries gets diluted, although at the political level the commitment of individual governments to forging defence ties with India in depth can be differentiated.

That India should be the world's largest importer of arms is a serious indictment of the state of indigenous defence manufacturing. India should have built domestic capability on an accelerated basis in view of the enduring combined threat from China and Pakistan and Western technology denial regimes applied to us. India cannot have genuine strategic autonomy without possessing an independent defence production base. We have, unfortunately, not been able to leverage our large-scale imports for obtaining the level of transfers of technology needed by us. Fortunately, the size of the Indian market has persuaded countries like France and Germany to reduce their defence supplies to Pakistan.

With the lifting of the nuclear sanctions on us and Western support for our membership of key technology denial regimes, meaningful technology transfers to us are now more possible in principle. The offsets policy can enlarge our domestic manufacturing base with participation by European companies, but unless the present 26 percent ceiling on foreign direct investment is increased to at least 49 percent, it would be on a sub-contractual basis, with serious technology transfers remaining elusive.

*

February, 2013

4

Dealing with the Neighbour from Hell: Slandering the Indian Army

Ambassador Prabhat P Shukla

Since the recent episodes on our side of the Line of Control (LC) in January 2013, there has been a spate of articles seeking to justify and somehow explain the Pakistani actions, even if many are prefaced with the pro-forma demurral that the beheadings – this time and in the past – were condemnable. Many of the spurious arguments used by the appeasers of Pakistan have been disposed of in earlier writings; one of the newer ones has been that the Indian Army has done similar things. Happily, Raksha Mantri Antony has denied these allegations, and so has the former Army Chief, Gen Malik. But this has not settled matters. Proof of the culpability of the Indian Army, as adduced in some sections of our media, is that Pakistan has lodged several such accusations against the Indian Army with the UN Military Observers Group for India and Pakistan (UNMOGIP) over the last decades. This latter body has, in turn, taken this up with India, but has received no reply.

There is a history to all this, and it would be important for the unbiased reader to be aware of this and draw correct conclusion regarding these kinds of arguments. There was a time when UNMOGIP played an active role along the Cease-Fire Line, as it was called before the 1972 Simla Agreement, and India was dealing with this body on a continuing basis. The last time that it played a substantive role was in 1965, especially in the run-up to the war that broke out in the autumn of that year. The events that led to war were, as usual, precipitated by Pakistani action in sending infiltrators across the LC, while denying any role in this. By now, this is Standard Operating Procedure (SOP), but then it was relatively new, having been done only once before, in September-October 1947.

Accordingly, both sides complained to UNMOGIP in August 1965. That body was then headed by an Australian, Lt Gen Robert Nimmo, who had been its head since 1950. He enquired into the charges made by both sides and submitted his report to the UN Secretary General, U Thant. The latter made a report to the full Security Council on 3 September 1965, and reported as follows:

> UNMOGIP received an Indian complaint of Pakistani shelling, on 1 September, of pickets and a battalion Headquarters in the Chamb area of the Jammu-Bhimber sector of the Cease-Fire Line. The complaint stated that at 0230 hours on that date one and a half Pakistani tank squadrons crossed the Cease-Fire Line in this area supported by artillery. Pakistani artillery was also said to have fired on a battalion Headquarters in the Punch area from 1630 on 1 September and on an Indian battalion Headquarters in the Jangar area. The substance of these complaints was subsequently confirmed by United Nations Military Observers. A Pakistani complaint reported that Indian soldiers had crossed the CFL in strength in the Kargil, Tithwal, and Uri-Punch sectors as reported above. Pakistan, in this complaint also affirmed the crossing of the CFL by Pakistan troops in the Bhimber area on 1 September as a defensive measure to forestall Indian action, asserting also that in this sector the Indian Air Force had taken offensive action against Pakistan troops. Also on 1 September armed infiltrators ambushed an Indian convoy at Gund north-east of Srinagar on the Leh road and both sides sustained casualties. On 2 September the Jammu team of UNMOGIP received an Indian complaint that Pakistan aircraft had attacked the road between Chamb and Jaurian during the morning of 2 September and that Jaurian village was in flames. The air attack on Jaurian village was confirmed by UN Military Observers. [*Emphasis added*]

The purpose of this long quote and the added emphasis is to demonstrate that the Indian complaints were confirmed by Gen Nimmo, while the Pakistani complaints were not. This is important, because, as mentioned above, the charges against the Indian Army in recent years rest on the record of Pakistani charges against it, and lodged with the UNMOGIP. It is another of Pakistani SOPs to make such false charges, and the events of 1965, which were subjected to comprehensive scrutiny by UNMOGIP and the UN Security Council, testify to this. Gen Nimmo died in January 1966 in Islamabad, apparently of a heart attack, this being the very day that the Tashkent Conference began. Prime Minister Shastri died at the end of the Conference.

There is more: this may be seen in the statement made by Secretary General U Thant, which again deserves to be quoted at length:

> In mid-June of this year [1965] for example, Gen Nimmo reported that during the five months, a total of 2231 complaints from both sides charging violation of the Cease Fire had been submitted to UNMOGIP. Most of these involved firing across the CFL [Cease Fire Line], although some concerned crossings of the Line by armed men. As of that date, 377 violations in all categories had been confirmed by the Observers....

The point to note is that there was a gross exaggeration in the number of incidents alleged to have taken place. This was at a time when India used to maintain contact with UNMOGIP, and there was the danger that charges would be proved false, as did indeed happen regularly. Today, when India no longer deals with that body's complaints, it would be tempting for Pakistan to make even more charges than in 1965. It is safe therefore to conclude that the charges being purveyed in the media today are wild exaggerations.

The Nimmo Report itself was never made public. The records show that Prime Minister Shastri wanted it made public, but found no support among the principal actors – USSR, USA and the UK. He acknowledged that the Report had some negative things to say about the conduct of India too, but its conclusions were unequivocal and placed the blame on Pakistan. It is probably not too late even now for our Ministries of Defence and External Affairs to upload these on their websites, and fulfil Shastri's wishes.

To sum up, what the record shows is that Pakistan has been habitually misrepresenting the facts to the international community, and it should not surprise anyone that this continues today. Both in terms of the number of charges, and, more importantly, in terms of the veracity of the allegations, the historical record shows that reports made by Pakistan to UNMOGIP were just not true. The dishonesty was taking place right from the start, of course, but they were being made even at a time when there was the serious risk of their being challenged and proven false. Today, India no longer has any truck with UNMOGIP, and it is therefore much safer to trump up charges against it. For Pakistan, it is a safe bet – India will not answer, and so the appeasers in India can repeat and endorse the allegation. Alternatively, India is forced to answer, and thereby brings UNMOGIP – and by extension, the UN – back into play on the Kashmir issue.

There is an important tail-piece to the 1965 episode described above. The Security Council meeting of 3 September was followed by a debate on 6 September at which the Indian Foreign Secretary, CS Jha, [and a representative of Pakistan] was also present. The speech of the Indian representative contains the following passage. He was responding to the Pakistani charge that India was in Kashmir as a colonial power:

> If there is colonialism, it exists in Pakistan. The Pashtuns, the Baluch, and the East Pakistanis, are being ruled without any regard to their civil rights, to their fundamental human rights and freedoms. This is colonialism as the world understands it.

Events since then, with the emergence of an independent Bangladesh and the on-going resistance in Baluchistan, certainly provide a ringing endorsement of the Indian Foreign Secretary's judgment. As to UNMOGIP itself, the fact is that Shastri wanted its numbers to be increased in 1965, so that it could do a more thorough job of monitoring. This did not happen, unfortunately, and after 1972, India stopped all dealings with UNMOGIP. The important thing is to see this to completion, and wind up the operations of the body on the Indian side, even if Pakistan will not agree to this on its side.

There remains the question of why the appeasers and pro-Pakistan elements are so gullible as to buy into any allegation against the Indian Army. The motive behind such reports requires to be examined and understood, so that the public at least is not misled.

*

April, 2013

5

Sino-Indian Stand-off in Ladakh: Implications and Options

Ambassador Satish Chandra, Vice Chairman, VIF

On April 15th, around 50 PLA soldiers intruded about 10 km inside the Indian territory in eastern Ladakh and erected a tented post there. Efforts to get the area vacated through flag meetings, activation of the bilateral joint secretary level mechanism set up to address such situations, and intervention of our Foreign Secretary with the Chinese Ambassador have so far failed. As a result, the Indo-Tibetan Border Police has established a camp 300 meters from that set up by the PLA troops leading to an eyeball-to-eyeball confrontation.

The problem has arisen because the 4057-km-long Sino-Indian border is disputed and because a common perception about the course of the Line of Actual Control (LAC) is lacking. This has led each country, with a view to bolstering its territorial claims, to undertake patrolling in areas perceived by the other to be on its side of the LAC. While such activity on our part has been relatively modest, China has each year engaged in hundreds of incursions into Indian territory. Such decades-long activity is not risk free as anything can happen when the armed personnel of two contending parties are in close proximity in a disputed area. Accordingly, we should have been much more proactive in seeking to resolve the border dispute or, at least, arriving at a common perception of the LAC.

The current incident is much more serious than earlier ones because it is the first occasion in decades when the Chinese are adamant about not vacating the area. Clearly China has decided to up the ante and this move constitutes yet another provocation that we need to appropriately address. Unfortunately, India has placed too much faith on the innumerable affirmations committing both countries to maintain peace and tranquility along their borders and to resolve their border-related differences peacefully as well as in the multi-tiered mechanisms to ensure that the channels of communication remain open at all times.

Such faith is misplaced as China has shown no desire to resolve our border-related differences. As recently as March 2013, President Xi Jinping in response to questions from the media asserted that "the boundary question is a complex issue", resolving it "will not be easy" and pending settlement, we should not let it affect "the all-round development in ties." China, obviously, does not want to work on the early resolution of the boundary issue with a view to keeping India off balance, to destabilise us and to choose the time and manner in which it would act against us.

The foregoing coupled with China's rapid military modernisation is naturally worrisome given its inimical approach towards India which is borne out by the following:

1. Rapid upgradation of infrastructure and force levels in Tibet along with India-specific military exercises;
2. Ratcheting up of claims to Arunachal Pradesh;
3. Non-grant of visas to residents of Arunachal Pradesh on Indian passports;
4. PLA presence in Pakistan-Occupied Kashmir;
5. Claims that Sino-Indian border is only 2000 km long, thus questioning the legality of our possession of the Ladakh sector;
6. Use of Pakistan as a proxy through grant to it of nuclear weapons related technology as well as conventional weapons;
7. Pursuance of a string of pearls strategy to strangulate India;
8. Opposition to India's efforts to secure permanent membership in the UN Security Council and in various multilateral nonproliferation–related export control regimes like the Nuclear Suppliers Group, the Australia Group, etc.

In view of China's overwhelming military superiority and inimical disposition towards India, we have the following policy options:

1. **Business as Usual Approach.** It is characterised by a casual military modernisation programme, timidity towards China calculated to avoid ruffling its feathers and a hedging strategy in our relationship with other major players in the region. This option is based on the hope that in the absence of any 'provocative' steps by India, China will not take any

aggressive steps against us. Such an approach smacks of appeasement and as history has shown will only encourage further Chinese adventurism.

2. **Reciprocal Military Buildup Coupled with Business as Usual Approach.** This would entail a focused China centric military buildup while continuing to appease it. While superior to a pure 'Business as Usual Approach', it will invoke China's ire without causing it to renounce its inimical policies vis-à-vis India. This is apparent from the fact that China is reported to have indicated that it will only vacate its recent incursion if India dismantles its fortifications along its borders.
3. **Firm Self-Respecting Policy.** This should be our preferred approach and comprise the following elements:
   (a) Rapid military buildup designed to inflict pain on China in the event of an attack on India; such an attack should invoke counter attacks on China's vulnerable points and its lines of communication both on land and sea. Our nuclear forces should be appropriately upgraded particularly the submarine vector. Specific attention must be paid to neutralisation of Chinese military superiority through asymmetric warfare and guerilla tactics.
   (b) Linkages with countries that are similarly threatened by China should be openly pursued and plans discreetly developed for reciprocal assistance in the event of Chinese aggression.
   (c) Inimical moves by China should not be brushed under the carpet and must be responded to firmly. In the instant case, we should set up camps in areas regarded by China as being on its side of the LAC but are in India as per our perception. Grant of stapled visas for those from Arunachal should not merely be the object of protest but cause us to issue stapled visas for Chinese from Sinkiang and Tibet.
   (d) We must play the Tibet card by allowing the Dalai Lama and the Kalon Tripa greater access to our leadership, ceasing to reiterate that Tibet is a part of China, being more supportive of human rights in Tibet and in Sinkiang at international fora, instigating moves in the UN for Tibetan independence, projecting that Tibet is the water tower of Asia and its mismanagement by China threatens the entire region etc.
   (e) While welcoming increased Sino-Indian economic ties we must ensure that trade is more balanced and China does not use it as a means to damage Indian industry and enter into sensitive sectors like telecommunications.

Adoption of such a policy will, of course, provoke painful Chinese counter-measures but it will in the long term make India stronger. A prerequisite for the adoption of such a policy is, of course, the need to clean up our act at home by providing better governance and ensuring rapid economic development.

*

June, 2013

6

India-China Relations: A Reality Check

Lieutenant General Gautam Banerjee, PVSM, AVSM, YSM

> "*One sided pursuit of peace and disarmament is a powerful incentive to the adversary to intensify its own pursuit of war*".
>
> – **Luttwak**

The Elephant's Dilemma

New Delhi's purportedly 'meek submission' to what is seen as arbitrary, at times blatant, affronts to India's national dignity that is regularly inflicted by Beijing, often comes to be lambasted by our strategic community. Common citizens too are dismayed when they find New Delhi bending-backwards to reconcile to Beijing's highhandedness, sometimes after lodging meek protest and sometimes allowing the arrogation to pass.[1] Many times, as in the matter of the Chinese People's Liberation Army's (PLA) muscle flexing at the Line of Actual Control (LAC), either the incidents are left unreported, or when that is unfeasible, down-playing explanations are advanced to soothe public consternation – a case of the victim holding brief for the tormentor![2]

In more disconcerting vein, there come grave provocations from China that amount to a sort of 'hostility' against our nationhood. Besides the mind-boggling nonsense of staking claim over the State of Arunachal Pradesh, occupation of the *Shaksgam Valley* in Ladakh, pumping up Pakistan with military, nuclear and missile capabilities – a brazen recourse to destabilise India – and negation of India's stance on terrorism go to exemplify Beijing's obsessive antipathy towards India.[3] In all cases, New Delhi suffers these inimical policies in stoic resignation. There is, therefore, good reasons for the criticism that our strategic community heaps upon the government of the day.

Governance in contemporary India is driven by economic considerations, as indeed it should be. However, there are signs emanating from policy-making confabulations that indicate that the other fundamentals of national security may be consigned to the sidelines in favour of 'interests' of the commercial conglomerate. Obviously, when tested under eternal political wisdom, that is a trend dangerous for the future of our nationhood. Even if the undertakings of national defence are suspended as a temporary trade-off in favour of economic-industrial take-off, as China did during the 1980s and 1990s, the governing establishment may not be absolved from its primary charter that mandates, not the promotion of business interests *per se*, but the provision of secure and sovereign environment for the people to flourish.

The purpose of this piece is, firstly, to suggest that notwithstanding the enchanting dream of ending geo-political rivalry through commercial connections, the *Sino-Indian relationship may remain contentious in the foreseeable future*, and secondly, to argue that *articulation of military power-backed diplomacy would be a hopeful option* for India to live in peace with an overwhelmingly powerful and pugnacious neighbour.[4]

Contentions Ever-Interminable

One comes across many theories to explain Beijing's compulsive hostility towards India. Experts aver that the root cause of China's aversion is the power-play of regional *leadership* – of the kind of that usually comes up between the largest and the second largest neighbours. Then of course, there is India's repudiation of China's *territorial claims* and China's piqué of Indian's solidarity with the *Tibetan people*. In economic terms, competition for *energy*, *water* and *mining* rights for strategic minerals, and China's efforts to secure its *sea lines of communication* are also identified as the points of contention. No doubt, all these irritants add up to reinforce the already existing mutual suspicion. However, with the kind of sabre-rattling that China is frequently at, there is no doubt that a powerful majority in the Chinese establishment is afflicted with a sense of apprehension vis-à-vis India. But then what might these apprehensions be, and what can India do about it?

The answer may lie in the weight of the contentious issues that cast a shadow of unease upon Sino-Indo relations.

Regional Leadership?

In the question of rivalry for *leadership* in the region, the verdict is clear. To state the obvious, China encompasses a vast geographical area and unlimited range of resources. Traditionally, it cradles an extraordinary level of socio-political as well as practical intellect, and has developed sublime forms of civic and military wisdom in equal measure. It is China's cultural strength that allowed it to preserve its sovereignty through the periodical shrinkages of political authority, never giving up its claims to rule over what China considered its domain and staking its 'rightful' status as a superior race of the 'Middle Kingdom'.

China's fortune is again on an up-curve as it is a rising power of mind-boggling potential. Its grip over all segments of its societies is pervasive and its technological, economic and military clout is galloping sure and fast. While lining up to do business with China and so keep their domestic economies on track, even powerful nations are compelled to be wary of the inevitability of security challenges emanating from the fire-breathing dragon. Indeed, there is little doubt regarding China's global ascendancy in the days to come; political thinkers are already articulating the idea of its role as a 'pro-active super-power'. In bilateral context, its lead over India on every aspect – political authority, structural stability, economy, science and technology and military power – is so overwhelming, and continuously increasing, that even a fleeting thought of closing the gap may be discarded outright.

In contrast, India, though an equally ancient civilisation, has not articulated a proportionate balance between spiritualism, socio-political wisdom and nationalism. All through its history, there have been short periods of powerful centralisation followed by long periods of political disintegration that invited cyclic invasions and foreign rule. Presently, even as India's economy improves and it emerges as an accommodative member of the global polity, it is yet unable to articulate its state-power to disperse such anti-national tendencies that emanate from within or without.[5] Thus, notwithstanding a vibrant democracy in play, armed rebellion has displaced the State in nearly one-fifth of the country. One third of its people remain malnourished while numerous groups of ethnic, linguistic, casteist, religious, business and political manipulators assail each other, and by default, harm national ideals. Meanwhile, inimical neighbours continue to sabotage its national interests, with impunity.

To be realistic, there is no way India may stake for regional leadership in the foreseeable future. Even if Beijing views India's growing strategic relationships with US, Japan, Australia, Vietnam, Indonesia, Central Asian States and Myanmar as 'ganging up' to contain it, it may seek remedy not in targeting India, but in controlling its own brusque and over-bearing manner of conducting regional diplomacy. Indeed, China need not slip into a banal believe that India could pose a challenge to its ascendency in any manner.[6]

But that 'ghost' of apprehension may be exorcised by the Chinese themselves; India can do little to clear that perception.

The Tibet Issue

The *Tibet* issue is a cause of concern that sets Beijing on the warpath. History records that the borders of successive Nanjing-Beijing empires have gone through many cycles of expansions and contractions. Thus in some periods, Beijing's imperialistic control extended westwards right up to Turkmenistan, while at other times, revolt emanating from outlying provinces caused the empires to shrink into just the *Han* populated areas of the *Hwang Ho* and *Yang Ze* River Basins.[7] Perhaps this ingrained memory makes the ruling communist regime extremely sensitive to situations in Tibet, Xinjiang and Outer Mongolia. Chinese leadership's avowed purpose being to perpetuate the stability of their autarchic rule, the simmering discontent in Tibet and world-wide solidarity with the Tibetan cause must be a cause of serious anxiety for them. Even its attempts to buy Tibetan people's loyalty through accelerated economic development have failed to silence the skeptics who see it as a step to cascade Han settlements and so alter the demography of Tibet. Besides, economic prosperity stokes the urge for freedom, and therefore, the "Free Tibet" movement will remain a serious worry for the Chinese leadership in the foreseeable future. India, in sheltering a Tibet Government-in-Exile, would continue to be viewed as an 'upstart challenger', a potential 'destabiliser', who needs to be 'kept in place'.[8]

There is really nothing that India can do about successive Dalai Lamas and their followers taking shelter in its territory. May be China could do something about its ways of dealing with these unfortunate people so that they do not have to escape to India. It could reconcile to India's compulsions in accommodating Tibetan refugees under the established international convention. May be New Delhi's support of China's causes in various forums even in the absence of any reciprocal gesture would someday satiate Beijing's complexes in this regard.

Here again there is little that India can do more than what it already does do to assuage China's fears.

The Territorial Dispute

India's repudiation of China's occupation of the strategically sensitive *Aksai Chin* and *Shaksgam Valley*, and outright rejection of the nonsensical claim over Tawang/ Arunachal Pradesh further add to the latter's consternation. Indeed, it is difficult to visualise India ceding territories to humour China's expansionist agenda, just as it is naïve to expect China to rid itself of its deeply ingrained instincts of expansionistic philosophy.[9] India, therefore, will continue to be a target for Beijing to vent its frustrations upon.

A reasonably acceptable solution, if at all it comes, would have to be at China's behest. Even then, given the hawkish instincts on either side, it may not be a settlement in perpetuity; revisionist elements would keep raising the issue when it suits them.

Water

The Tibetan Plateau is the major source of sweet *water* that sustains life in the South and East Asia. No doubt, diversion of such waters to enliven its heartlands is an enticing prospect for China. But when considered in light of international riparian laws and the Middle Kingdom's compulsive urge to secure great power status, of which display of sense of responsibility is an essential ingredient, the dream may encounter major hurdles. China will have to contend with the fact that diversion of waters from the *Brahmaputra*, *Sutlej* and *Indus* rivers would affect many other neighbours, and that coalescence of a coalition of victims of its highhandedness, even if it is made up of smaller and weaker nations, would be detrimental to its interests.[10] Thus, even if technological complexities, enormity of investment, decades of construction and environmental consequences may not deter it, and if the global political equation continues to remain favourable to China during those decades, any arbitrary diversion of waters by China may not be beyond contest.

In the overall context therefore, China may not find India as the sole stumbling block on this issue; in India, it would continue to be a cause of discomfiture though.

Strategic Encirclement?

What is described as China's '*string of pearls*' strategy – that is, establishment of naval facilities surrounding the Indian Peninsula in alliance with littoral countries – would certainly strengthen its *sea lines of communication* as well as *mining* prospects in the India Ocean; it would also enhance its economic and diplomatic clout. Indeed, China is free to seek political arrangements to create this 'string' as its wants to, but there is much concern that this 'string' would lead to 'encirclement' of India. No doubt that 'string' would pinch, but only if India fails to invest in sea-power and take advantage of the strategic situation of the peninsular India that is best situated to control the Indian Ocean.

Rationally viewed, factoring facilities for naval replenishment located on foreign shores thousands of nautical miles away from mainland China as unassailable 'military bases', from where flotillas of the People's Liberation Army Navy (PLAN) would supposedly set about to impose adversities upon other users of the Indian Ocean, may cause less anxiety when tested in light of the scales of naval forces and logistics that would be necessary to that purpose. It may take China four to five decades of continuation of favourable internal and international order to realise that purported goal, howsoever delightful that ambition might be to a compulsive hegemon.[11] Besides, it would be an entire lot of nations whose interests would be equally threatened by China's dominance over the Indian Ocean.

This issue therefore would be a common concern among many nations, India included, that needs resolute preparations over time to manage.

Competition for Strategic Resources

There may be a case to view the issue of race for resources just as a business competition that is ever-present in all deals at all times. Such rivalries may not lead to enmity *per se*.[12] Besides, securing global sources for supply of assured *energy* and strategic *minerals* for one country does not imply that the other may have to starve; the architecture of economic exploitation of natural resources is so intimately intertwined across the globe. The concern that India would jeopardise China's energy hunt, or in securing its sources of energy China will cause India to be shunted out, may not, either way, be so overwhelming.[13]

The trade race may, therefore, be allowed to gain momentum without acrimony.

Compelling Observations

We may, at this stage, conclude this part of discussion with the observation that Sino-Indian relationship is marred by such fundamental in congruencies which cannot be resolved at India's instance without compromising its core values. New Delhi has to wait and hope that Beijing will someday be rid of its anxiety over India taking what it believes to be its pie, but lot of water must flow out of *Tsang*

Po before that. Till then, *the relationship will continue to be contentious and we will have to live with a long haul of unilateral antagonism, sometimes in latent form, brazen at other times.*

Keeping the 'Dragon' at Bay

Beijing's growing acts of diplomatic hostility, even to the extent that the understandings reached in the past – the peace and tranquility agreement 2005, for example – are sought to be repudiated through deliberate acts of negation, must remain a potential source of trouble for India.[14] As, therefore, stakes in geo-politics rise, China's insidious muscle flexing along our entire Northern borders, across the Indian Ocean region and even on international waters should be expected. We are also aware of the fact that Pakistan would continue to serve as China's proxy detractor against India. What however remains unstated is that Beijing is also well placed in promoting internal trouble within parts of India, when it wishes to. Even India's industrial sector could be choked by Beijing-instigated economic exclusions, and there would be none to restrain it, busy as most of the powers would be in finding crumbs to peck at from its courtyard.

So at the receiving end of one-sided antagonism from a great and powerful neighbour, what does India do to keep the 'dragon' off its back? How do we, as many strategic thinkers opine, keep China's predatory instincts in check while concentrating on our own economic progress? Let us examine this aspect.

We may start with what enchanting rhetoric we may *not* fall prey to.

Lure of Complacency

First, we may not take China's rhetoric of "peaceful rise to power" on face value: firstly, because in geo-politics, power never comes peacefully, and secondly, the peace Beijing speaks of is but a peace on its terms.

Second, we may not be fixated to the view that integration of Taiwan is China's sole focus. Presently, that goal remains farfetched, whereas Tibet is a 'live' issue in contention. Settlement of the Tibet issue will bring it a step closer to integration of Taiwan. Therefore, possibility of a situation when Beijing may bolster its politico-economic measures with military power to overwhelm the Tibetan refraction is real. India will invariably be embroiled in that conflict in some manner or the other.

Third, growing bilateral trade may not be a harbinger of dispute resolution. History bears testimony to the fact that good business does not come in the way of politico-military confrontation.

Fourth, the claim over whole of the Arunachal Pradesh may not be seen just as a bargaining posture. Such rhetorical claims, when repeated over decades, tend to get crystallised into national aspirations. When that happens, even authoritarian regimes are unable to back out against popular pressure.

Lastly, we may not dismiss those experts who have recently expressed the possibility of another Chinese 'attack' on India. Of course, as expected, the manner of the offensive may differ. In any case, we have to do better than repeating our gullibility's of the pre-1962, post-Kutch 1965 and pre-Kargil kinds if we do not wish to suffer another visitation of misfortune.

Thus, in the context of China's adversarial posture, New Delhi has to convince Beijing to limit its uncontrollable expansionist urge to nothing beyond a ritualistic war-dance.

Options Oft Articulated

Will a *tit-for-tat* exchange work? Asking Beijing either to move out the PLA from Occupied Kashmir or face the prospect of the Indian Army moving into *Aksai Chin*, for example? Or by sallying out to damage some huts and paint some boulders across the LAC? Can India indulge in such charade without poking Beijing to up the *ante*? The obvious answer is that such a bizarre 'game' may make a subtle gesture, nothing more, but worse, it might invite a reaction that India would be hard put to absorb.

Can New Delhi impose such a regime of trade restrictions that it starts hurting China's economy? By all accounts, such a step may cause some losses to China, but its counter-effect on Indian economic progress may be many times over. After all, the weaker gets trampled first.

Growing economic inter-dependency could be thought of to marginalise the hawks in Beijing, mainly the PLA and the rank communists. This may be a good option provided the economic benefits are equitably balanced, not biased against India. Besides, it needs to be appreciated that notwithstanding encouraging prophecies, economic bindings have seldom prevented one State from undermining the other. Conversely, in its efforts to keep the trade equation in her its, China may find another cause to be nasty.

Strength of human resources bolsters national security. Can we bank upon that to stand up to Beijing's arrogance? Well, that could be possible if we could maintain our lead in mathematical genius, English language, scientific temper and strong civil institutions that we had inherited at independence. Sadly, that lead has been lost, more or less; China catches up fast when she wishes to, while India tends to entangle herself in endless arguments and agitations, nepotism and mobocracy, divisive compromises and farcical politics. This option therefore is contingent upon India reinventing its societal strength – it is a faraway option.

Possibly, India can leverage common cause with the United States, Japan, Vietnam, Australia, Indonesia, to name just a few, to blunt China's predatory tendency. Can such a leverage be accomplished without provoking China, something that wisdom tells us to better avoid? Can we prevent such collaborations with the 'like-minded' parties – no saints themselves – from undermining our interests in some other manner? Arguably, it may be possible to forge such a leverage, though it would be a tight-rope act, liable to misfire.

What about retaliatory measures in Tibet? Can India stoke Tibetan resistance in the same manner that China uses Pakistan to tie knots around it? That indeed would be a strong leverage to exercise. But what if China retaliates by promoting Maoist and North East insurgencies; she had been doing so earlier even without any provocation, after all? Obviously, this extreme option may be reserved as a recourse only in war, with due preparations to handle the consequences.

The preceding discussion leaves *military deterrence as the sole practicable, and profitable, recourse to keep China on friendly terms.*

Role of Military Power

We know that obduracy of an overwhelmingly powerful neighbour may not be contained by reconciliatory or collaborative diplomacy alone. Beijing's arrogance will rise in step with its progress and power – this is already evident. Considering its ever-present roots as discussed above, Sino-Indian confrontation of some kind or the other is inevitable. Given China's philosophy of using military might as a catalyst of political ambitions, it is imperative for India to wield such military power that would motivate Beijing to seek its goals through peaceful means. Indeed, that is what our political leadership has sought to do all these years since 1962. But with the military institution frozen in obsolescence and afflicted with debilitating 'hollowness', can India's military power continue to pay its 'deterrence-dividend', or even dissuade our great neighbour's innate urge to grab territories? The answer, as honest analysts aver, is '*no*'.

Further, given that our goal of socio-economic uplift precludes the practicality of competing with China's military prowess, India may not hope to ever acquire that level of military power that could defeat a *full-spectrum, all-front, total war* that the PLA's doctrine espouses, even if that strategy is sought to be camouflaged under the beguiling terminology of "limited war under conditions of informalisation".

A 'Smile and Gun' Option

From the preceding discussion, it emerges that given the compulsions under which it has to carry the burden of statecraft, the courses adopted by New Delhi in keeping the overbearing 'dragon' at bay have to be double-nuanced. Indeed, it makes sense to promote political and economic engagement, sometimes reconciling affronts with petulance and showing occasional resolve.[15] However, since Beijing is no exception in respecting the power of gun, that stoicism needs to be backed up with an efficient military machine that could 'bite' painfully even when bound. *India could work towards that level of military preparedness which, even if it may not prevail, would make a clash of force prohibitively dear to China.* History tell us that it is possible to do so at a cost that is affordable and a pace that is adaptable. Indian strategists may therefore have to come to terms with the aforementioned restraining dispensations, and yet devise strategies that would deny free run to the PLA should Beijing decide to settle her pique with force.

But insight also tells us that the Indian system of administrating its military institution restricts rather than sponsors such exceptional strategies. Our political culture remains in oblivion of the nuances of cost-efficient management of military organisation and development of strategic articulations, while the burden of defence policy making is consigned to a school of pretending strategists made up of bureaucrats, scientists and auditors – in exclusion of sanctified representation from the military intellectuals! As the show of smug satisfaction among the polity and the media over raising of two army divisions, or positioning some aircraft on the North-East frontier, or successful launches of missiles – all half-measures, titillating but overall lopsided – indicates, innocence of the profound nuances of war-fighting seems to pervade the entire state-apparatus. Consequently, even while maintaining the third largest army in the world, the nation remains bereft of the advantages expected and dividends accrued. That is a sad situation.

Engaging with China

Friendly engagement with China is a necessity that would work only if it is cemented with the backing of military strength. A comprehensive revamp – transformation, so to say – of the Indian defence establishment is therefore overdue. This, however, may be possible only if there is firm resolve in our politico-bureaucratic system to nurture military expertise, foster synergy between India's numerous defence and quasi-defence establishments and respect the time-lines of force-modernisation.

This condition does not prevail today.

NOTES

1. New Delhi's reconciliation with issue of 'stapled visa' to the residents of J&K, blocking the Asian Development Bank loan for Arunachal Pradesh and whimsical response to the threat of deluge along Paree Chu in Himachal Pradesh are some examples. Diplomatic protests, when lodged, are disdainfully dismissed by Beijing, mostly so.
2. Instances of damaging Indian bunkers, shooing away bonafide graziers and preventing track construction work near the LAC to proceed are known. Besides, of course, there are ever-increasing violations of the LAC. India's attempts to explain away these violations to its citizens as "differing perceptions of the alignment of LAC between the two sides" do not really wash since the Chinese have consistently avoided specifying their 'perception' of the LAC and so settle this irritant till the border issue is resolved.
3. Since 2006, China 'clarifies' that the entire Arunachal Pradesh ("Outer Tibet" is the newly invented nomenclature!) belongs to them. Imagine an international boundary, running not along the watershed of massive Himalayan Ranges, but over and across its reverse foothills! That is a glimpse of 'Chinese logic'! In the case of Shaksgam Valley, one squatter has gifted its trespass to another! The mischievous deal has gone a step further: Chinese Army is now operating in Pakistan Occupied Kashmir.
4. China and India have never been neighbours. Tibet has always occupied that place independent of the ever-changing Sino-Tibet political equations, till communist China completely subsumed Tibet nationalism in the 1950s.
5. Arguably, the eulogistic chants of India being an "economic power" or even an "emerging super-power" notwithstanding, she is actually just a "business destination" for the developed nations to rake profit from. It is the lure of profit that causes the developed world to lip enchanting adulations over India's supposed "success story".
6. Of course, China too faces numerous problems. But it is in control and is prepared to keep it that way, notwithstanding from some China-watcher's wishful predictions of a gathering trouble.
7. All this while, the vast belt of territory starting from Manchuria in the North, and covering what are called Inner Mongolia, Quinghai, Gansu, Xinjiang and Tibet regions in the West, had enjoyed freedom or subjugation – at varying degrees – at one time or the other. It was only during the early Manchu rule that the map of the empire appeared to be somewhat close to what China controls today, or lays claim upon.
8. Recently, the instinctive mindset was revealed when commenting on India's 'Agni V' missile test, a Chinese mouthpiece accused India of 'entertaining visions of imposing regional hegemony', a status that was, by implication, considered to be reserved, by divine consensus, for China alone.
9. Ironically, the communist regime fully identifies with its much decried imperialist past. Thus, the communists claim the largest areas that were ever controlled, or even trod upon, by Beijing-based empires at any point of time. By this logic India could claim Pakistan, Afghanistan, Myanmar etc, the Britain may claim half the world, and every other country may claim every other's territory!

10. As political philosophers have contended, even the most powerful hegemons are conscious of a virtual 'red line' which when crossed, invites self-doom. Beijing will ignore that 'line' at its peril.
11. A static international order is nearly impossible to imagine. Besides, 'encirclement' of the Cold war era is invalid in today's world. Granting a foothold for naval replenishment does not necessarily mean that hostile acts against another country will find auto-endorsement.
12. India opted to purchase fighter aircraft from the French stable, much to consternation in the US. And that did not lead to a duel.
13. Economic and societal survival of nations that export and import energy and other minerals is so inter-wound that any major disruption in the cycle will devastate societies of both categories. The effect will be global – it will lead to a kind of global chaos.
14. We may recount three cases of Beijing's diplomatic duplicity. One, when asked as to why wasn't its territorial claims raised before the late 1950s, Zhou en Lai replied that "the time was not ripe"!; two, the volte-face on Beijing's stance on Sikkim; three, claim over all of Arunachal Pradesh and invention of the term "Outer Tibet". *Indeed,* it is hard to reconcile to a great nation indulging in such undignified tricks.
15. Instances of either versions of reactions are one, 'ignoring' the recent episode of visa denial to an officer hailing from Arunachal Pradesh and going ahead with a truncated delegation on military exchange, and two, petulant 'reconciliation' with PLA's move into Pakistan Occupied Kashmir by simply stating that the matter was 'being watched'. Conversely, 'resolve' was shown in going ahead with explorations in the South China Sea, rejecting Beijing's 'warning'.

*

August, 2013

7

China's Defence White Paper, 2013: Assertions of A 'Super-Power' in Making?

Lieutenant General Gautam Banerjee, PVSM, AVSM, YSM

Promulgations of a Super-Power

In April 2013, the People's Republic of China (PRC) released her eighth *Defence White Paper*, titled as 'The Diversified Employment of China's Armed Forces'. This exercise has been undertaken bi-annually since the early 2000s, and is in consonance with China's inexorable claim to super-power status that brings with it an expectation among the international community that the contender would want to enunciate her visions and goals for them to take note of the coming dispensation. Rise of PRC being an issue of global focus, the White Paper has been, and is being, analysed from various angles by eminent experts.

PRC's past record of dealing with the other stakeholders of the Asia and Pacific Region instils amongst the latter, considerable degree of apprehensions as to her future intents and initiatives. China's Defence White Paper is therefore a document to be studied and thoroughly analysed against regional considerations. This call is more addressed to India, a nation that has had the misfortune of being incessantly targeted by PRC, as exemplified by its policy of propping up Pakistan as her proxy to undermine the Indian nationhood, blatant nuclear proliferation, brazen territorial claims, undiplomatic gesture sometimes crouched in niceties sometimes not, and pincer movements astride the northern highlands and southern oceans that would invariably impose strategic constraints upon India.

No doubt, when viewed objectively, most of the PRC's agenda – discounting her anti-India machinations in covert as well as ominous mode – appears to be in tune with her economic compulsions. Indeed, China's inroads into Africa, Latin America, Myanmar, Indian Ocean littoral States and the Pakistan Occupied Kashmir, when shorn of background experiences of her past behaviour, seem to be justified on pure economic grounds. However, when considered in the backdrop of the compulsive *pan-Han* sense of superiority and hegemonic demands of supreme entitlements, the contents of the White Paper turn complex and forbidding. It is therefore necessary that the articulations enunciated in the White Paper be tempered with the Chinese leadership's cultural instincts before factoring these into India's policy-making inputs. There may thus be a case to briefly recall China's ruling culture before delving into the pronouncements of the White Paper.

Accordingly, it is proposed to delve into the pronouncement made in China's latest Defence White Paper in the backdrop of PRC leadership's cultural outlook. The matter has been discussed under the following Sections:

- Section 1: Cultural Dimensions of China's Statecraft;
- Section 2: PRC's Strategic Vision;
- Section 3: The Government-Party-Army Interdependency;
- Section 4: Analysis of the Pronouncements of the Defence White Paper.

SECTION 1
CULTURAL DIMENSIONS OF CHINA'S STATECRAFT

The manner of conducting statecraft and formulation of defence strategy are determined by a nation's cultural construct, particularly when it is so sublime as China's culture is. Therefore, discussion on certain aspects of her cultural inclinations would help understand the pronouncements of the Defence White Paper better.

A Sense of Superiority

China's ancient civilisation is distinguished by its elaborate record keeping of nearly six millennia and consequently, a tradition of continuity that is not seen in other civilisations of the past. It was so that the successive generations of the venerated scholar-administrators (mandarins) of imperial China continued to subscribe to the neo-Confucian state-culture that saw itself as 'superior' among the 'barbarians' all around. The exaggerated *sense of superiority* over other peoples and her presumed *right of exclusive entitlements* therefore permeated as an innate characteristic of the Chinese State. This characteristic was evident not only under the neo-*Han* rule, but also when China was ruled by dynasties of alien ethnicity –

pan-Chinese people, so to say, who, upon ascending to power, found it useful to adapt to the well-established tradition of Confucius-influenced, superior Han culture.

Notwithstanding the notion of communist equality, this complex remains at the core of the modern pan-Han psyche; if repudiated, the average Chinese finds it strange that others may not necessarily defer to his ordained status of exclusivity.

The Imperative of Peripheral Control

Territories ruled by the Chinese Empires have traditionally been categorised under two distinct parts: the '*core*' or inner areas and the '*peripheral*' or outer territories. The former is a vast landmass of ethnic Han and neo-Han homeland situated among the West-East river valleys – the Yellow, Wei, Huai, Han and Yangzi River Valleys. Over the past millennia, this core area has been the cradle of the great Han civilisation while being ruled by dynasties of Han as well as foreign ethnicity. Beyond that core area, the Manchurian Provinces, Inner Mongolia, Xinjiang, Qinghai, Tibet and parts of Gansu, Sichuan and Yunnan constitute the peripheral territories, inhabited by peoples of distinct ethnicity and culture whom the Han considered as 'barbarians'; at some points in time, Mongolia, Korea and Vietnam too had been considered as parts of the Empire.

Relationship between the core and the periphery has ever been fluctuating between two extremes. The peripheral powers – the *Huns, Kitans, Jurchens, Turks, Uyghur's, Mongols, Manchu's* and *Tibetans* – had at times accepted China's suzerainty while at other times they professed independence, even hostility, inflicting frequent attacks and devastations upon the core areas. It was so that imperial China, from the time of the *Song Empire* in the 10th century, learnt the lesson that enjoined the State to exercise firm control over these territories as an imperative for maintaining internal stability and order. Ever since, the struggle to exercise that control had engaged imperial China, till the situation stabilised somewhat in her favour during the early part of the *Qing Empire.*

That institutional memory is so deeply ingrained that successive governments of China continue to consider 'integration' of peripheral territories as a fundamental plank of stable nationhood.

Fear of Internal Instability

Riven by an unending stream of 'barbarian' attacks from the nomadic inhabitants of the peripheries, internal revolts, infighting among the contenders of throne, reign of the warlords and civil wars, breakdown of internal order has been a recurring feature in China. Besides, she has been subject to repeated invasions from Japan and European powers. All these events have been extraordinarily violent and destructive, repeatedly ravaging the society and the State. Chinese consider those catastrophes to be the main cause of weakening of the imperial China and the 'centuries of humiliation' that she was obliged to suffer during the past two centuries.

Having vowed not to permit such helplessness to displace their march towards a destined super-status, China's communist leaders are wary of slackening control over their people, even if permitting economic liberalisation to keep them satisfied and engaged. Obviously, even hints of emergence of internal chaos, whether instigated internally or from outside, are to be responded with firm clamp down – like it happened in the Tiananmen Square in 1989 and recently in Tibet. That is one principle that the PRC leadership would not compromise – their survival depends on it.

Rewarding Loyalists

Confucian ideology ordained that having to use violence was anathema to China's blue-blooded cultural superiority and a failure of noble statecraft. It was so that notwithstanding the near continuous chain of warfare imposed upon the Chinese heartland by the 'barbarians' of the northern steppes and western highlands, the Empire had been rather generous to these inimical stocks once these had submitted to the Empire's suzerainty. Indeed, it was a result of that tradition that there were times when the rulers of neighbouring ethnic nations demanded to be accorded vassal status for the lure of highly valued 'gifts' from the Empire, taking to violence if that demand was not met!

Today that tradition is manifested in PRC's solidarity with her client States, Pakistan and North Korea included, who wear their love and loyalty towards the PRC on their sleeve.

Regional Horizon

Unlike European powers, America and Japan, China has not been reckonably successful in seizing profound control over regions beyond her periphery – probably on account of her unending struggles to keep her core and peripheral territories in order. However, China's ruling establishment recognises that the present socio-economic dispensation entails that:

- Firstly, economic uplift of the people is mandatory for the Communist Party to survive;

- Secondly, path of economic progress is paved by control over outlying reservoirs of natural resources;
- Thirdly, secure access to resources comes from super-status and military strength;
- And lastly, to secure the nation's destiny, the Communist Party of China (CPC) must remain in power.

Accordingly, PRC's pressing urge to lay hands on territories beyond may be seen as a pre-requisite that she is committed to enforce.

Comments

A succession of vicious internal conflicts during the past century or so caused the aforementioned cultural instincts to remain contained within the core of Han politics. Even then, these instincts did manifest in China's past dealings with Korea, Vietnam, India and Japan. Since the 1980s, when PRC warmed up to its power potentials, the State had been restrained by its supreme leader, *Deng Xiaoping*, from showing hegemonic tendencies; the statesman had enjoined the leadership to "...observe calmly, secure our position, cope with affairs calmly, hide our capabilities, and bide our time ...". The recent events, however, indicate that the period of "bide our time" may be at its last leg.

This situation brings into focus certain indicators of the PRC's strategic vision.

SECTION 2
PRC'S STRATEGIC VISION

The manner in which a nation chooses to build up and articulate its military power is determined by its native strategic vision. It is so that in case of China, even as she transited through the periods of monarchical autarchy, a short republican regime, the *Guomindang* governance and finally its displacement by communist rule, the tradition of imperialist thinking and domineering statecraft has continued to flourish amongst the CPC leadership. As the confidence level and status of PRC grows, these instincts are apparently crystallising into an overt strategic vision of a complexion that her neighbours may have reasons to be wary of. Wisdom therefore dictates that indicators of that vision, as discussed in the following paragraphs, may be taken note of.

Integration

China's communist leadership has opted to subscribe to the imperialist urge of integrating the peripheral territories – Manchuria, Mongolia, Turkmenistan, Tibet,

Yunnan, the China Sea islands etc. – with the core of Chinese mainland. There may not be reasons to dispute that quest. However, in fulfilment of that self-ordination, they lay claim upon *any* piece of land that had *ever* been under *any* form of imperialistic control for *whatever* length of time, and then unfolding such claims at the 'opportune' moment as her 'persuasive' power grows. That such brazen ideas, if conceded, would destabilise the entire world, does not seem to matter to the 'superior' race and their sense of 'entitlements by right', even if it must be conceded that like any other state-apparatus, there are different schools of ideologists within the CPC. At the present juncture, the hawks seem to dominate.

Expansionism

Since the millennia's past, barring her relatively brief engagements with Mongolia, Korea, Indo-China, Nepal and Myanmar, China has traditionally confined its urge of 'unification' to its 'peripheral territories'. Among these incessant efforts, there were three prominent phases of the unification process: during the *Sui Dynasty* in 589 CE, the *Song Dynasty* in 960 CE and *Qing Reunification* of the 17th and 18th Centuries. However, weighed down by incessant troubles caused by wars, revolts and recurring calamities, seldom ever in her history has China found herself prepared to look beyond her northern steppes or the westerly Tibet-Turkmen plateaus to establish her control. Even *Kublai Khan's* (Yuan-Mongol Dynasty) attempts to dominate the China Sea in the 13th century and the 15th century six-voyage maritime exploits of Ming Admiral *Zhen who* did not change that focus. Presently, however, PRC has broken from her past imposition to lay claims over lands and seas well outside her peripheral territories. As a corollary, she is intent on building up her military might as it must befit a super-power, including a blue water navy.

Nationalist Surge

So far the expansionist urge had been confined amongst the hawkish policy makers who were generally not accountable to the citizens. Being excluded from the right to question, the citizenry too was non-committal in the matters of State policies. Lately, however, there has been an officially sanctioned surge of nationalist fervour among the common citizens – a fervour that may coalesce into a popular demand that the ruling regime may find difficult to control. Thus *inter alia*, the State may have to commit to expansionism even if it wants to recuse at any stage. As evidenced from the situation created by the State in Pakistan, this is a dangerous portend.

Committed Perceptions

Lastly, in the intermix of neo-Confucian, Sun Zsu-Bangfa and communist culture, the Chinese are smug in perceived perfection of their versions of 'established facts' and 'logical conclusions'. Political manoeuvres and application of military power being synonymatic to them, the contemporary CPC leadership is not averse in exerting force, or many variations of demonstration of force that they adopt, to convince the intransigent to back off from confrontation, as they did in the China Seas and recently in Tibet. Besides, it may opt to view even non-military gestures of a targeted nation as 'provocation' which may leave them 'no choice' but to launch military forces to execute what is termed as 'counter-attack', and if that attack is resisted by the victim, to launch, 'reluctantly' of course, an all-out 'counter-attack in self-defence'.

Similarly, taking liberty with interpretation of established facts, selective repudiation of international norms and reversal from past understandings are considered to be fair political strategy, to be unfolded "when time comes". Indeed, 'peace' is professed by enjoining the target country to let PRC take what she wants, while 'talks' are meant to display its 'magnanimity' in sparing some parts of the grab provided the victim shows its ready appreciation. Interactions reveal that in all seriousness, the Chinese find it strange that most subjects of their 'friendly' overtures find their naturally 'simple and straight forward' claims to be contestable. No doubt, most powers subscribe to such machinations but the communist regime beats them by her sheer arrogance.

Comments

Having discussed the state as well as strategic culture of the PRC leadership, it may be worthwhile to discuss the status of the People's Liberation Army (PLA) in the overall objectives of the State. The necessity emerges due to the fact that under the Chinese dispensation, the State, the Party and its military institution are so inseparably integrated that for comprehensive examination of the Defence White Paper, it would be obligatory to look at what the CCP expects of the PLA.

SECTION 3
THE GOVERNMENT-CCP-PLA INTERDEPENDENCY

Rarely, if ever, one comes across examples of a modern, powerful State in which the government-military integration is so intimate and overbearing as it is in the PRC. Of course, that is due to the monolithic bonding between the CCP and the

PLA, wherein the PLA has ever been the CCP's *executive arm*, both in military as well as civic matters. And with the CCP and the State having become synonymic, that bondage stands sealed. Indeed, in the Chinese scheme of matters, military force is not only meant to fight a war *after* a stage when all other alternatives have failed to work, but it is also an intrinsic element of the entire politico-diplomatic process *right from the beginning* to send messages to the adversary through military postures and actions – firing missiles, concentrate troops, conducting exercises, etc., for example.

More than that, the PLA has been built up by the CCP-State as an asset that is to be unleashed to secure, by force or by enforcement, such political objectives that it has set for itself, stoically sacrificing its soldiery if that would promote the Party's cause – as it was evident in Korea, Vietnam, and even in the botched up Cultural Revolution. It is in this context that deployment of *People's Militia* in implementation of massive social, economic and engineering schemes, commitment of *People's Armed Police Force* (PAPF) in controlling revolts in peripheral provinces and modernisation of the *regular PLA* to promote the nation's sovereign 'will' have to be viewed.

Traditionally, a bonding of interdependency among the triumvirate of State-Party-PLA has been nurtured by PLA's informal right of access to top Party posts. As the following lines reveal, that situation has seen certain reckonable changes of inconsistent nature during the recent years.

Firstly, with the passing away of the iconic communist-military professionals of the Civil War era, top Party posts are no more the exclusive domain of the military brass. In fact, military representation in the CCP Politburo, its Standing Committee, even the State as well as Party Central Military Commission, is on the decline. This development is in line with the following one.

Secondly, the State having discarded the classical communist agenda in favour of economic development, the rank of die-hard communism-dedicated military brass has been succeeded by a hierarchy that is thoroughly professional by the modern standards. The contemporary military brass, while remaining communism-oriented on face, are of necessity, committed to cost-efficient management of a gigantic military establishment and its numerous military and civil mandates. That is an exacting task by itself, rendered furthermore complex when the PLA's committal to sweeping modernisation is factored in. Expectedly, their role in Party responsibilities may be singular no more, nor may they have the time or opportunity to be the exclusive 'pillars' of the Party in future. There is therefore a hint of the lord-serf kind of communist-soldier bondage turning into formal civil-military relationship.

Thirdly, survival of the regime – which is communist in form – being the primary agenda, the CCP leadership may have reasons to be wary of the new generation PLA's readiness to blindly submit to its ordinations. Since by practice communist regimes ride on their military institution, the military's reluctance to intervene in favour of such regimes – in Romania and Russia for example – may have made the CCP leaders uneasy. Evidently, the alarm had been palpable when seen in light of widespread dissatisfaction, even protest, among the PLA officers before and after the Tiananmen Square crackdown. It may therefore be envisaged that in tune with global tendencies, the Party may not continue to take PLA for granted – like a sheep to provide wool when alive and meat when dead.

As the society flowers, display of ideas and actions outside the Party Line would not remain confined to what today is called as 'dissidence'. CCP therefore would do everything to keep a firm grip on the PLA. One mean to do so would be to accommodate PLA top brass in the policy-making bodies and accord due respect to PLA's concerns. The other mean is to divest the PLA of its gargantuan civil industry and its part-soldiers, and right size it into a professional military force. Indeed, this effort has been going on since the past two decades or so, but as it happens in dealing with human concerns, the process remains tentative and distracted. The first solution may strengthen the school of hawks while the second requires the PLA-Militia to be kept meaningfully committed till the PLA transforms into a purely military force. The concept of 'diversified employment' may be rooted to the second condition.

Fourthly, in contrast to the aforementioned trend, the State-CCP continues to be dependent on the PLA, one, to attain global super-status, two, to maintain internal stability, and three, to progress civic-economic developmental schemes. In fact, execution of projects and implementation of schemes under military norms of conduct is found to be preferable in distant underdeveloped areas, to keep to fast-track schedule, limit corruption and foster accountability. This preference manifests in the practice of enrolling project-dedicated professionals and technical experts into the PLA-People's Militia and subject the project-implementation to an overarch of military law. Indeed, PLA appears to be the lead institution in giving shape to the CCP's national vision, at least till parallel civil institutions are firmly in place. No doubt, civilian institutions are being built up and strengthened to implement all aspects of State policies, but the time when the military will confine itself to what it is supposed to – just train, and fight when necessary – is yet a long way off. It is in this context that the pivotal role of the PLA and the People's Militia under the stewardship of regular officers comes to prominence.

In the overall context, the Government-CCP-PLA matrix seems to be in a flux. Consequently, international observers, particularly those of the wary neighbourhood, are concerned as to the military charter of the emerging super-power. The PRC recognises that concern and as it behoves an emerging super-power, assuages the stake-holders through open dissemination of the State's mandate to the PLA. The Defence White Paper is a demonstrative expression of that mandate.

SECTION 4
ANALYSIS OF THE PRONOUNCEMENTS OF THE DEFENCE WHITE PAPER

Honed over thousands of years of statecraft, messages of the Chinese State, to be comprehensively understood, have to be factored with its postures, gestures, timings and linguistic synonyms. The Defence White Paper therefore may be better dissected in the backdrop of the cultural and strategic dimensions of China's policy formulations, and tempered with the CCP-PLA linkage which must have played a part in its articulations. Having discussed that backdrop, the stage is set to evaluate the pronouncements of the Defence White Paper.

Notably, the White Paper specifies the PLA, PAPF and the People's Militia as distinct entities, 'armed forces' being the combined terminology to refer to these. Obviously, the PLA Army (PLAA), PLA Navy (PLAN), PLA Air Force (PLAAF) and PLA Second Artillery Force (PLASAF) are clubbed under the nomenclature of PLA.

The Title

The White Paper is titled as 'The Diversified Employment of China's Armed Forces'. Indeed, given the Government-CCP-PLA interdependency, the title needs no revelations, except that the armed forces may be expected to play greater role in implementation of the concept of 'integration through stability and development' in the troubled regions of Tibet and Xinjiang. It could also point to the role to be played by the PLA Navy in gaining incremental grab of over the thirty odd islands in the China Sea which PRC considers to be in the 'hands of foreigners' (sic), besides helping out with exploration in her claimed expanse of continental shelf and making sure that her overseas investments are not tampered with.

The Preface

In the Preface, apart from 'diversified' employment of China's armed forces to ensure 'security guarantee', assistance in national development and contribution to 'world peace' and 'regional stability', the White Paper professes the following intents:

- Reiteration of PRC's strategic choice of 'peaceful development' and a 'defence policy that is defensive in nature';
- Repudiation of hegemonism and military expansion, and pursuit of comprehensive, common and cooperative security through mutual trust, benefit, equality etc.;
- Buildup of powerful armed forces in conformity to China's status, security needs and development interests.

The White Paper then goes on to elaborate upon the matters aforementioned in five parts. These elaborations and comments thereof are discussed in the following paragraphs.

Part I: New Situation, New Challenges and New Missions

This part points to 'increasing hegemonism' and emergence of complicated security challenges. Interestingly, it complains of 'some neighbouring countries' of forging military alliances to 'make trouble' against China's territorial sovereignty and maritime rights. Mention in passing has also been made of the threats posed by 'three forces, namely, terrorism, separatism and extremism', existence of security risks to China's overseas interests and an international competition to gain 'strategic superiorities' in outer space and cyber space.

Needless to state, at the first instance, this part of the narrative appears to be mindboggling in its hypocrisy and conforms to the innate characteristics of the Chinese State, as discussed earlier Sections. At the same time, it raises hope that unlike other super-powers of the past and the present one, China will actually rise to that status peacefully, without having to de-stabilise the neighbourhood.

The narration then moves to China's 'dramatically' growing national strength 'to safeguard her national unification, territorial integrity and development interests'. This description is covered under four headings, as follows:

- *One*, a broad vision of China's 'national security strategy and military strategy' is enunciated, which aims at '*winning local wars* under the conditions of informationisation, joint employment of all Services and arms and *active* planning for the use of armed forces in *peacetime* to deal effectively with various *security threats*' (sic);

- *Two*, a firm resolve to is expressed to 'unswervingly' implement the strategy of 'active defence', prevent aggression, contain *separatist* forces, safeguard border, coastal and territorial air security, protect national maritime, outer space and cyber space rights and interests;
- *Three*, mention is made of enhancing the quality of national defence 'mobilisation' and 'reserve' force building';
- *Four*, 'diversified' employment of China's armed forces to support the country's 'peaceful development' through 'integrated civilian-military' schemes, is touched upon.

The description is signed off with a statement, "*We will not attack unless we are attacked; but we will surely counterattack if attacked*"!

At the end of this part, the State-CCP's dependence on the PLA as the lead institution to push economic interests and development in outlying regions is asserted. Besides, commitment of China's armed forces in disaster relief, security of her overseas interests, 'merchant vessel protection' (the term may be an innocent version of 'Sea Lines of Communication'), and UN-mandated coalition operations, including joint training, to foster world peace is reiterated. These commitments are to be undertaken in conformity to 'universally recognised norms of international relations', to ensure 'legitimacy of operations involving foreign countries and militaries' (sic).

Comments

To the target readership of the White Paper, this part is most significant. The matters to take cognizance of are as follows:

- The narration confirms the regime's deep seated fear of *internal instability*. However, the CCP may reconcile to the fact that the remedy may be in her, not the outsider's, hands;
- The moot point to ponder is as to what threat to her security, territory, rights etc. might China envisage, and why, and in what manner; whose *aggression* does she intend to *win* against in a *local war* by her strategy of *active defence* which calls for *national mobilisation* and deployment of *reserves* over and above the world's largest armed forces? Of course, it must be conceded that every sovereign country enjoys the right to build up its military institution in the manner desired, but surely, that build up may not rob the neighbourhood of their joy;

- The brave pronouncement of "*...will surely counter-attack...*" may also be aimed at China's reputation of engaging with superior powers regardless, and so foster a psychological deterrence to 'self-deter' the chosen adversary(s).
- As for the PRC's pronouncements regarding its global commitments, these are understandable matters in light of China's super-power aspirations. Hopefully, unlike the preceding insinuations, these pronouncements may not chill the neighbour's spine if the PRC leadership desists from their habit of professing their unique interpretations of the universally recognised norms.

Viewed in light of her past behavior with those nations who do not subscribe to subservience to China's bidding, the narration in this part may be forbidding.

Part II: Building and Development of China's Armed Forces

This part of the Defence White Paper lists out the broad features of the current organisation of the armed forces of the PRC which includes the People' Armed Police Force (PAPF) and the 'People's Militia'. These details, and much more, are already known to the strategic community. Indeed, evaluation of the defence force-structure of PRC is a separate exercise in itself. Therefore, in the present instance, it may suffice just to underline some of the organisational aspects which find PRC's formal acknowledgement through this White Paper. These aspects are:

- Commitment to build an 'informationised military force structure' and new types of lean, joint, multi-functional and efficient combat forces, obviously with Chinese characteristics;
- The 850,000 strong PLA Army (PLAA) stands organised into seven Military Area Commands (MACs), with 18 Combined Corps, additional independent formations and reoriented from theater defence to trans-theater mobility;
- The 235,000 strong PLA Navy (PLAN) stands committed to maintaining PRC's sovereignty over its territorial seas along with its maritime rights and interests. Towards this end, the endeavor is to accelerate its modernisation to develop blue-water capabilities, that would impart capabilities of strategic deterrence and counterattack;
- The PLA Air Force (PLAAF) consists of 398,000 officers and men who form part of one 'air command' integrated with each of the seven Military Area Commands. PLAAF focuses on reconnaissance and early warning,

air strike, air and missile defence, and strategic projection capabilities;

- The PLA Second Artillery Force (PLASAF) forms the core of China's strategic deterrence. Capable of carrying out nuclear counterattacks and precision strikes with conventional missiles, its purpose is to deter other countries from using nuclear weapons against China;
- The People's Armed Police Force (PAPF) deals with emergencies, combating terrorism and participating in and supporting national economic development;
- The Militia is a backup force of the PLA. It is structured to undertake support role in joint air defence, intelligence, reconnaissance, engineering, communications, transportation and equipment repair, as well as to provide reserve units for combat, logistics and equipment support. At usual times, it engages in socialist modernisation drive, maintenance of social order and emergency rescue and disaster relief operations.

Comments

This part alludes to PLA's success in breaking free of its ideological burden of 'protracted people's war' with mass armies. Initiated by China's military thinkers, this was a process that commenced in 1960s but was soon diverted from its course by the domineering 'Long March' leadership. The thinkers could find their feet again only in the aftermath of their Vietnam experience, and then the theoretical inquisition began. The new military doctrine was finally adopted after the jolt the Chinese strategic community suffered when they realised in the wake of the Gulf War in 1991 as to how incapable the PLA was in relation to its strategic goals and how inferior it was terms of modern war-fighting capabilities.

Though the topic is beyond the scope of this paper, it would be in order to mention the key doctrinal parameters that the PLA has adopted. PLA accedes to the fact that it will have to fight a superior enemy (unmistakingly, the United States) and the theatre ('War Zone') could be the China Sea (*localised*). Thus motivated by its proven military wisdom, PLA aims to gain early initiative in fighting off a technologically superior force in a fast, short and intense war (*active defence*) as far *forward* as possible. In that, PLA intends to deploy lean, modern, and highly trained 'packet of excellence' formations in conjunction with 'information warfare' enabled (*informationised*) forces (*Chinese characteristics,* to wit) to exploit the vulnerabilities of high-technology dependent adversary and thus create an asymmetrical advantage. Knowing themselves to be nowhere near catching up with the sole competitor, Chinese strategists bank on missile units to find some sort of parity in *localised* exchange. Finally, it is implicit that even if catching up with the United States military remains a long way off, the PLA has already become a military power of disproportionate capabilities in the Asia-Pacific neighbourhood.

The resolve to structure a lean, highly professional and efficient PLA, commitment of PLAP in fostering internal stability and the Militia's role in infrastructural development are also reiterated in this part. New nomenclatures used to define the higher defence organisation and field formations are noteworthy.

Part III: Defending National Sovereignty, Security and Territorial Integrity

This is a rhetorical part. It calls upon PRC's armed forces to defend China's land borders and sea areas against 'foreign invasions, encroachments, provocations'. Towards that end, pronouncements are made regarding recourse to 'resolute nuclear counter-attack' if China 'comes under nuclear threat' (sic). The importance attached to inter-Military Area Command training and exercises, the fulcrum of PLA's current doctrine, is also highlighted.

Comments

Notably, the rhetoric gives rise to two considerations. These are:

- The rhetoric is directed, not just at the PLA, but also the PAPF and the Militia, all combined being referred to as the 'armed forces'. May be, like the PLAN and PLAAF, PAPF and the Militia are also coming of age. This development could be in tune with the new relationship between the CCP and the PLA, as discussed in Section 3 above;
- Viewed in the backdrop of recent statements made in various forums, the narration may be a reiteration of PRC's stance that it would not give up its territorial claims while expecting that the victims would stay away from seeking protection by 'ganging up'. Thus, the claims must be resolved peacefully – in favour of China, of course.
- There have been some discussions on the White Paper not reiterating China's commitment to the principles of nuclear 'no first use' and 'no use against non-nuclear adversary'. This is significant. However, with the PRC's propensity of interpreting situations in its own unique way, this omission does not really matter. A target may always be pronounced as 'own territory occupied by playing tricks by villainous forces', and an 'attack' may always be invented to 'justify' launch of 'resolute counter-attacks'.

The experience so far is that the excellence of Chinese statecraft would ensure that PRC does what it intends to do. Elements of doubt over that excellence, however, emerge when considered that, firstly, by her nuclear proliferation, China has undermined her own status, and secondly, by her brusque mannerisms, she is driving the lesser powers to seek protection in alliances.

Part IV: Supporting National Economic and Social Development

As the heading suggests, this part elaborates upon the armed force's 'subordination to national reform and development'. This role is to be achieved through 'participation in infrastructure projects, ecological-environment conservation, new socialist rural area development, and by taking solid steps to support poverty-alleviation initiatives, give financial aid to education and provide medical service support' (sic). Citing notable examples, the armed forces are enjoined to *participate* in national development, emergency rescue and disaster relief and to *protect* national development interests, while being mandated to *maintain* social harmony and stability according to law.

The narration then proceeds to allude to the new law, promulgated in 2009, which mandates the PAPF with 'maintaining social stability' against emergencies and 'counter-terrorism', besides reiterating the PLA's mandate of safeguarding maritime rights and overseas interests.

Comments

The narration in this part is in tune with the cultural backdrop as discussed in earlier Sections. The reckonable inferences are:

- One, the State's dependence on the armed forces in governance over peripheral regions, already an established communist practice, has substantially increased. With the armed forces subordinated to 'maintenance of social stability', that is actually a political role, the dependence seems to be complete. This express dependency may be on account of an urgency to integrate the separatist influenced regions through development, and absence of effective civil institutions to secure that end;
- 'Counter-terrorism' referred to is the PRC's description of violent expression of ethnic or cultural dissidence among the non-Han people; there is nothing more to it;
- The purported 'safeguard of maritime rights' may be nuanced with, firstly, identifying with territorial claims, and secondly, muscle-flexing to usurp

control over these;
- Having acquired vast overseas ventures, it is natural that the intent of protecting these, particularly in the event of the host States turning hostile, must be made clear. Further, it may be inferred that in so doing, those international obligations which may be in consonance would be fulfilled.

This part shows that China is yet far from her goal of global super-status and that her civil institutions are but nascent, contrary to the hallmarks of that status. It also indicates that she intends to march on resolutely – she will.

Part V: Safeguarding World Peace and Regional Stability

Citing an impressive list of its participation in global military peacekeeping, disaster relief and medical assistance, this part conveys PRC's resolve to use its armed forces to 'staunchly' uphold world peace and regional stability. It declares its intent to participate in regional and international security affairs, including safeguarding the sea lines of communications, and play an active role in international political and security fields. Towards this end it seeks, by means of joint training, to increase cooperation and mutual trust with the armed forces of other countries.

Comments

The narrative of this part is in consonance with China's out-reach to global super-power status and the expectations that status generates among the comity of nations.

Overall Impression

The White Paper is the latest elaboration of the 'Historic Missions' of the PLA as it was spelt out by the President of PRC and Chairman of CCP and CMC in December 2004. The mission was enunciated as follows:

- To perform the role of an 'important force' in safeguarding the Party's 'ruling' position;
- To 'guarantee' the safeguard of the period of 'strategic opportunities' for national development;
- To provide 'strategic support' in safeguarding national interests;
- To play role in upholding world peace and 'mutual development'.

Issuance of the Defence White Paper is an act of grace, so to say, for a great country that must emerge as a global power soon on the strength of its vision, capabilities and resources. Looking at it in isolation from the doings of the past seven decades of communist rule, it is a document that could assure the lesser powers in the neighbourhood of China's noble intent, letting them chart their destiny in the manner they may choose to. Perceptible experiences of PRC's external policies, however, cast a shadow upon such hopes. After all, it is difficult to reconcile with that State's institutional practice of propagating lies and misrepresentations crouched in abusive language, export of violent rebellion, territorial aggression, illegal nuclear proliferation, etc. – the list of outrages is long.

Even as PRC's climb to super-status is leveling out, there is no easing out of the arrogance and mal-intent, as exemplified by announcements of outlandish territorial claims, acts of brazen diplomacy and intermittent needling to show as to who is the 'boss'. It seems that the Chinese leadership is on a mission to seek retribution from the neighbouring countries against what inimical acts that China's past tormentors had inflicted upon her.

It is certain that China's deeply ingrained wisdom would tell her leadership that causing alarm among the middle rung powers in the Asia and Pacific Region may not be the best way to stardom. Tormentors do not make super-powers.

*

November, 2016

8

Realising the 'Make Defence Equipment in India' Dream by First Nurturing: In-house Human Resources

Lalit Joshi

Introduction

The Defence Procurement Procedure (DPP) 2016 was unveiled by the Ministry of Defence (MoD) in March this year incorporating most of the recommendations of the Committee of Experts (CoE) constituted by MoD for 'Amendment to DPP-2013 Including Formulation of Policy Framework'. Efforts to indigenise defence procurement have been made by the MoD for more than two decades now but have yielded limited benefits as echoed in India's enormous defence import budget. The preceding DPPs issued since 2002 are testimony to the fact that mere issue of a new DPP cannot guarantee success. India still imports 70 percent of its arms requirement and has the dubious distinction of being the World's top arms importer (SIPRI report, 2015).

DPP 2016 is distinct in one important aspect from earlier versions wherein continuity of tenure and nurturing of human resources have been emphasised for the first time in the Project Management Units (PMU). An earnest implementation of this suggestion across the Acquisition process will be a game changer for achieving the 'Make Defence Equipment in India (MDEI)' program and will require laying out a detailed roadmap and action plan. In absence of a definite strategy, the proposal to consolidate the knowledge of human resources may remain in paper, severely impacting success of MDEI program. While sufficient energy and resources have been expended to constantly revise the DPP and generate expediency, transparency and probity in defence procurement, the subject of dealing effectively with lack of insufficient domain knowledge of personnel involved in procurement process has not been addressed. This paper attempts to deal with the issue.

In his paper, 'Operationalising DPP 2013', Air Vice Marshal Manmohan Bahadur has said,

> There is a major issue of non-availability of resident expertise in the acquisition process amongst the designated personnel, both civil and military. In the military there is no systematic cadre management of such human resource, thus, more often than not, an officer gets posted to the acquisition branch from any place, may be from a field area, without knowing anything about the intricacies of procurement. A similar situation is prevalent in the MoD, where inter-ministerial transfers are governed by career progression imperatives rather than by the yardstick of domain expertise.[1]

Given that the provision of logistics support for our armed forces typically represents well in excess of 50 percent of the defence budget, the relative absence of skilled human resources in defence procurement ruefully highlights the lack of Human Resources Development (HRD) culture in the country. Will DPP 2016 achieve self-reliance in the defence sector by improving the defence acquisition process? Well it can, if the available skilled human resources are reorganised and the execution of task of consolidation of human skills in defence procurement which has not yet begun in earnest is given highest priority.

What can be done differently by the Government this time to achieve the aim of DPP 2016? This paper attempts to present a framework for realising indigenisation by reorganising, redirecting and rationalising the existing trained and motivated human resources in the defence Services and MoD without raising any new establishments. The paper draws wisdom, expertise and contents heavily from the CoE report and DPP 2016. What has been added is a practicing defence logistician's perspective and suggestions that will enable actual implementation of the intentions of the committee and DPP 2016 for realising the MDEI program. To begin, let us dwell into the aim of DPP and the MDEI framework as elucidated in DPP 2016 and CoE report to understand the magnitude and complexity of task envisaged for the Human Resources (HR) involved in the process.

Aim of DPP 2016

The primary aim of DPP is to provide requisite defence materiel to the armed forces in the desired quantities in the desired time frame to enable them to perform their tasks efficiently. However, it must also pursue the long-term goals of self-reliance in design, development and production of equipment required for defence to provide strategic depth. The procedure should embody the key ingredients of a fair, transparent, efficient and accountable system. It should build and foster trust among its constituents.[2]

A MDEI policy for the defence sector should ideally aim to reverse the current imbalance between the import of defence materiel and its indigenous manufacture without adversely affecting the requirements, capability and preparedness of the user. Since all the indigenous capacity cannot be built overnight, a graduated approach needs to be taken starting with a conscious shift in favour of the Make in India category and significant increase in the indigenous content. At the same time, to ensure that 'Make in India' concept does not become just 'assemble in India', it is necessary to develop the capability for design and development and capacities for manufacturing, as well as the ability to service, maintain and upgrade a given system.

The unequivocal emphasis placed by the Government on 'Make in India' concept, brings the defence sector at the cusp of an unprecedented opportunity for the Indian defence industry and the international players in the field. India's rise as an economic power, her requirements of defence preparedness and her vibrant industrial base together have the potential to convert the MDEI program into a reality with its spin-off in other sectors as well. The responsibility to enable and strengthen this process and help create an eco-system where design, research and development (R&D), manufacturing, maintenance, upgrade and export capabilities thrive, lies on the shoulders of HR under MoD. However, it must be noted that the military and civil acquisition cultures are different as they are associated with non-profit and profit-related objectives respectively that represent a significant management challenge to balance. A successful resolution of this conflict is the key to indigenisation and delivery of logistics support over the many decades after the platform or equipment has been successfully introduced into service.

Critical Tasks Envisaged under DPP 2016 and CoE Report

The DPP has a clear objective to create conditions conducive for the private industry to take an active role in MDEI program, to enhance the potential of Micro, Small and Medium Enterprises (MSMEs) in indigenisation and broaden the defence R&D base of the country. It goes into details to the extent of outlining processes for setting up of test facilities for qualification of defence equipment (in the interim recommending use of Test facilities of Quality Assurance (QA) organisations and the Defence Research and Development Organisation (DRDO) by private industry), user trial evaluation for equipment and systems developed by private industry, incentives for the private defence industry for enhancing R&D spend and exports promotion and skill development at all levels.

Single-Window Approval for Vendors. One of the problems faced by the private industry, particularly the MSMEs, is the absence of a one-stop shop for information and facilitation in MoD. The creation of industry facilitation desk will give the prospective participants adequate support to review and enhance their capabilities in areas of their competence, if necessary by forging collaborations with foreign Original Equipment Manufacturers (OEMs). The 'single-window system' will help the aspiring vendors in clearance of project proposals to meet the regulatory and compliance requirements. This would be done by maintaining two-way communications with private industry through regular interaction, information exchange and facilitation in areas of licensing, test facilities and discharge of offsets. A routine matter like delay in payment for invoices rendered can become an extremely frustrating exercise and can be particularly debilitating for MSMEs.

Facilitating Use of Trial Venues of Defence Services. The area of field evaluation trials has been identified as one of the most critical delay factors in the acquisition chain in DPP 2016. At present, Services and DRDO have complete control on the trial avenues with no obligation to private industry. Formal procedure and processes need to be put in place to facilitate the private industry in this respect, on payment basis. A vibrant Defence Industrial Base (DIB) must necessarily include large, medium and small scale industry enabling utilisation as well as consolidation of the national manufacturing base. Fostering a constructive, long term partnership is a strategic imperative to minimise dependence on foreign vendors. Larger and sustained production volume of any system leads to optimisation of cost as well as improved production efficiency. The MoD departments or any integrator for that matter must work together to achieve the MDEI objective.

Vendor Selection. Transparent selection procedures would be set in place for selecting strategic and development partners. Participating industrial entities thereafter need to be integrated into a system which requires long-term relationships (defence materiel life span can last 30 to 40 years) for maintenance, repair, overhaul, product support, upgrades and follow-on purchases. A robust vendor rating system needs to be put in place and frequent changes in vendors discouraged since the order quantities are limited and there being only one buyer, the induction of a new vendor in an established supply chain can only be done at the cost of the one already within it. Time is also expended in certifying new vendors and undertaking quality checks of their products.

Accessibility of Acquisition Departments in High-Security Zones. The CoE highlighted another genuine difficulty of the industry in accessing the various offices in MoD, being located in a defence security zone. Personnel in the organisation work cheek and jowl with colleagues who deal with very sensitive matters and the mindset is one of secrecy and great caution. This 'sense' percolates to the procurement personnel who are wary of meeting with people 'outside the system'. A change in the location where vendors don't feel harassed to obtain security clearance to interact with officials will send a clear message about the government's honest intentions as well as actions to implement MDEI program. The vendors are least enthused to visit even lower formations and units due to high-handed attitude displayed at the gates for security checks. There is a requirement to sensitise governance to such an extent that vendors feel welcome and not dependent upon its largesse. After all it's a mutually beneficial contract, business and partnership. This is not to say that security procedures and probity would be given the goby.

Data Sharing. The scope and magnitude of tasks envisaged under the DPP is vast and complex. The Indian private industry's participation in defence sector is in its early stages and it needs time to understand, assess, make a suitable business case and respond to meet the specific capability requirement of the Services. It is therefore considered essential that the requirements of specific equipment, system and platforms or their upgrades are shared with the industry at stages of preparation of the Technology Perspective Capability Roadmap (TPCR), development of Services Qualitative Requirements (SQRs) and fielding the five-year Services Capital Acquisition Plans (SCAP). The private sector has to be accorded a level playing field and a data centre must be established under the aegis of 'digital India' manned by dedicated and responsible staff. Such a data centre would cater to the needs of all the stakeholders and provide a digital meeting place which by itself is a herculean task but needs to be attended to expeditiously. The procurement procedure must reduce bottlenecks and time lines. Data on concepts such as Life Cycle Costing (LCC) and Performance Based Logistics (PBL), under which the OEM is paid to provide an outcome such as the operational availability of a particular platform or piece of equipment, need to be shared.

A Case for Formation of an Acquisition Department (AD) for Defence Procurement in MoD

One primary impediment to implementation of DPP in the past has been deficiency in domain knowledge of personnel dealing in defence procurement. It is a truism that the officials, whether they are in MoD or in Services HQ, are not trained to deal with the intricacies of defence procurement. Their expertise is built only through their own adaptability in related appointments.[3]

In the existing system, the personnel learn the nuances of defence procurement on the job after being posted there. The postings are generally for a period of three to four years and thereafter a replacement is posted in who may also be alien to the procurement procedures at the center. The learning and experience gained by the outgoing person gets dissipated immediately as he is mostly sent to perform an entirely different task. Frequent rotation of personnel causes frequent snapping of links and inadequate maintenance of historical database leading to difficulty in benchmarking of costs that is vital for procurement of equipment. Due to lack of continuity, policies and guidelines are being regularly altered on the basis of individual assessments of the nation's need for armed forces.[4] The procurement projects also keep getting varying degree of importance that ultimately causes either delays or a dead end. We have right people available but their placement has been flawed.

Therefore, it is recommended that the organisation provides opportunity to manpower gaining experience and interest in procurement departments to continue working there and not dissipate this advantage to meet other perceived and superficial requirements of tenure and rank-based posting policies. A competent team will gain in confidence. Once a base is created, the many tasks envisaged under DPP 2016, like applying single-window clearance concepts in defence procurement, can begin. The knowledgeable team will effectively handle the OEM and industry bodies by virtue of domain knowledge resulting in transparency and probity in defence procurement.

In the USA, through a 'Congress Mandate', the government maintains a base level of 1,45,000 skilled work force for dealing with the defence deals, and the UK has 6000 personnel trained for procurement. In the absence of an exclusive defence acquisition organisation in India, a number of committees on acquisition reforms as well as the CoE have recommended establishment of similar procurement organisations. However, in the Indian context, even permanency in postings policy has not been successful as experienced from the performance of the DRDO, Defence Public Sector Units (DPSUs) and the Armed Forces Civilian Employees (AFCE) who number over 12,000 under the office of the Joint Secretary (E/CAO), MoD.

A beginning has been made to address the personnel management issues in DPP 2016 wherein MoD has to establish Project Management Units (PMU) that will be headed by two star rank officers or equivalent and staffed appropriately with professionals having adequate knowledge and experience on projects under 'Make' procedure. The Head, under each service headquarter, will have a tenure of three years and the staff positioned in PMUs shall have longer tenures to ensure continuity during execution of projects. The PMUs can also hire expert practitioners from domains such as finance, legal and technology, from public and private sectors. This is the most radical step taken by the Government wherein availability and need for consolidation of in-house expertise has been acknowledged and that should lead to formation of an Acquisition Department in the process. To overcome the skill deficit, the CoE also made recommendations for setting up a defence manufacturing sector skill council, initiating a joint MoD and industry-sponsored internship programme, a university programme for military engineering, skill development through the offset route and setting up of tool rooms around defence industry clusters for India.

The constitution of the Defence Acquisition Wing and decision-making Boards which resulted out of earlier DPP revisions reflected a deep desire to bring about greater synergy in procurement but have been unable to reduce imports by India. Even the CoE's belief that greater integration of Services within the MoD has taken place after the series of initiatives taken as a result of the recommendations of the Group of Ministers in 2002 is factually an overassessment. The best and oldest democracies in the world have retained firm civilian control over their armed forces not by isolating them but by integrating them within the central edifice of government and involving them in national security decision-making process. The feedback from the Services and industry reflects that the overall procurement process from request for proposal (RFP) to Signing of Contract is still very prolonged, owing to impediments attributable to delays in technical and field evaluation, resolution of complaints and rigidity of adherence to SQRs. The process delays deprive the Services from acquiring the envisaged capability as per schedule and also enhance the risk to the industry in terms of cost of maintaining idle capacity and manpower. On the positive side, the industry remains very enthusiastic about their participation in defence sector given the preferred categorisation in favour of 'Buy (Indian) and Buy & Make (Indian)'.

The AD may establish an Integrated Acquisition Management (IAM) model that involves taking a holistic systems approach of equipment management from "womb to tomb". IAM includes integration at the inter-services and national level. IAM guides in developing material and a support strategy that optimises functional support, leverages existing resources, and guides the system engineering process to quantify and lower life cycle cost and decrease the logistics foot prints, making the system easier to support.

The statement made by General V P Malik during Kargil war that *"we will fight with whatever we have"* summarises the logistics preparedness and extent of IAM existing in our armed forces. In absence of IAM, in a case, Oxygen-cum-Communication Masks worn below the helmet by the pilots of the Air Force and Army Aviation were procured independently by the two Services. The Army procured the Mask ex-import at four times the cost at which it was procured by the Air Force indigenously. Similarly, Sniper Rifle for Special Forces was obtained by the Army and Air Force independently, which resulted in avoidable excess expenditure.[5] In 2003, the Army took almost a year to evaluate Underwater Diving Equipment while the same had been acquired by the Navy much earlier in 1999.[6] Such dichotomies are a result of lack of a central authority that coordinates the activities of various entities making up an acquisition and supply network leading to a situation whereby each is responsible for arranging and managing a contract in isolation.

Only a dedicated, empowered and exclusive Acquisition Department can understand the nuances of procurement process in Defence as highlighted in the preceding paragraphs. However, the establishment of a new framework for Acquisition Department as recommended by the CoE may take long time and efforts and success still may remain elusive. In the Indian work culture context, it is considered that creation of a new specialised Defence Acquisition structure in MoD may not give desirable benefits and we may end up with creating another setup for parking additional idle HR. A study of existing structures in other countries would be certainly beneficial, but we will have to design our own distinctive AD organisation by reconfiguring the existing human resources through an internal mechanism. When the AD is staffed with experienced and willing people available in-house, the organisation will be bestowed with the benefits of experience gained by them during line function.

We do have formal institutions of training for workforce at induction level and throughout their career, which have trained people with requisite skills in diverse fields of technology, trial procedures, commercial negotiations and legal issues in contractual matters, estimation of costs, financing structures, project management and data analysis. But frequent rotation of personnel in Departments of MoD disrupts continuity and communications required for nurturing specialisation in procurement. What is required is an empowered and skilled HR group that would take informed decisions. In the existing setup, a temporary executive doesn't feel comfortable to even take decisions on even minor deviations from SQRs at technical or field evaluation stages, thus setting the acquisition clock back by many years. This leads to an oft repeated criticism that such entities work in their own silos, leading to conflicts and delays. In absence of continuity of personnel in acquisition departments in MoD, many decisions have at times adversely impacted defence procurement. Last year, the MoD had to retract one of its orders on revision of financial powers when the procurement became extremely difficult even for routine supplies. According to MoD spokesperson, "This was required in view of the demand of the Services for restoring inherent powers since it was creating problems in their day-to-day functioning and showing up in low expenditure trend."[7]

Roadmap for Inducting Skilled Human Resources in Acquisition Department

The importance of human resources in the defence procurement has been adequately covered in the CoE report, according to which defence production process must be built on robust full spectrum capable human resources ranging from the research to the operation level. From the inputs, it is apparent that India at present does not have a structured framework and a robust system to prepare its HR to address all issues connected with building and sustaining defence systems.[8]

Actually, the impasse of non-availability of trained manpower is quite easy to fix as MoD personnel are experienced and well motivated to learn new skills. Once a person gets posted to a procurement-related appointment he/she acquires adequate on the job training and experience. What is lacking is consolidation of the domain knowledge and work experience gained in the procurement function due to posting out of staff after a limited tenure based on a rigid belief that rotation of personnel is necessary for career progression and service requirement even at the cost of the primary task for which he is employed.

The CoE has stressed on requirement of a greater convergence between the departments in MoD that can be achieved by consolidating and enhancing the existing capacities and core competencies of HR available under the Departments of Defence (DoD). The procurement executive tasked to execute MDEI, in an efficient and timely manner, must have in-house professional expertise in provisioning and procurement disciplines, comprehend complex procedures, work in harmony, and have continuity of tenure and the ability to obtain outside professional advice when needed. He should be subjected to capability assessments from time to time.

There is deficiency in core domain knowledge because no one organisation or person ever has taken a long-term ownership in MoD and the defence sector. But who is going to be responsible for taking the ownership for execution? Raksha Mantri (RM)? Yes, but thereafter who else in a frequently rotational appointments policy. Whenever a new RM takes over the ownership, he may not find a competent team to support him. By the time he gets a fair understanding of the organisation, someone else in his team may be changing places because a similar transition is happening in the lower hierarchy! There is utmost need of listing and addressing the HR issues, where the real bottlenecks and red tape occur.

To implement the suggestion, an institutional mechanism will have to be created under the top leadership to curb the home biases and turf wars. A reliable team under the RM may be formed for implementation of the new Human Resource (HR) policy to achieve the aims of DPP 2016. The Integrated Defence Staff (IDS) Headquarter (HQ) can be the nodal agency. HQ IDS is the nominated nodal agency for jointmanship in MoD which integrates policy, doctrine, war fighting and procurement. It is an institutional framework for higher defence management and functions as principal arm and secretariat to the Chiefs of Staff committee and has also been involved in discussions to simplify the acquisition process.

Sufficient organisational structure exists in the IDS but it too lacks the domain knowledge in procurement due the similar constraints of continuity, lack of attitude for collaborative functioning and authority that has stymied the implementation of DPP. A competent team when formed can establish a cell for imparting education and training in defense procurement. Similar model will have to be replicated by each service HQ for meeting their requirements. The team will be focused on directing and regulating the placement of right people for the right job. A domain knowledge qualified, confident and strong team can bring in the benefits of synergy between multiple agencies involved in defence procurement. It would be sad if we become slaves to the procedures and systems to the extent that indigenisation and DPP 2016 become casualties.

However, it must be realised that one of the causes outlined in most case studies is the pitfall in implementation process. Poor implementation has always been the bane of Indian Administration and if we are able to overcome this drawback with requisite determination and honesty of purpose, there could be a ray of hope for the Services.[9] Indians have not been found wanting in promulgating perfect policies. Very often, new policies get made the moment a new Commander is appointed but implementation has always been tardy. That's because execution is a different ball game and requires in depth understanding of policies, domain knowledge and whole hearted participation from people. Unless people are well trained and confident, even good policies will not produce the desired results.

Nurturing Human Resources for Acquisition

The existing acquisition structure involving Service HQs, Acquisition, Technical and Financial Managers all working under the Director General Acquisition where the final decision is taken in a hierarchical manner having defined roles for the Defence Secretary, RM and the Cabinet Committee on Security at the apex, is fine as on now. However, what is required is strengthening the organisations by inducting the heads in the aforesaid structure from in-house HR. Care should be taken to ensure that enough talent is nurtured in a healthy HR environment in MoD departments. This should be possible by inviting people to join the AD organisation and giving them continuity of tenures to develop domain knowledge in their field of specialisation. Availability of empowered HR can also be accomplished by organisations when they are given a measure of autonomy and flexibility to devise their own procedures for activities that would enable them to better perform their allocated functions. Both the Departments of Atomic Energy and Space have benefited immensely from such dispensations.

In place of the multiple systems that exist today, MoD may plan to standardise on a single best of each solution (best of breed) HR platform. 'Best of Breed' is the strategy of selecting the best product of each type (and integrating them yourself), rather than selecting one large integrated solution from a single vendor. A single platform that natively integrates various HR application processes and data virtually eliminates the need for manual and costly systems integration as the processes and underlying technology are pre-integrated to help in better internal and inter-departmental talent mobility, improved ability to quickly respond to changing business needs and better workforce alignment to overall strategy.

In the existing system, the people appointed for working in the acquisition directorates are put through some training as soon as they assume their appointment. The learning centers like Defence Services Staff College (DSSC),

College of Defence Management (CDM) and National Defence College (NDC) too could introduce the subject of capital acquisition in their curriculum. Each Department under MoD also has their respective Material Management Institutes, imparting exhaustive training on Acquisition process. But the knowledge and experience dissipates soon due to frequent rotation of personnel on the job. Precious time is lost in the process and the acquisition cycle gets sluggish or collapses.

The CoE expects that when Indian National Defence University (INDU) becomes functional, training and research will get requisite attention. The INDU proposal is meant to augment existing military education and provide the intellectual underpinnings for 'jointness' among the Departments of MoD and that requires new ways of thinking and building networks of trust that reach across narrow bureaucratic and service silos. The draft bill for the proposed INDU has been recently placed in the public domain. While the intent to seek comments is a good sign, the draft bill is a stark illustration of deeper infirmities in thinking about both national security and higher education.[10] Unless we focus on core issues, we are likely to get overwhelmed by peripheral issues like what kind of campus or infrastructure would it entail or who would be the president of the university or what would be the share of the MoD Departments in the organisational structure?[11]

To create an institute of national importance, the Government should invite the few who by interest and hard work develop some understanding of Acquisition process but may have been posted out as if to emphasise that expertise is a dangerous thing. INDU must make conscious efforts to learn about best practices in professional military education from other countries. Unless these steps are taken, the INDU will become another costly retirement home and another babudom masquerading as deep thinking, which would defeat the entire purpose of this endeavor.[12]

Change in Mindset

The CoE report reflects a need for mindset change in MoD to bring transparency in defence procurement process, a critical component of Defence Logistics. 'Logistics' embraces a significantly broad spectrum of acquisition, support and disposal challenges besides the storage and physical movement of material (and its associated information).[13]

It is important to understand the mindset of people who form the backbone of an organisation. In India, older and more senior people expect their juniors to show deference in body language in allowing their superiors to initiate discussions and in listening attentively without interruption or revealing any sign of impatience. Indians, among themselves, are incredibly conscious of their social status and would have fought off very stiff competition to get there.[14] These constraints, aggravated by Alice in Wonderland prioritisation, make it difficult for the Indian system to advance more than a handful of policy priorities in parallel. Risk aversion is a guiding principle. By adopting best management practices developed in the west while keeping the Indian sensibilities in mind, a beginning can be made.

Indians tolerate corrupt individuals rather than correct them and anticipate out of turn rewards.[15] The work environment in the government organisations discourages people to take initiative and just by being compliant one can continue to earn his salary and promotion due to which ownership of tasks and lack of expertise in job have become the main casualties. Due to our historical practice of the caste system that believes that all men are not equal, a stigma is attached to chores like cleaning and low-wage jobs. Focusing on HR in Defence Logistics, the committee emphasised that an environment should be built in which decisions can be taken with courage. Courageous acts are based on trust, and over the years trust has taken a beating. It is only with trust that results will be achieved. It is necessary to address the dilemma of those who are trained and prepared to take decisions in the overall interests of the defence preparedness of the country, but who would not be prepared to do so in an atmosphere vitiated by allegations of corruption wherein everyone in the hierarchy is looked at with suspicion. Measures of confidence building need to be institutionalised. The CoE underlines the need to alter the management structures of organisations under DoD, imbibing a 'hand holding and nurturing' DNA for procurement executive rather than a 'hands off' approach where meetings with industry personnel are looked upon with suspicion.

Importance of Research

The Cambridge dictionary defines research as 'a detailed study of a subject, especially in order to discover (new) information or reach a (new) understanding'. There is a requirement for all the faculties involved from existing institutions and think tanks to interact and conduct seminars regularly on Acquisition policy. Our think tanks and research institutes like Institute for Defence Studies and Analysis (IDSA), United Services Institute (USI), Centers for Air Power, Land, Maritime and Joint Studies (CAPS, CLAWS, NMF, CENJOWS) are involved in developing curriculum and undertaking case studies on policy analysis but very few researchers are working on historical and contemporary issues to improve the acquisition system. Also, most researchers have little or limited line exposure to this complex activity which limits their work.

Utilisation of Skilled Personnel Seeking Premature Release from Service into Acquisition Department

In March last year, answering a query raised in the Rajya Sabha, Defence Minister Manohar Parrikar said that the armed forces faced a shortage of over 11,000 officers. One primary reason of shortage is the fact that a large number of officers are seeking pre-mature release from the Services. For over three years now, one officer from India's defence forces has quit each day.[16]

Career growth means different things to different people. For some, promotion within the organisation means much; for others it may mean accepting a new assignment elsewhere or achieving the larger goal in life, like fulfilling family objectives. For them, career mobility is not always about moving up and they are happy with their current position and may deliberately forego promotions to meet personal needs.[17] A large number of service personnel seek premature release from the Services at a very young age to meet their family commitments that can't be fulfilled due to frequent postings to distant and difficult places and also because of its strict hierarchical and pyramidal structure. Most possess vast experience and welcome assignments of responsibility, but at their place of convenience, and excel in them. Conscious of their self-respect, they put in extra effort to ensure that no fingers are ever raised at their commitment and dedication. They bring with them tremendous knowledge and experience required by the organisation. The AD must tap and invite such people having rich experience in the acquisition process and who would like to continue in the job. Besides reducing attrition in the Services, this will encourage people to follow their interests and take advantage of the growing opportunities in the acquisition process and thus contribute meaningfully to the growth of the defence services.

Integrated Human Resources System (IHRS) for the MoD

It is fair to assume that in the acquisition process dealing with a range of diverse and complex issues the decision making must be based on performance and measurable outcomes and not on beliefs, opinions, or arbitrary preferences. In the defence services, the personnel biases are removed by virtue of well-established embedded training program and most men are motivated, knowledgeable and disciplined. The need of the hour is to ensure that these well-trained personnel are integrated with an efficient acquisition system for battle readiness and economy of effort and that can be achieved by an Integrated Acquisition and Human Resources System (IAHRS).

Skill, knowledge, abilities and experience are only useful when right man is positioned at the right place. Best of IAM practices will not be executed if HR is not competent. IHRS will look for versatile talent to groom leadership potential. It is the man behind the machine who will play the dominant role in any future battle and integrate IAM with IHRS, when he is well trained, motivated and nurtured. The concept of 'Management of Defence by Committees' has to be dropped.

The Integrated Human Resource System (IHRS) includes functions of Human Resource Management (HRM) and Human Resource Development (HRD). The HRM includes traditional functions of personnel and administration such as personnel data file, job evaluation, compensation, benefits, security, safety and health. It also has an important focus on recruitment, staffing, performance appraisal, promotions and training. The aim of HRD on the other hand is to create a climate that enables every person to discover, develop and use his or her capabilities to the fullest extent in order to further both individual and organisational goals. It includes, planning of organisational structures to respond to strategic imperatives, building of organisational culture and monitoring of personnel attitudes and developing inter personnel communication and participation of individuals in management. HRD goes much beyond the Personnel function, which is usually confined to job administration like postings. Due to changing values emphasis has shifted to trust, openness and exploration which are looked after by HRD. HRD tries to find out the strengths existing in an organisation, and then consolidates and strengthens them. HRD places premium on the dignity and the potential of the people and is the answer to problems of waning loyalty and declining commitment.

The culmination of all HRD effort is to foster a climate conducive to self-development. One of the benefits that could be expected is to get people off their defensive postures, to be less uptight and more open to criticism because they have arrived at an honest estimation of their self through introspection. Of course it doesn't mean that HRD is superior because it is proactive, and Personnel function is inferior being reactive. Both are complementary to each other. HRD's role will be to create an environment that facilitates idea generation and execution. It should harness the individual's brilliance within the organisational framework, or else he will move out to start his own venture as supported from the fact that a large number of skilled personnel are seeking premature release from the defence services.

Conclusion

A promising course of action for realising the MDEI program and 'self-reliance' in defence industry, which doesn't even require any additional spending or raising of a new establishment, has been suggested here based on the expertise and long work experience in the logistics field in defence services. The paper brings out a comprehensive road map that recommends a complete understanding of the aim and critical tasks envisaged under DPP 2016, formation of an Acquisition Department and inducting skilled and motivated human resources in the Department by first identifying, nurturing and integrating the available personnel in the MoD.

The recent policies of the Government like Make in India, Skill India and Digital India are good initiatives to create a defence industrial base that India can be proud of. However, it will require a shift in the organisational culture and reorientation to work which cannot be achieved without an empowered, skilled and confident human resources. Only an experienced, motivated and regulated team can understand and resolve the nuances of defence procurement and the much-touted offsets policy. Indigenisation can get wings when the importance of domain knowledge in acquisition process is recognised and human resources are nurtured.

NOTES

1. AVM Manmohan Bahadur, Operationalising DPP 2013.
2. Chapter 1, DPP 2016.
3. Gen N C Vij, Unravelling DPP 2013.
4. Brig Vinod Anand, in his paper, Private Sector as Partner in Attaining Self-Reliance.
5. Lt Gen (Dr) V K Saxena, DPP 2016 – An Enabler not a Show Stopper.
6. Brig Vinod Anand, Integrating the Indian Military: Retrospect and Prospect, *Journal of Defence Studies*, IDSA.
7. *The Indian Express*, 25 December 2015.
8. Para 6.4.02 of Committee of Experts Report for Amendment to DPP-2013 Including Formulation of Policy Framework.
9. Gen N C Vij, Unravelling DPP 2013.
10. Devesh Kapur and Anit Mukherjee in an article on INDU in *The Hindu*.
11. Arjun Subramanium in his article 'A place of study for India's scholar-soldiers'.
12. Kapur and Mukherjee, op. cit.
13. Defence logistics: an important research field in need of researchers; International Journal of Physical Distribution & Logistics Management, March 2013.
14. Charles Ashcroft, Air and Naval Adviser UK.
15. Live Mint article, 14 October 2016.
16. Yogesh Kumar, News Information Service, *Times of India*, 12 Aug 2015.
17. Lt Col Yogesh Nair, *USI Journal*, Vol CXL, No 582, 2010.

August, 2017

9

India Needs Structural Changes to Remove Uncertainty in National Security

Brigadier Narender Kumar

The Situation

Thucydides had said, "Peace is a temporary truce in a war that is continuously going on." India is at war since 1947 as no nation has fought so many conventional and sub-conventional conflicts post World War–II as India. Incidentally, each of these wars were different from others. Wars that were imposed on India were conventional wars (1962, 1965 & 1971), local war (Kargil), proxy war (Jammu & Kashmir, or J&K) and sub-conventional conflicts (insurgency in the North East and Left Wing Extremism, or LWE).

Being a young nation, the Indian politico-military leadership had little knowledge of science and art of war fighting, and that was acknowledged by Nehru post-1962 debacle when he said, "We made a mistake by not building military capabilities."[1] Building capability is a military science and employment of that capability is an art inherent to military leadership. Therefore, political and military leadership should be in sync with each other to identify what capabilities are required and how that capability should be leveraged to achieve national security objectives.

When the first Commander-in-Chief of the Indian Army, General Sir Rob Lockhart, went to Nehru with a formal defence paper that needed a policy directive from the Prime Minister, Nehru had exclaimed, "We don't need a defense policy. Our policy is *ahimsa* (non-violence). We foresee no military threats."[2] Nehru was convinced that India faced no threat and even if it existed it could be dealt with diplomatically and by the principles of *Panchsheel.* But the myth was exposed when India was forced to fight the first war in 1947-48 itself and then three conventional wars in a period of one decade (1962-1971). Nehru had refused to lay down a defence policy for his passive notions, but for some unknown reasons even the successive political leadership of the country refrained from spelling out a defense policy or a National Security Strategy (NSS). As a consequence, formulation of military strategy has dithered and a military doctrine continues to remain a distant reality. Whereas ratification of both these documents by the National Security Council (NSC), to build military capabilities and to guide military actions during peace and war, are essential, in the absence of these principle government policy documents, the big question remains, 'defence preparedness and capability building – for what'?

It is beyond comprehension that in spite of the number of wars India has fought and military crisis it has faced in the last seven decades, India has not put in place a functional Higher Defence Organisation (HDO) that can deal with issues of national security in a structured manner. Thus, voids exist in policy formations related to national security, capability building, defence reforms, defence planning process and robust border defence.

Credible military capabilities dictates the military actions against a given security problem. Temptation to play with luck in the matters of national security is a dangerous policy. A nation must take military recourse against a security threat, firstly, after other options are exhausted, and secondly, when it is sure that it is in a position to build up the response with speed and sustain it even if the conflict escalates to a theatre or full-spectrum war. Rushing military as first respondent when there are border defence forces in place is an unwise strategy and suggest lack of understanding of principles of war and capability building; once military is deployed, taking a step back is seen as strategic surrender, but pulling back border defence forces is not seen with the same prism.

National security needs a structured and professional approach and cannot be left to the bureaucracy at the Ministry of Defence (MoD) and part-time political heads. Major fault lines that exist in the national security system are:

- A *HDO* and its components are in place but the functioning is ad hoc with no clear agenda to deliberate and periodically review the defence preparedness and capability building. NSS and Strategic Defence and Security Review (SDSR) are basic documents that would determine as to what capabilities are required in the near or distant future. In the absence of such systematic approach, the nation has not been able to build basic threshold capabilities to deal with the local wars in the immediate near future, theatre wars in next two to five years and full spectrum wars in next 10 years.

- There is no *military advisor* integral to Prime Minister's Office (PMO), NSC, and even National Security Council Secretariat (NSCS). As a result the decisions on defence related issues are taken through inputs received from MOD which at times may not be in consonance with the Services Headquarters. As a result, the Cabinet Committee on Security (CCS) and NSC both are deprived of vital professional inputs and assessment on defence preparedness. Risk assessment on vital national security issues is conspicuous by its absence. Acquisition of weapon systems and equipment has become a tool for diplomatic engagement and that is not a good idea to build capabilities. Acquisition of 36 Rafale fighter aircrafts and weapons and equipment acquisition of approximately $10 Billion from Russia is an example of this policy.
- India has handled *short-term* threats and crisis reasonably well. What has been the biggest problem is the capability building to deal with long-term threats. The NSC has fallen short of expectations to identify the capabilities required for building threat cum capability-based force for predictable and unpredictable external and internal threats.
- National security is one of the most vital functions of the government. It needs political direction, professional inputs and regular reviews, whereas in the Indian context it is left to the military to manage with whatever budget is left over from the other priorities of the government to meet the external and internal challenges. Gen VP Malik's statement during Kargil war that "We will fight with whatever we have" is a sorry state of affairs that exist in the system even today. The French Chief of Armed Forces resigned over defence budget stating, "In the current circumstances I see myself as no longer able to guarantee the robust defense force I believe is necessary to guarantee the protection of France and the French people, today and tomorrow and to sustain the aims of our country."[3] It is not necessary for a chief to resign but professional integrity does call for transparent and frank audit of military capabilities and what the armed forces can do within the *budget constraint*. The political leadership and nation should know about the capabilities so that nation does not live on a false hope.

- *Border defence* is split between Ministry of Home Affairs (MHA) and MoD. Border management forces look at borders from police perspective whereas Line of Actual Control (LAC) and Line of Control (LC) require military approach given the sensitive nature of the unresolved border disputes. Border management forces should ideally be equipped and trained for defending the borders during war because primary objective of deployment of these forces along LAC/LC is to seize initiative from adversary if situation so warrant. Since the hierarchy of border management forces is from police, therefore the troops are neither equipped nor trained to undertake proactive actions to position itself in an advantageous position for subsequent offensive or defensive operations during hot war scenario. A mindset of peacetime responsibility is a dangerous outlook. Another glaring fault in border defence is that the command of the border management forces will be shifted from police to Army at most critical period when transition from peace to war takes place whereas the command of troops during transition from peace to war should be stable so that it does not create turbulence. But in the current system turbulence is inherent and there is uncertainty because troops will be under the command of those military leaders with whom they have neither trained nor established a bond of comrades in arm. As a matter of principle, changing the horse in mid-stream is against the principles of war. The fault does not lie with Central Armed Police Forces (CAPF) or its leadership but the fault lies with the political system that has brought this turbulence in the system due to lack of understanding of national security.
- Ministry of External Affairs (MEA) and military should be in sync with the emerging threats to national security. The current *inter-ministerial interaction* is cosmetic in nature and except occasional briefings by operational directorates, exchange of views and intimate interaction is minimal. Whereas diplomats serving in missions abroad should have intimate knowledge about the ground situation and existing military capabilities, or else how can they leverage national power to protect vital national interests. Whether one is uniformed or in civvies, greater understanding can only come when one physically interacts with the geography, and those who defend these geographical boundaries.

The Way Forward

There is a need to understand that wars are political in nature and politico-military leadership matters in preservation of national interests because ultimately that makes the difference in outcome of a war.[4] Thus there is a need to have intimate relationship between military and political leadership. This relationship cannot be indirect because military ultimately is employed by political leadership to achieve political objectives. No army can achieve political objectives without requisite military capabilities hence there is a need for a functional HDO that can assist political leadership to build military capabilities to serve the interest of the nation. The U.S. military had been completely refurbished after the debacle of Vietnam War[5] because political leadership realised that the existing structures and capabilities were inadequate to serve US interests any longer. Defence Reforms and restructuring of HDO in Indian context is long overdue. India should learn lessons from modernisation of PLA, Syrian War and Hezbollah-Israel war. Lessons from Syrian crisis is that one should deal with the problem of war when war isn't imminent.[6]

The way forward to bridge the fault lines are as under:

- HDO is an apex body responsible for the security of the nation and to guide the national security strategy. It can minimise the danger of misjudgment, miscalculation, escalation and unintended consequences in modern warfare.[7] *Review of HDO* is paramount; it requires restructuring so that decision time is reduced and the inputs received through decision support system are pragmatic and plausible. Such input can only come when HDO has professional representatives at NSC, PMO and NSCS level. There is a requirement of HDO and its components to meet regularly to preview the agenda of national security. If there is periodic review of defence preparedness by HDO, then India would not be in a state when ammunitions stocks fall dangerously[8] against the Minimum Acceptable Risk Level (MARL).
- SDSR must be carried out once in every five years and NSC should review it annually to carryout course corrections in defence planning process and prioritisation of capability building. SDSR will set the stage for capability building and draw attention of the political leadership to risks and opportunities in near future. SDSR will guide defence planning process, capability building, military strategy and doctrine. Indeed, *SDSR is one of the primary charter of NSCS* and one of the most important

document to guide the future strategies in matters related to national security.

- There should be a system of *debate on risk assessment* before adoption of a strategy that has impact on national security. It must lay down military, political and diplomatic impact before a major military posturing or manoeuvre is undertaken. Situation such as in 1962, and to some extent in Sri Lanka, can be avoided if such a system under NSCS exists; else decisions taken in a state of excited political mind are likely to cause serious reversals and could compromise national security.
- There is a need for deeper *coordination between MEA and Services Headquarters*. Indication of development of capabilities required for future challenges should come from the diplomats deployed in missions abroad. Inputs from the MEA along with that of the external intelligence agencies should be validated by the Services and projected to the NSC.
- Fragmented approach and divided command of border defence is an artificially created fault line. Current *system of border management* of unsettled borders is flawed that needs to be junked and the capabilities should be upgraded to border defence; there should be unity of command and homogeneity in training, equipment and ethos.

Prevailing international security scenario is extremely complex and vulnerabilities to the national security are no more restricted to geographical proximity nor purely military in nature. Contemporary and future wars are unrestricted in space, duration, resources and tools. Preparation for war under such scenario is the responsibility of political leadership because they have to dictate as to what capabilities are required to meet national security objectives. There is no harm in admitting that India has failed to keep pace with the security challenges it is likely to face in near future. The reasons could be political, economic or diplomatic, but one of the prime reasons is lack of strategic and military understanding by the political leadership. This has further been compounded by the fact that bureaucracy has insulated the political leadership which too has avoided facing tough questions on national security issues.

The Doklam standoff should act as reminder to the nation that it is more important for the political leadership to directly interact with military in peace time to understand the nuances of capability building and war fighting. This assumes significance because future wars are going to be complex, lethal and damages will be irreversible. Perforce, there is a need to incorporate professionals in planning, policy making and audit of capabilities.

Conclusion

The current Doklam stand-off is an opportunity to integrate political and military leadership and to set a foundation for structured response to crises in future. If a nation desires that it must retain ability to dominate and control situations, it must develop capabilities that give it strength to negotiate, from not under fear or coercion, but from position of strength. JF Kennedy said that "Never negotiate from fear and never fear to negotiate".[9] It is opined that the CCS has handled short-term threats reasonably well but the biggest problem lies in capability building. That is the charter of NSC – to oversee the defence planning process and support it with dedicated budgetary support.

If a local war with China is just one stand-off away and limited war with Pakistan is just one terror strike away, in that case it is vital for India to focus on development of military capabilities in an earnest manner, without further delay and political passivity.

NOTES

1. Nehru and the Indian Armed Forces 5th Lecture - by General J N Chaudhuri, 5th May 1973. Accessed from https://www.cambridgetrust.org/assets/documents/Lecture_5.pdf on March 19, 2017.
2. How Nehru, Menon conspired against army chief Thimayya, *Hindustan Times,* Feb 13, 2016
3. Simon Carraud and Michel Rose, France's armed forces chief resigns after clash with Macron over budget cuts, *Reuters* World News, July 19, 2017.
4. James Jay Carafano, 5 Big Lessons from the First Gulf War, *The National Interest,* August 10, 2015.
5. Ibid.
6. Ronald Glossop, What Lessons Should We Learn from the Crisis in Syria? Citizens for Global Solutions, August 30, 2013.
7. Mark Thompson, 50 Years Later: The Lessons of the Cuban Missile Crisis, Accessed on July 22, 2017 from http://nation.time.com/2012/10/22/50-years-later-the-lessons-of-the-cuban-missile-crisis/, Oct. 22, 2012.
8. Shaurya Karanbir Gurung, No improvement in Army's availability of ammunition: CAG, *The Economic Times,* July 22, 2017.
9. Mark Thompson, 50 Years Later: The Lessons of the Cuban Missile Crisis, Accessed on July 22, 2017 from http://nation.time.com/2012/10/22/50-years-later-the-lessons-of-the-cuban-missile-crisis/, Oct. 22, 2012.

*

May, 2018

10

Constitution of the New Defence Panel Chaired by the NSA

G. Mohan Kumar

Recently, the Ministry of Defence (MoD) has constituted a Defence Planning Committee (DPC) chaired by the National Security Advisor (NSA) with the objectives of: (1) Drafting a national security strategy; (2) drawing up a capability development plan; (3) working on defence diplomacy and (4) improving defence manufacturing in India. Sub-committees are to be constituted for each of the subject matters above and the Committee will include the representatives of the Ministries of Finance (MoF) and External Affairs (MEA).

One wonders why such a committee is necessary in the first place when there is a full-fledged body, namely the National Security Council (NSC) and its Secretariat which can easily be tasked by the Government to draw up the National Security Strategy. A National Security Strategy has to be very comprehensive with defence strategy as a very important sub-set of that. It has to touch upon all aspects of national security be it internal security, cyber security, natural resources security, energy security, and so on, thus covering a variety of sectors all of which may not necessarily be related to the security forces.

If the MoD has used the term 'National Security Strategy' to mean a National Defence Strategy, then this work could have been entrusted to a committee of defence experts, who after assessing the security threats arising from our main adversaries and the challenges the country is likely to face in the Indian Ocean Region, could have dwelt on the overall defence strategy to be adopted for approval by the Cabinet Committee on Security. Based on that approved defence strategy, a comprehensive capability development plan could be drawn up by the MoD.

While it is appropriated that the capability plan be based on the security (defence) strategy, it appears that the decision to constitute this new Committee is an attempt to defer further the appointment of the Chief of Defence Staff (CDS) or a Permanent Chairman of the Chief of Staff Committee (PCCOSC), or to shelve the very idea. Expert committees like the Kargil Review Committee as well as the Naresh Chandra Committee had gone into the need for comprehensive defence planning and integration of the three Services with regard to capability development. These committees, after careful consideration, had recommended the appointment of a CDS, or a PCCOSC. In the scheme of things, it will be the responsibility of the CDS/PCCOSC to prepare comprehensive defence plans by taking a balanced view of the competing requirements of the three Services and optimising the defence expenditure. Here the role of the CDS/ PCCOSC is purely intellectual and not so much operational. He is expected to be a level-headed person who by virtue of his seniority and experience would ensure that better sense prevails among the Services by putting breaks on unreasonable demands of each service and by calling a spade a spade. The apprehension that the office of the proposed CDS/PCCOSC will have too much power vested in it is totally misplaced if the MoD is clear about his role as narrated above.

It is well known that the Long Term Integrated Perspective Plan (LTIPP) already lays down the capability development plan with a 15-year perspective. However, weakness of the LTIPP is that it is nothing but an ambitious wish list of capabilities without a realistic correlation with the actual availability of funds. In its present form, it remains an ideal roadmap without any linkage to funding or rational force structures. It calls for great clarity of thinking and unity of thought to create a tri-services integrated capability plan out of the LTIPP. This can be done only by someone like the CDS/PCCSOC who can analyse the projected requirements of the Services critically and objectively and arrive at the optimum force structure that could provide the maximum teeth to tail ratio within the available resources.

That is an exercise which calls for tremendous co-ordination and comprehensive inter-services dialogue which can be effectively moderated only by someone of the stature of the CDS/PCCOSC. It is not something which can be deliberated upon by a committee as constituted by the MoD which does not have the requisite expertise. Of course, once the capability development plan is in place, there will be the need for a committee consisting of the MoD and Ministry of Finance (MoF), for the PMO to approve a 15-year acquisition/infrastructure budget, and for the MoF to own up the same and provide funds in the annual budget as per a 15-year roll-on plan. For this plan to be effective, non-lapsability will have to be conferred on the defence budget. Here the role of PMO will be that of a moderator to ensure that the MoF does not renege on its commitments.

As regards defence diplomacy, a committee had been constituted in the year 2016 to evolve specific strategies relevant to India's interests. This Committee was chaired by the then Deputy NSA and included various experts. The report of this Committee is available with the MoD and the least it can do is to implement these recommendations. But in defence diplomacy, we have limitations of our own – inadequacy of funds and lack of a strong defence industrial base to cater to the requirements of friendly countries in a satisfactory manner which can counter our resource-rich adversaries like China or a combination of China and Pakistan. Unless these issues are addressed, defence diplomacy will remain a story of unfulfilled commitments.

As regards defence manufacturing, there are no magic solutions and constituting a committee is certainly not one of these. For the defence industry to be innovation based and to be an engine of growth, the basic requirement is change in mindset. There is no doubt that India's defence manufacturing dream will remain unrealised till the private sector gets into the act in a big way and gets involved in big projects. The main reason is that in defence manufacturing, technology is a formidable challenge. The private sector, by virtue of its flair for innovation and reverse engineering, will be in a much better position to crack the technological challenges and induct competent technologists from the open market.

Therefore, the MoD needs to move ahead boldly with the strategic partnership programme. However, the fate of the single-engine fighter aircraft plan, which had been deliberated upon at the highest levels before it was initiated through a 'Request For Information', is an example of how the bureaucracy could play the procrastination game and how the Services can acquiesce in it despite their reservations. The sad truth is that in the prevailing political atmosphere, no one wants to invite flak from our 'socialist' political class by batting for the private sector lest it should be termed as another egregious example of crony capitalism!

Leaving aside strategic partnerships, the MoD's acquisition wing badly needs a revamp to make it contribute meaningfully to the Make in India dream. Unlike advanced countries, our defence acquisition system is totally fragmented without any linkage to the industry or product and technology development. Restructuring of the Acquisition Wing which had been gone into by the Pritam Singh Committee of Experts has not been acted upon, ostensibly on the unconvincing ground that it would require creation of more posts. In the MoD, creation of posts can be expenditure neutral if it is done imaginatively by redeployment of Services personnel. A country like USA has more than 150,000 professionals handling defence acquisitions. France and UK have tens of thousands of such professionals. For a country of India's size, would another few hundreds or even thousands be too many people?

The MoD's production arms, namely the Defence Public Sector Undertakings (DPSU) and the Ordnance Factory Board (OFB), need to make fundamental changes in their approach to manufacturing by being efficient integrators and by allowing a vibrant eco-system of Micro, Small and Medium Enterprises (MSME) to thrive. The OFB's departmental structure, which is a sad legacy of the East India Company era, needs to be dismantled at the earliest to make way for a vibrant corporate structure. Departmental procedures which have their roots in the Government Financial Regulations are not conducive for improved productivity, efficiency and quality management. Reform measures which were recommended in the Raman Puri Committee's report have been stymied thanks to the lukewarm, half-hearted approach by the Department of Defence Production. Even in its present form, the OFB is far from having at least a long-term vendor policy to encourage the eco-system of small and medium industries. There is no real example in the recent past of a product designed independently by the private sector getting long-term support from the OFB.

The same holds good for the Defence Research and Development Organisation (DRDO), which unlike the Atomic Energy and Space departments, has not lent wholehearted support to the private sector by outsourcing its research and development requirements. The DRDO still spends a fortune on in-house development of sub-systems and parts on 'built-to-specifications' projects without involving the private sector significantly. Similarly, there has to be dynamism in the productionisation of newly developed products through fast proto-type development in which the private sector can also play a key role. The same applies to DPSUs like the Hindusatn Aeronautical Limited (HAL) which have always suffered from production capacity constraints. The HAL, besides its own manufacturing, may do well to licence some of its products like the Advanced

Light Helicopter, Light Combat Aircraft and the Light Combat Helicopter to the private sector so that the armed forces do not have to wait interminably to get their legitimate requirements.

In short, the MoD already has a wealth of sane advice which has accumulated over the years. What is required is not the rigmarole of another committee, but bold decision making.

*

August, 2018

11

US-India 2 Plus 2 Dialogue: Significance of Strategic Partnership

Lieutenant General Gautam Banerjee, PVSM, AVSM, YSM

> *"Want of foresight, unwillingness to act when action would be simple and effective, confusion of counsel until emergency comes ... are the features which constitute the endless repetition of history"*
>
> **– Anon**

Defence Industry and Defence Preparedness

A nation's industry is built upon a strong base of pure sciences and its translation into technology, all the three sprouting up essentially to meet economic demands. In case of India, poverty had limited the domestic markets for high-technology quality products while trade protectionism did the same in the international arena. The result was that the indigenous industry got stymied in meeting low-end demands, the basic foundation of pure sciences was left to stagnate leading to brain drain, and research and development remained stifled in low priority.

As for the defence industry, India's post-independence policy of repudiating military power as an instrument of statehood led to a situation when India's vast World War II era defence sector infrastructure was unable to catch up with modern defence technology. Eventually, rising threat to India's national defence led to her having to import, at heavy cost and under impinging conditions, most of her defence weaponry and equipment to match, to a minimalist extent, the aggressive neighbours. But since the fiscal ability to import modern military hardware could not be sustained, the Indian defence forces have been over time reduced to well below their designated capabilities.

More disconcertedly, India's lag in modern science, technology and industry, particularly that in respect of defence industry, is so vast that it would take generations to catch up, provided a concerted thrust towards that end is sustained over the coming decades. Given the other challenges confronting India, that condition appears to be difficult to fulfil even as the threat to India's security keeps rising.

India's Strategic Insecurity

India's weak foundations of scientific temper and industrial capacity at the time of independence, and exclusion from access to Western repositories of modern technology thereafter, has brought India to a condition of most disconcerting strategic insecurity. Indeed, it would not be any exaggeration to state that there is no other globally significant country whose national integrity stands so severely threatened. For India, it is a case of triple whammy, so to say.

The first whammy arises from two of her militarily powerful, innately aggressive next-door Northern and Western neighbours choosing to gang up to undermine India's territorial integrity as an objective matter of their national objective. The second one arises from the more powerful of the duo usurping India's centrality in the Southern waters of the Indian Ocean while using its massive economic strength to adversely influence India's traditionally Indo-centric neighbours. The third whammy comes from India's combination of misdirected defence industrial policies, archaic defence acquisition process and meagre defence allocations all of which has translated into a debilitating military 'hollowness'.

It is that context that the issue of substantial US-India Defence Cooperation needs to be examined.

US-India Defence Cooperation

At no time in her independent existence has India been so assiduously courted for 'comprehensive strategic partnership' by any of the international players, let alone by a global super-power. The reference here is to the US describing India as a key contributor to her power-politics and embracing the latter into a new two-by-two (2 by 2, or 2+2) ministerial dialogue, the purpose being to 'enhance strategic coordination' between the two democratic and freedom promoting nations in order to 'maintain peace and stability in the Asia-Pacific Region'.

Not that there had been any dearth of such intent in the past among the ever-active shapers of international dispensation, but the offers had remained firmly repudiated by the Indian leadership's idealist, and arguably practical, principles. No doubt, those principles have brought many accomplishments to an India that had been rendered destitute by centuries of exploitation. But it is also undeniable that the isolation from closer connections with the advanced world has prevented her from catching up with the runaway sciences, technologies and industrialisation of the modern era. Even if that was done under certain understandably genuine reservations, India continues to pay the price of closing such options.

Obviously, the US offer is anything but philanthropic. In the American strategic calculations, India could play a key role in the continuation of her super-power status in general and the security provider's role in the Asia-Pacific Region at a lesser cost in terms of men, material and finances. The key consideration here is that US-India defence cooperation offers to India a ready route to close the aforementioned generational lag that afflicts her science, technology and industry sectors. Indeed, defence cooperation with the most advanced defence industry would enable India to skip many steps of the time- and cost-intensive ladder and so to secure lateral entry into higher levels of research, design and production of modern military hardware.

No doubt, the American are not naïve to offer their frontier military technologies, and what is shared would remain a step or two behind the latest. But even then, lateral entry by skipping more numerous steps of design and development would be no mean advantage either. Further, accorded the right focus, a 'step-behind' technology would open up avenues to develop indigenous finishing algorithms and designs commensurate to Indian requirements and customised to secrecy parameters.

There would be unwarranted conditions and demands from the stronger partner of course, but astute measures can always be adoptable to limit the issues of mutual differences. That in fact is necessary, because if repudiated too long and too irritably, the opportunity of gaining out of the strategic partnership might pass, while the super-power looks to alternate options.

The Course of US-India Defence Cooperation

The quest for substantive Indo-US relations began in 1995 with signing of an 'Agreed Minute on Defence Relations'. After a decade of stagnation, a 'Defence Framework Agreement for the US-India Defence Relationship' was signed in 2005. This document focused on defence trade, joint exercises, personnel exchanges, collaboration and cooperation in maritime security and counter-piracy operations, exchanges between each of the Services, etc. As a sequel to that Defence Framework Agreement, the 'Defence Technology and Trade Initiative' (DTTI) was initiated in 2012, the objective being to facilitate collaborative defense co-production of modern weapon systems with American technologies. The salience of DTTI is that it would make it possible to modernise India's defence forces and defence industry – the former by import of modern weaponry to the extent unavoidable and affordable, and the latter by collaborative research, technology acquisition and industrial cooperation. Inter alia, that level of DTTI partnership would also strengthen the two economies.

Meanwhile, there arose a constituency of naysayers who saw red in the very mention of strategic partnerships and interest-group alliances, and tried to mar that ever proven political option into an electoral xenophobia. The resistance flows out of political apprehensions of compromising with India's 'military neutrality', raising the major defence supplier, Russia's piqué, and adverse effects of the American 'Asia Pivot' Strategy on the current Sino-Indian relations. That line of thought is also reinforced by the instances of US defecting, in self-interest, from commitments made. A more informed, practical and mature policy making, instead of baulking in fear and self-doubt at the very mention of strategic partnerships, would rather focused upon the clauses of such alliances and make sure that these serve Indian interests as much as that of the partner's.

After two decades of dithering, in 2015, the Defence Framework Agreement was renewed for the next 10 years. Under this renewed Agreement, the following 'pathfinder projects' of joint development and production were identified:

- Intelligence-gathering and reconnaissance modules for C-130J Super Hercules,
- Mobile electric hybrid power sources for aircraft,
- Chemical, biological warfare protection gear,
- Modern unmanned aerial vehicles (UAV), Raven.

Subsequently, two more collaborative development and production projects, and four government-to-government science and technology cooperation projects, have been identified – the fields of cooperation are expected to expand hereafter. The defence cooperation may thus turn into a robust foundation for the 'Defend India' and 'Make-in-India' initiative.

Beginning the early 2000s, the US proposed a set of three defence-related 'Foundation Agreements'. One of these, the 'Logistical Exchange Memorandum of Agreement' (LEMOA), was signed after the 'conscience keepers' breast-beating evoked no interest among the polity, and operationalised in 2016. As the name suggests, this Agreement covers provision of logistic cover to each of the partner's forces from their respective support infrastructure. No promise of coalition military action, basing foreign troops or concession from sovereignty contentions are made.

Present Status of Defence Cooperation

Presently, the US is pressing for finalisation of the other two foundation agreements, namely: the Communications Compatibility and Security Agreement, or COMCASA (earlier named as Communications and Information Security Memorandum of Agreement, or CISMOA); and the Basic Exchange and Cooperation Agreement (BECA).

The COMCASA, as the US elaborates, is needed to be in place to permit India to fully harness the capabilities of communication security equipment meant for exchange of classified military information and installed on military platforms that she imports from the US. The BECA, on the other hand, provides for collection, processing and sharing of geospatial information between the two militaries. This in fact is the most significant field of cooperation because in the modern dispensation, competent military deployment and usage of modern weaponry envisages comprehensive and updated geospatial mapping.

Like any instrument, while the three foundation agreements offer far-reaching advantages, military as well as civil, to either of the nations, they are also liable to misuse. India finds the terms of COMCASA as impracticable on account of her rather extensive Russian defence connections and the related agreements which must be inviolable. Similarly, the BECA is found disagreeable as it would open up India's own geo-spatial data bank to American scrutiny. Thus there is the doubt over India's sovereign freedom. But the issue here is not on points of disagreement; it is to find mutually accommodative solutions, and that hurdle should, as it has been in most instances, be surmountable.

Many official level confabulations later, in August 2017, the US mooted the offer of 2+2 Dialogue, and packaged it with the remarkably grand gesture of referring to the region as 'Indo-Pacific', and renaming its Pacific Command as 'Indo-Pacific Command', or USINDOPACOM. Semantics apart, the 2+2 Dialogue proposes to raise the level of confabulations from Secretary to Ministerial level.

What America Wants

As stated above, the American outreach to India after so many decades of mouthing soothing rhetoric alongside a deliberate policy to overlook of relentless assault on Indian nationhood comes from her inescapable needs. At no time in recent years has the terms of America's global supremacy and power wielding interests have been so brazenly ignored and defied by, besides a host of innately anti-America forces, her business partner of five decades, China. Even her enchanting protégée of seven decades – Pakistan – has been misleading her, with her tacit overlook of course. Presently, even a resurgent Russia is finding the duo's company rather agreeable. Thus the current situation, wherein the American dispensations are exploited to undermine her interests, obliges the US to look for dependable and capable allies to maintain her global leadership. Finally, with the coming of the Trump Administration, it is apparent that the US is intent on wriggling out of her opportunist clients' geo-political blackmail and invest in more dependable relationships.

The situation is aptly summarised by what a notable Washington D.C.–based conservative think tank, the American Enterprise Institute (AEI), states in its recent report titled 'An American Strategy for Southeast Asia'. The basic points of arguments in the Report are:

(a) The United States should adopt a 'comprehensive strategy for Southeast Asia with security, economic, and governance components to defend her interests and ensure peace and stability in the Indo-Pacific region';

(b) Southeast Asia, 'a region comprised of 635 million people in 11 countries which has been increasingly affected in recent years by China's growing economic and military might' holds geopolitical importance on account of the sea lanes that pass through it, and the resources which it contains.

(c) 'China's claims over the South China Sea and its military build-up on man-made islands pose a security threat not only to her Southeast Asian neighbours, but also to American interests in the region, given the potential of drawing the U.S. into the territorial tussles'. Further, 'A free and open Southeast Asia is crucial if the United States wants to achieve her broader goals in the region'.

(d) The Trump administration has modelled an Indo-Pacific strategy in an effort 'to manage China's militarisation in the South China Sea and the Indian Ocean, and growing Chinese economic power with its multitrillion-dollar Belt and Road Initiative in Eurasia and Southeast Asia'. US pledge, at the ASEAN Foreign Ministers' meeting in Singapore, of $290 million in aid of 'security funding' for Southeast Asia as a counterbalance to China's plans to step up her engagement in the region is a concrete step in that direction.

Conclusion

Exploited and undermined by her beneficiary regimes, the US policy makers have been, for the past two decade or so, intent on forging strategic partnerships with mature, law abiding and stable powers. Rising appreciation of the Indian manner of statecraft, as evidenced by a regular sequence of India-favourable gestures, pronouncements and partnership initiatives are the result of that policy.

Given her mounting strategic vulnerability on the one hand, and the huge technological lag on the other, it is important for India to find avenues to co-develop and co-produce, even import when necessary, modern defence hardware. For that, should there be manageable accommodations to be made in the US-India defence cooperation initiatives, that must be acceptable in the interest of national defence in an increasingly vicious, predatory environment. Needless to state, that does not absolve the Indian defence policymakers from going all-out in the ultimate goal of strengthening, expanding and building up indigenous defence research, development and production. In fact, defence cooperation with advanced military powers would have to be but a process of that reaching that objective.

National defence, and its corollary, the call for 'military necessity' needs to be attended to with all alacrity. India needs US' partnership to modernise her defence industry while US too needs India to sustain her premier status in the region. That is an equation that India would let loose at her peril.

*

June, 2019

12

The Top Four Ministers Need to Work in Harmony to Help Build New India

Arvind Gupta

One striking feature of Modi Sarkar's new cabinet is that the top four jobs of Home, Finance, Defence and External Affairs are now occupied by new incumbents. They will bring their own visions and styles of functioning to their portfolios. Enjoying the trust of the Prime Minister, they, as members of the Cabinet Committee on Security, would need to work as a team to fulfil Prime Minister's vision for New India.

India is facing, as it has in the past, complex internal security challenges handling which requires holistic political, economic, and law and order approaches. Kashmir is an example. The BJP manifesto has spoken about removing Articles 370 and 35A of the Constitution. If this goal is realised, the situation in Kashmir would change forever. The repercussions of such a move would need to be carefully assessed.

The *status quo* in Kashmir cannot continue indefinitely. Bold, well-considered moves are needed. Assembly elections are due in J&K. Kashmiri pundits evicted from their homes under the shadow of the gun thirty years ago continue to await their return. Cross-border infiltration, incidents of cross-border terrorism, alienation and radicalisation amongst the Kashmiri youth remain persistent. The divide between Jammu and the Valley is deepening. The new Home Minister would have to devise a proper strategy to deal with the delicate situation in Jammu and Kashmir.

The framework agreement signed with the Nationalist Socialist Council of Nagaland (NSCN)-IM during the tenure of the previous government has not yet resulted in a proper settlement of the Naga issue. The situation cannot be allowed to fester indefinitely. While a lot has been done to gain an upper hand over left-wing extremism, the Maoists remain active inflicting damage on the security forces from time to time. Radicalisation, inspired by the Islamic State (IS) type of extremist ideologies, is increasing and palpable. Suitable de-radicalisation measures will need to be devised to deal with this very serious problem.

The Home Minister may also like to have a closer look at the capacities of the institutions governed by the Home Ministry. A number of suggestions were made in the last term of the Government regarding strengthening border security, coastal security, counter-terrorism mechanisms, building a National Intelligence Grid and so on. India still does not have a national counter-terrorism centre. The Home Ministry's budget has increased rapidly crossing – 100,000 crores for the first time. Yet, police force modernisation, police reforms, and training of para-military forces lag behind. Image of the police in the public is low. In the meanwhile, old policing methods are no longer effective for new age crimes and law and order situations. Police personnel have to be tech-savvy and sensitive to people's problems. The old mindsets must change. The problem of corruption among police personnel needs to be tackled.

The Home Minister may also like to have a deeper look at the structure of the Ministry of Home Affairs (MHA) itself. Is it organised suitably to deal with contemporary internal security challenges which arise from radicalisation, unemployment amongst youth, uneven population growth, regional imbalances, environmental degradation, unplanned urbanisation, natural disasters, extreme weather events, nexus between drug trafficking and terrorism, cyber space, internal migrations, farmers distress, violence against gender, social media-inspired campaigns, et cetera? The plain answer is 'no'. Our mindset is too old and structures too rigid to deal with these challenges. There are hardly any experts in the MHA who can provide inputs to the Home Minister based on such disciplines as psychology, behavioural sciences, anthropology, linguistics, etc. Modernisation of the Home Ministry is urgently needed. The new Home Minister should look into this aspect with the help of experts and not be guided solely by the bureaucrats.

The Finance Minister would get down to the task of preparing the first budget of the new government amidst slowing growth in the last three quarters. Government's welfare schemes, on the basis of which it won the mandate of the people, would need to be continued, extended and deepened. Resources for a hundred plus welfare schemes would have to be found and sustained. Stress on the banking sector would need to be relieved. The requirements of the Ministry of

Defence (MoD) for higher defence budget would have to be met. At the same time, rural development, agriculture, small industry, skill development, education and health, to name a few, require greater resources.

The Finance Minister would also have to keep an eye on the current account deficit which cannot be increased beyond its present level without damaging the economy. There are already demands from various quarters for the simplification and reduction of the GST. Raising new resources will be a major task for the Finance Minister. The Government would need to take suitable steps to revive private investment and increase foreign direct investment in the country. The economy would have to become more productive and competitive.

The last five years have shown time and again the need for deep reforms in the defence sector. It is an open secret that defence budget as a share of the GDP (about 1.6 percent) has fallen steadily in real terms and is not good enough to sustain modernisation of the Armed Forces. Procurements are becoming more expensive by the day and in the long run they are unsustainable. Indigenisation of defence production has not got the required boost. The 'Make in India' program in the defence sector has not yet taken off. Procurement procedures remain lengthy and tortuous. The strategic partnership reform announced in 2016, which would have brought the private sector into defence production in a big way, has faltered. There is not enough money to buy new equipment after meeting the existing commitments.

The security environment has altered rapidly. If India has to take on the challenges of China, Pakistan, and the threats arising from the Indo-Pacific region, it needs to do far more on defence. The cyber capabilities of the defence forces need to be enhanced. Defence diplomacy has to be stepped up by bringing in new ideas. The relationship between the MoD and the Armed Forces needs to be made more harmonious and synergetic. The decision on the appointment of the Chief of Defence Staff (CDS) must be finalised at the earliest.

The new External Affairs Minister, a confidant of the Prime Minister, has been handpicked to steer India's diplomacy. As former Foreign Secretary, he is well-versed with the opportunities and diplomatic challenges the country faces. No doubt he will hit the deck running. The global and regional environment is highly uncertain. In the next few weeks, a hectic diplomatic engagement agenda is awaiting the Prime Minister. Indo-US relations have seen headwinds in the context of trade and economic relationship. US sanctions have also impacted India's relations with Iran and Russia. The connectivity agenda of the Government, launched in the last term, remains incomplete. The neighbourhood, the extended neighbourhood and relationships with the great powers will be the top foreign policy priority for the Government. The Indian media would be closely watching the possible meeting between PM Modi and Pakistan PM Imran Khan on the sidelines of the Shanghai Cooperation Organisation (SCO) summit. The Government is unlikely to give up its firm view that talks and terrorism cannot go together.

Ties with China are never without problems. India would have to look carefully as the Chinese push to penetrate the Indian telecom market with Huawei's 5G technologies which have raised concerns over the world. Will the new government be able to persuade the Chinese to agree on a border settlement, or a clarification on the Line of Actual Control at least? How will India deal with the growing influence of China in its sensitive neighbourhood? China's Belt and Road Initiative is reflective of its geo-political ambitions. These questions were always there. They take on new meanings as the global balance of power changes.

If India's economy slows down, India's options also diminish. The Ministry of External Affairs (MEA) would need to see how India's vast markets can be leveraged to meet India's interests. Diplomacy has to be a combined effort of MEA, MoD, MHA, Ministry of Finance (MoF), Ministry of Commerce and other sectoral ministries. The potential of Indian culture in building 'New India' has been under-utilised. The MEA should impart a strategic dimension to public diplomacy. The role of the Indian Council of Cultural Relations in strategising culture needs to be reexamined in this context.

The National Security Advisor (NSA) has been playing an important role in the critical aspects of India's diplomacy, particularly relating to the security aspects. A trusted aide, he has been a trouble shooter for the Prime Minister. It remains to be seen whether the NSA's role will change in the new government.

The National Security Council (NSC), set up in 1999, has been underused. In most countries, NSCs have become important institutions, bringing about coordination and a measure of monitoring the implementation of strategic programmes. The NSC could provide much-needed coordination amongst various ministries, particularly when it comes to the issues of threat perception, scenario building, crystal gazing and ways and means to deal with multiple challenges. It is hoped that NSC would become more active in the second term of the Government.

In today's day and age, no Minister or Ministry can work as an island. The four top ministers have to work together to realise the Government's agenda of New India.

July, 2019

13

Kargil War: Recollections

Ambassador Satish Chandra

Review of the Kargil War

The Kargil War was fought from May through till 26 July 1999 across a trans-Himalayan front of about 150 km at dizzying heights of up to 18000 feet in what was the most inhospitable and unlikely battleground in history. The relatively rapid expulsion of the Pakistani forces from these areas which had been occupied by them through deception and stealth in early 1999 constituted a major military success for India. The credit for this goes largely to our soldiers – both officers and men.

This victory did not come cheap. It is estimated that over 500 Indian officers and men made the supreme sacrifice and over 1100 were wounded. The Pakistani casualty toll was much higher and easily double that taken by India.

My perspectives on the Kargil War are largely informed by my having been the Member Secretary of the Kargil Review Committee set up in end July 1999 to review the events leading up to the conflict and to make recommendations to safeguard national security against such armed intrusions. Given this remit, the Committee did not look at how the conflict was handled post 26 May 1999.

My appointment as Member Secretary of the Committee was driven by the fact that I was Secretary, National Security Council Secretariat (NSCS), and as such not only had security-related responsibilities but also had the requisite staff and office resources to effectively service the Committee's requirements. Had the Committee been left to itself to fend for its office and staff resources, it would not have been able to complete its work as expeditiously and efficiently as it did with the support of the NSCS. In fact, this model of utilising the capacities of the NSCS for security-related work became a trend setter. It was thus also utilised as the secretariat for the Group of Ministers set up for reviewing the national security system and over the years took the lead in many cross-cutting security-related issues on which there was diffidence of one or another institution to take the lead.

The Committee functioned in a spirit of openness and transparency. It not only engaged in debate within itself but also with those in the strategic community including even officers in the NSCS who were helping out in its work. This was in large measure due to the persona of its other constituents notably the late Mr K Subrahmanyam, the Chairman, and doyen of India's strategic fraternity, the meticulous Lt Gen KK Hazari, former Vice Chief of Army Staff, and the late Mr BG Verghese, one of our most respected and versatile journalists. One would be remiss in not also mentioning the role of the National Security Advisor, namely Mr Brajesh Mishra, in enormously facilitating the task of the Committee. As a result of his whole-hearted support, the entire national establishment opened itself to freely interacting with the Committee and to answering all its queries. Furthermore, he gave the Committee a complete carte blanche in developing the report as it pleased and without the slightest interference. Indeed, even though he knew in advance through me that the Committee had decided to recommend that the office of the National Security Advisor (NSA) and the Principal Secretary to the Prime Minister should not be occupied by the same person as done by him, he made no effort to effectuate any change in the recommendation.

The Committee consciously desisted from wasting time and energy in fixing responsibility on individuals, choosing instead to work in a cooperative mode with all concerned to tease out the lessons that could be learnt from the Kargil experience. In the process it had in-depth interactions with scores of political leaders including the highest in the land, military personnel at all levels, intelligence officials, relevant civil servants, journalists etc. It also made a number of field visits particularly to Jammu and Kashmir including the area of operations. On the basis of this arduous and extensive exercise, the Committee published its report on 15 December 2015 – less than five months after having been constituted. Credit must be given to the Government for having made this report public as this was not the norm at the time and as there were some things in it which did not sit well with the Government. The report was also tabled in Parliament. It is, however, a pity that the voluminous annexures and appendices to the report were not made public by the Government despite the Committee's request that this should be done with appropriate security deletions where necessary.

The main elements of the Committee's report, apart from its recommendations, included, *inter alia*, the nature of the Pakistani action, its authors, its motivations, our response, our so called intelligence failure, and speculation on whether or not the Kargil War could have been avoided.

Pakistani Action

Stealth, secrecy, and deception were the hallmarks of the Pakistani intrusions in the Kargil. The exercise, accordingly, was undertaken with virtually no movement of additional formations from outside the sector and with no extraordinary dumping of stores and ammunition. It also involved only around 2000 men across a front of about 150 km in shallow depths of 5-9 km. Movement of these personnel was undertaken in deep winter, viz, from January to April 1999, when patrolling by our forces was virtually impossible and when some posts were traditionally vacated. Finally, the Pakistani forces came in fancy dress masquerading as militants in order to create the fiction that the action was being undertaken by freedom fighters and not by the Pakistani Army.

The Kargil intrusions were part of a plan formulated in the 1980s but never executed. The author of this exercise was Gen Musharraf who had been made the Army Chief by Nawaz Sharif in October 1998 over the heads of two other Generals. Even within Pakistan knowledge of the operation was confined to a small coterie of Generals around him on a need to know basis. Neither the Air Force nor the Navy were kept in the loop. It is uncertain as to how much Nawaz Sharif knew, though the Committee took the stand that "the balance of possibility suggests that he was fully in the picture." It further asserted that he was at least aware of the broad thrust of the plan when he welcomed Mr. Vajpayee in Lahore in February 1999.

Clearly, the Pakistani intrusion was well planned and executed and it completely surprised India. By end of April, the Pakistani forces had occupied all the high points across a 150-km front without detection. Furthermore, even after detection in the second week of May, we believed that what we confronted were militants and not the Army. It was not till a few weeks later after active engagement that we realised that what we were up against were not militants but the Pakistani Army. It is true that there were some militants amongst the Pakistani infiltrators but these were in the nature of support elements. It was estimated that the bulk of the intruders were regular soldiers and the militants were no more than, perhaps, 30 percent of the total force.

I may mention that as Chairman Joint Intelligence Committee, I came to know that something was afoot in the Kargil Sector only in the second week of May when officials from two intelligence agencies claimed that they had reports about ingress of Pakistani intruders into India. This contention was vehemently denied by officials from two other intelligence agencies. While these agencies were in the process of arriving at a reconciled position, the matter became public. In retrospect, we know that the Army had some information of the intrusions in the first of week of May itself though it assessed these as a militant and not a Pakistan Army intrusion.

Pakistani Motivations and Assumptions

Pakistan's Kargil adventure was motivated by the desire to internationalise the Kashmir issue as a nuclear flashpoint and encourage third-party intervention; to alter the LC and use the areas captured as a possible trade off against Indian positions on Siachen; to interdict the Srinagar Leh road; and to provide a fillip to the insurgency in Kashmir. The main assumptions behind this move were as follows:

1. Early third-party intervention would take place in Pakistan's favour thereby enabling it to retain possession of the areas captured by it enabling it to bargain from a position of strength.
2. Its nuclear capability would obviate any larger Indian riposte across the International Border (IB) or even the use of air power.
3. India would not be in a position to mount a swift and resolute response due to a variety of factors.

In the event, these assumptions were off the mark barring possibly India not countering with a cross IB retaliation and its restrained use of air power.

If Pakistan took India by surprise in terms of its occupation of the Kargil heights by stealth, India equally took Pakistan by surprise with its swift and effective retaliation, compelling it to vacate aggression. Indeed, if one looks back over time, this was not the first time that Pakistan underestimated the firmness of Indian response. This happened in 1947, it happened in 1965 when we crossed the IB, it happened during the 2016 surgical strikes, and it happened at Balakot. Miscalculations by Pakistan about the Indian reaction occur in part because its military is fairly contemptuous about "Hindu" India's ability to respond firmly and in part because India has usually reacted with caution and restraint even to the most serious provocations like the 1993 or the 2008 Mumbai attacks.

India's Response

After initial detection of the intrusions in the second week of May, Indian response was prompt and effective. A comprehensive set of actions was initiated to establish contact with the intruders, to fix the extent of the incursion and to contain it. Adequate troops and firepower were moved in. It was, however, only after some encounters that we realised that the bulk of the intruders were regulars. By the last week of May it was decided to also deploy the Indian Air Force (IAF), though it was restricted from crossing the Line of Control (LC) and thus made to operate in a straitjacket. Appropriate covering moves were also undertaken by the Army along the IB and the Western fleet was augmented by elements from the Eastern fleet not only to keep Pakistan from further mischief but also placing it on notice that India was intent on ensuring that it pulled back. Pakistan's efforts at negotiating were rebuffed and the message given was that it must first vacate aggression. India's firm and unequivocal moves were well understood and respected by the international community. In the event, they secured Pakistan's total retreat from the positions occupied by it on Indian soil by 26 July 1999.

I may mention that through the course of the Kargil conflict, both the NSCS and a National Security Advisory Board (NSAB) sub-group were separately providing inputs to Government of the actions we needed to take. There was considerable anxiety that dislodging the Pakistan Army from the Kargil heights through frontal action would not only be time consuming but would also be costly in terms of the casualties we would take. Accordingly, the NSCS suggested that India should open another front either along the LC or the IB in order to impel Pakistan to vacate its aggression in the Kargil Sector. The NSAB sub-group, on its part, recommended heavy air bombardment of Pakistani forces across the LC. In the event, neither of these suggestions gained traction and we engaged in a conventional slugfest with Pakistan in the Kargil Sector, taking heavy casualties. However, we got them out much sooner than anticipated due to the valour of our Armed Forces and good leadership. The diplomatic factor was, no doubt, at the back of the minds of our leadership which, perhaps, rightly felt that the diplomatic support that India enjoyed would diminish if we crossed the IB or even the LC.

India's so called 'Intelligence Failure'

Through the Kargil conflict and its aftermath, much was made of India's so called intelligence failure both in terms of the long delayed detection of the intrusion and in terms of the fact that for a long time we felt that the intrusion had been undertaken not by the Pakistan Army but by militants. It is, of course, a fact that India was caught unawares and to that extent there was a failure of intelligence. But due consideration should be given to the fact that detection of such an intrusion was extremely difficult in the absence of high-quality surveillance equipment and inability to mount effective patrols due to extreme weather conditions.

Furthermore, the intrusion was virtually impossible to foresee as it defied logic being a high-risk–low-reward exercise which carried within it the seeds of its own defeat and to which prudence militated against: High risk, because having been launched in the height of winter it was prone to heavy weather-related casualties, which in fact occurred as evident from the diaries of captured Pakistani soldiers. Also early detection of the intruders and their consequent elimination was always a probability, which, luckily for Pakistan, did not happen. Low reward because the intrusion could not possibly have been sustained for meaningful follow-up action as it was carried out by a relatively small number of troops from within the sector in order to avoid detection. Induction of formations from outside the sector would have entailed detection but not doing so resulted in the intrusions having a limited shelf life. Finally, sustainability of such an intrusion required an enormous logistic effort which Pakistan could not deploy in stealth. Accordingly, Lt. General (Retd) Ali Quli Khan, one of Pakistan's most professional generals, while dubbing the Kargil War as the "worst debacle" in Pakistan's history, went on to state that its "conception and planning at the highest level had been poor – in fact, so poor that the only word which can adequately describe it is unprofessional. We all know that the main duty of the high command is to ensure that with their meticulous planning they create conditions whereby their junior combatants can fight easily. This was certainly not done at Kargil. It is also fairly obvious that the Kargil Operation was not conceived in its totality... and brought ignominy to Pakistan."

As far as the Committee was concerned, it primarily held the Research & Analysis Wing (R&AW) responsible for the intelligence failure as it had not detected a change in the deployment of battalions in the area, and more specifically, the addition of one battalion to the force level normally deployed there. It held Military Intelligence (MI) responsible to a lesser extent for not detecting the intrusion on the grounds that it should have been able to pick up the forward moves undertaken.

Could Kargil have been Avoided?

The Committee felt that Kargil could have been prevented had the Indian Army plugged every possible loophole across the LC and guarded every square inch of territory. This was naturally not done as it would not have been cost effective militarily or politically. Above all, the Army must never be used as a border guarding force and should only be used for war fighting. Using it in a border guarding role will diminish it and adversely affect its war-fighting capability.

Recommendations

The Committee made around two dozen recommendations. The single most important one of which was to undertake a thorough review of the national security system in its entirety by an independent body of credible experts.

This recommendation was accepted forthwith and a Group of Ministers chaired by the Home Minister was constituted in April 2000 to undertake the review of the national security system in its entirety. In order to facilitate their work, the Group of Ministers set up four task forces chaired and peopled by experts from outside the system to make recommendations in areas of intelligence, internal security, border management, and higher defence management. On the basis of the inputs submitted by the four task forces, which took into account the recommendations of the Kargil Review Committee, and following detailed discussions with them and lengthy internal deliberations, the Group of Ministers submitted a report containing around 350 recommendations barely a year after it had been set up. This exercise constituted the most exhaustive review of the Indian security system ever undertaken. The CCS, in its meeting of 15th May 2001, accepted all these recommendations barring those pertaining to the setting up of a Chief of Defence Staff (CDS).

This was unfortunate as the appointment of a CDS would have made for much more effective defence management. Specifically, a CDS would have provided single point military advice to the Government, administered the strategic forces, promoted greater "jointness" in the armed forces, and enhanced the efficacy of the planning process through intra- and inter-service prioritisation. It is my clear impression that Prime Minister Vajpayee himself had nothing fundamentally against the setting up of a CDS but was prevailed upon to postpone a decision in the matter by elements in the Congress which were against it. Accordingly, he made known to us that a decision on this issue must await a political consensus in the matter. The aversion of the Congress to the CDS became evident as the subsequent UPA Governments stymied all efforts to revive the idea. It is, therefore, ironical that the Congress manifesto today calls for the setting up of a CDS. One hopes that the Modi Government 2.0 would now bite the bullet and set up a CDS absence of which detracts from the optimal performance of our defence forces.

Implementation of the Group of Ministers recommendations were monitored by the NSCS on a quarterly basis and around 50-60 percent were implemented. Had all the recommendations been implemented with sincerity and despatch, India would have been much more secure than it is today. Specifically, we would have a populace and ruling class more disciplined and committed to the national cause, better policing, and better control on illegal migration, narco-trafficking, money laundering, and gun-running. We would also have more effective media management, better grip on crime and the coercive elements of State power notably the police, and the paramilitary forces, and the military would be better equipped and more effective. Indeed, I am convinced that had all the recommendations been implemented, 26/11 would never have happened and the many other terrorist incidents which have since occurred would have been avoided.

Specifically coming to the other recommendations made by the Kargil Review Committee, some were implemented and some were not. Some that were implemented include the setting up of an exclusive technical-intelligence organisation modelled on the US National Security Agency which took the form of the National Technical Research Organisation (NTRO), establishment of a Defence Intelligence Agency (DIA), acceptance of a two-stream approach – civil and military – for downloading and analysing imagery, acquisition and development of high quality Unmanned Aerial Vehicles (UAV) and satellites, integration of the Armed Forces Headquarters with the Ministry of Defence, and the establishment of an institutional mechanism which took the form of the Intelligence Coordination Group for the purpose of coordinating the work of the intelligence agencies as well as tasking them and evaluating their functioning.

Notable amongst the recommendations not implemented was the call for reduction of colour service from 17 to 7-10 years and diversion of the released manpower to the paramilitary formations, enhanced defence outlays, publication of a white paper on India's nuclear weapon programme, publication of authentic accounts of the 1965 and 1971 wars as well as of the Kargil Conflict, review of information policy to develop structures and processes to keep the public informed of vital national issues, the undertaking of credible measures in J&K to win back alienated sections of the population, and the adoption of a declaratory policy that violation of the LC's sanctity would meet with retaliation in a manner, time and place of India's choosing.

In conclusion, on the 20th anniversary of the Kargil War, there could be no better tribute to the gallantry of our brave hearts than for the Government to re-dedicate itself to India's safety and security. Towards this end, it would be well advised to undertake a comprehensive review of the progress achieved in the implementation of the recommendations made for security reform over the years, address the areas of difficulty where it has not been possible to implement these recommendations, and chart a plan of action for the future.

*

PART 2

DEFENCE PREPAREDNESS

September, 2012

14

Strategic Posture along China–India Borders: Is India Prepared?

General NC Vij, PVSM, UYSM, AVSM

The Context – Strategic Scenario

China's rise as a major international actor is certainly a defining feature of the strategic landscape of 21st century. It certainly has ramifications for the entire world but most definitely for the Far East and for India. If China has to emerge as a global power, it must first establish its unchallenged supremacy in its immediate neighborhood. India is the only country in the region which is somewhat of a competitor on both economic and military fronts. So it has got to be put in place; only question is, as to when?

As far as offering a justification to the rest of the world, the Chinese have evolved a widely publicised strategy of "Counter Attack in Self Defense", which is a multipurpose formulation that they use to describe most instances where China has initiated the use of force; that means that the PLA will launch the "first strike". China's 1962 War with India and Border War with Russia of 1969 fall under this category. Some people may still argue that China gains nothing by attacking India but so was said even before 1962 War.

Militarily, economically or politically, what time slot suits the Chinese the most? This could be within the next 3-5 years block or later, wherein the Indian Armed Force's level of preparedness and readiness for war are issues of hot and active debate in the country. Presently, the saving grace is that the Chinese themselves are nowhere close to their 'desired level' of modernisation and are only half way through to their modernisation programme. Alternatively, this could take place after 2020-25 when they will be fully ready and the capability gap would have increased exponentially between the two forces should we continue our modernisation programme on this sluggish pace!

To understand the level of threat posed by the Chinese in either of these two contingencies, we need to first analyse their level of preparedness.

CHINA: LEVEL OF MODERNISATION

Goal – Mission of the People's Liberation Army (PLA)

China is pursuing a long-term comprehensive military modernisation programme designed to improve the capacity of the PLA to fight and win, what they call 'local wars of short duration under conditions of informatisation' or high-intensity, information–centric military operations (note the word 'Short Duration' because it has implications for us). Local wars can also be interpreted as 'Regional Wars' as the character used for local wars can also mean regional wars.

It is the President Hu Zintao, who had articulated a new guidance for the PLA in 2004 to include missions extending beyond China's immediate territorial interests. The aspect of readiness to operate beyond immediate territory has its obvious portents. Even more importantly, Chinese leaders see this modernisation as a central component of their strategy to advance China's national development goals in the first two decades of the 21st century. The implications are obvious.

Since Taiwan retains their principal priority focus, their modernisation programmes assign priority to forces deployed opposite Taiwan, the South China Sea (SCS) and the Eastern Sea. Work on troops deployed in Tibet Autonomous Region (TAR) comes next but almost concurrently. The desired timeline of the Chinese to attain full preparedness level is 2020, but there are slippages, so it can easily go on to 2025 or so.

Budgetary Allocations

This is the most important part. The estimates about China's Defense Budget, as per the US and Taiwan, are pegged at approximately 180 billion US dollars for the year 2011. Three aspects which merit being emphasised in this regard are:

(a) Our budget is in the range of 36 billion US dollars. Funds for modernisation amount to only 12.87 billion US dollars.

(b) Even if one was to overlook the widened gap over the last few decades and make an assessment only from here onwards, the budgetary gap between the two sides will increase to over a trillion dollars worth of equipment in the next six years, i.e., 2018, and subsequently even more at the present rates of allocations.

(c) And even more significantly, the Chinese are incurring this level of expenditure when:
   (i) More than 80 percent of their weapon systems are being produced indigenously at much lower costs.
   (ii) On the other hand, with virtually no indigenous production, India is paying two to three times the cost of the equipment because of imports.

So the conclusion is obvious, that the gap between the two countries will exponentially increase with passage of time.

Now a quick analysis of the individual force structures of the Chinese.

Ground Forces

These forces were quite antiquated in the nineties. Even today:

(a) They suffer from significant shortcomings in command and control, air defence, communications and lack of combat experience.
(b) From mid-2011, they have begun the process of transforming parts of their forces into modular combined arms brigade-focused force structure. This concept is yet to be tested on the ground especially in the hills.
(c) Presently, growing numbers of modern heavy-armour, long-range strike Artillery and increased range air defense weapons are entering service in selected units, primarily those which may be deployed opposite Taiwan. The upgradation includes T-99, third-generation Main Battle Tanks, new generation amphibious assault vehicles and multiple rocket systems. Z-10 attack helicopter is a significant addition, even though the Aviation Wing itself with the Army formations is of recent origin.

Total Force Levels Available in TAR for Operations. 13 and 14 Group Armies from Chengdu Military Region and 47 and 21 Group Armies from Lanzhou Military Region can be deployed. 21 Group Army is designated as an offensive mobile force.

Infrastructure. Briefly stating:

(a) The PLA can concentrate up to seven divisions in TAR within one week; 12 divisions in 20-30 days because of the Qinghai–Tibet Railway or

QTR (Golmud to Lhasa – 1142 km and passes over 16640 ft at Tanggula Pass in Kunlun Mountain Range). Both the QTR and the oil pipe line will be vulnerable to interdiction operations from both ground and air.

(b) What is equally significant is that the Chinese can mobilise a Rapid Reaction Division into Lhasa within 24-36 hours and deploy up to two to three heli-lift battalions. Provided they can attain the air superiority of the kind required to carry out heli-borne operations, this is a sizeable threat and needs to be catered for.

(c) At the Nagqu Logistics Base, they are in the process of building up the handling capacity of 3.1 million tons, which is sizeable.

The Second Artillery Corps

This force is peculiar to the Chinese Armed Forces, wherein they have concentrated most of their rocket artillery and missiles systems. We have these types of force under different organisations but in much lesser numbers, which is a crucial shortfall.

This force also has 450-500 nuclear weapons. The Taiwanese estimate that this number will increase to 800 in this decade. These nukes are over and above what the Navy and Air Force have. This force will also be used for what they call 'resolute counter attacks', in both conventional and nuclear type of scenarios. They have also acquired Tactical Nuclear Weapons in large numbers.

There are many conflicting views about the use of Tactical Nuclear Weapons. The North Atlantic Treaty Organisation (NATO) forces had found during the Cold War that the numbers required for various contingencies were exorbitant and also were not commensurate to the desired outcomes, and thus their employment remained somewhat questionable. In our case, in the mountains, the efficacy of these tactical nukes may be further restricted, but this aspect needs to be studied in depth by the Indian Army. It is quite on the cards that the adversary may have very little compunction in the use of the Tactical Nuclear Weapons.

Navy

The Chinese are primarily focusing on anti-air and anti-surface warfare capability and also developing a credible 'at-sea' nuclear deterrence. This force is being transformed into a leaner force equipped with more modern multi-mission platforms.

The PLA Navy has 79 Destroyers/frigates and 50 submarines. The Air Craft Carrier (KUZNETSOV) will be functional by end of 2012 but the air component will take at least 5-7 years more to be effective. In the long run, the Navy will develop but its capability for carrier-based operations will remain of limited nature. That would limit them to operate in only the South China Sea and the Eastern Sea up to first and second chain of islands. Indian Ocean will be outside their capability for foreseeable future provided Indian Navy develops as per the plans and in desired timeframe.

The Chinese submarine fleet is also developing fast and the JIN Class (JL2) submarines (2-3 years away yet) will provide its Navy the first credible sea-based nuclear capability. This program has faced many delays already. They have presently two nuclear submarines and five more will be added in next 5-7 years.

The Chinese are developing DF-21D, the so-called 'Carrier Killer' and anti-ship ballistic missile (with a range of 1500-2700 km) which will also be a part of China's nuclear deterrence forces. It can also fire chemical warheads and Electro Magnetic Pulses (EMP) with maneuverable warheads. It will however take quite some time before these are operationally effective. They have also developed extensive mines and torpedo denial programmes under the 'Anti Denial and Anti Access Doctrine' for a Taiwan scenario. Overall, the Navy is still a work in progress.

Air Force

The PLA Air Force is in the nascent stages of developing 'ballistic missile defense' and an 'air-space integration' needed for early warning. One most noteworthy point is that in the nine airfields that they have in Lanzhou and Chengdu Military Regions, there are no worthwhile hardened shelters for their aircrafts and they will thus be vulnerable.

The PLA is also continuing to modernise its ground-based air defense forces with the introduction of new medium range Surface-to-Air Missiles (SAM). It has acquired multiple battalions of S-300 (Latest Russian SAMs) and is also negotiating for SAM–400 in large numbers. In foreseeable future, they will have the capability for net-centric operations and robust electronic protection. This is an area in which India needs considerable improvement.

The Air Force has a sizeable air fleet of 490 aircrafts of Second and Third Generation, which include J-10, SU-27 and SU-30. J-20, a fifth-generation stealth aircraft, is being propagated as a game-changing offensive weapon in the making. However, it is still in proto-type model. Badger TU-16 Bombers from Russia are being upgraded and Unmanned Aerial Vehicles (UAV) are being imported from Israel. Airborne Warning and Control Systems (AWAC) and mid-air refueling capabilities are still being built up.

The level of education of the pilots, the leadership qualities etc. are under serious debate in the Chinese Air Force. Presently, they lack the capability to take on forces with good standard of training like the Indian Air Force (IAF), but are fast moving in that direction.

Areas of Excellence for Asymmetric Warfare

Command, Control, Communications, Computers, Intelligence, Surveillance and Reconnaissance (C4I2SR) is being developed in a big way to:

(a) Enable commanders to respond to complex battlefield conditions with a high level of agility and synchronisation.
(b) Will also lead to greater integration amongst the three Services.

Chinese will continue to enjoy an edge over us in this field for quite some time.

Space and Counter-Space Capabilities

In this field, the Chinese have deployed satellites which enable real-time transfer of data to ground stations. They are also developing multi-dimensional programmes to limit or deny the use of space-based assets by adversaries. These provide them capabilities of laser and micro-wave jamming. Effort will also be to jam the adversary's command and control and the fire-control systems. These programs are however still facing challenges and their satellites are generally suffering from malfunctioning.

Cyber Warfare Capability

Intrusion and data theft are being used to collect strategic intelligence. The Chinese can also try and disrupt the enemy's essential services like air, railways and bank services etc. and business continuity processes. This is causing great concern to the US and all other countries in the region.

Threat from Electro-Magnetic Pulse

The US is fearing the possibility of tactics of nuclear warhead bursts in the atmosphere to create an electro-magnetic pulse attack with the intention to temporarily or permanently disable the electronic circuits. They are looking at this seriously and India also needs to expeditiously build up counter-capabilities in this regard.

Nuclear Aspects

Whereas the US, NATO countries and the Russian have exercised great reductions, the Chinese are continuing to develop their nuclear arsenal. Even more worrisome is the fact that the use of nuclear weapons is being built up as a part and parcel of their strategy for furtherance of military operations.

China's stated 'No First Use' policy is not explicitly stated and it commits them to nothing. There are questions as to whether 'demonstration strikes' or 'high-altitude bursts' would constitute a first use or not. It appears that they will have no hesitation in the first use of Tactical Nuclear Weapons. In any case, there is hardly a doubt that against Taiwan, this policy of No First Use will not be applicable.

THE INDIAN SCENARIO

Role Envisaged for the Armed Forces

It is learnt that both China and Pakistan are fine-tuning their strategies to impose a war on two fronts against India. Thus, in case a war breaks out, a 'two-fronts scenario' will be almost a certainty.

In such a contingency, the Indian Armed Forces will need to generate a punitive deterrence capability vis-à-vis Pakistan and optimal dissuasion vis-à-vis China. More simply put, it means that we must have a 'superiority ratio against Pakistan and optimal parity against China'. With our present force levels, that is a far cry, and that is why it is high time that the Government of India issues the directive for raising of the Strike Corps. Argument that any rising of force level will cause concern to the Chinese is naïve and puzzling to say the very least, especially in view of the fact that the Chinese have built up far more potent and threatening capability in the TAR.

We also need to prepare for unified operations in all five domains, i.e., Land, Sea, Air, Space and Information/Cyber. The preparatory work on operational plans also needs to be carried out jointly. We must also build up reserves in ammunition, missiles, spares and ancillaries for a minimum period of 60 days of warfare at an intense rate in a crash timeframe. These shortages remain one of the biggest areas of weakness. All other aspects warranting improvement have been projected by the three Services to the Ministry of Defense and work on them must proceed with a sense of urgency.

Conflict Scenarios: Possibilities

Let us very briefly examine the two possible conflict scenarios and the possible outcomes.

A War in Next 3-5 Years. A balanced analysis of the Chinese Armed Forces will show that:

(a) Their Armed Forces are still in varying stages of transition.

(b) Since their priority focus of development is towards Taiwan, there are still many facets of weaknesses in TAR.

(c) Their Navy does not presently have the capability to take on the Indian Navy in the Indian Ocean. This capability is not likely to be achieved over next 10-15 years.

(d) We can certainly choke them in the Malacca Straits, with some changes in our Navy's priority of allocation of forces opposite the two adversaries. The proximity of Andaman and Nicobar Islands to Malacca Straits offers us tremendous advantages in terms of effective air-sea operations against the Chinese.

(e) Our Air Force has the advantage of operating from the ground level in the North-East, which provides them far greater endurance. We also have huge advantage in terms of number of air fields. There is a strong possibility of the IAF inflicting heavy losses on the Chinese Air Force in TAR in the first 72 hours itself, as they lie in the open.

(f) Chinese capabilities in asymmetries operations are still developing, especially in the mountains. Also, the efficacy of modular mountain brigades in the mountains is still to be tested.

(g) Finally, Chinese themselves are seriously examining and attending to the problems of their lack of combat experience and also leadership abilities at junior and senior levels. That acts as a huge 'force multiplier' for us.

Progress of Operations. The assessment being offered here pre-supposes that the Strike Corps will be in place over next two years and all the shortages in ammunition, missiles and spares would have been made up. These are operational imperatives and not open to questions. In such a case:

(a) The terrain and the ground offer us the biggest advantage.

(b) For the first 20-30 days, we can generate near equal parity in forces, which will deny them the required force superiority for attack and render their operations most difficult and sluggish.

(c) With some changes in the grand strategy in the mid-term, there is a possibility of being able to create up to two Dual Tasked Divisions for the North-East and Ladakh Sectors in a certain time frame, e.g. after their task on the other front is done. Similarly, artillery allocations will have to be freshly planned.

However, most importantly there is a requirement to carry out joint planning for such operations on priority by all the three Services together in the same fashion as we have done for some other contingences. With all such preparations, we should be able to hold our own and leave the adversaries baffled.

Conflict Scenario after 2020-25

By this period, the Chinese modernisation programmes would have fully fructified. On our side, if the projected shortfall of equipment worth 155 billion US dollars for the three Armed Forces is not made up in these 8-10 years, the potential gap between the opposing sides would have increased exponentially, posing grave risks to Indian security.

Even more than the Conventional Operations, the asymmetric warfare will pose grave threat. Therefore, we must focus on the following aspects with renewed vigor:

(a) Technology must be the buzz word.
(b) A much higher degree of proficiency in aspects related to the informatisation, like C4I2SR, counter cyber operations, optimum utilisation of space assets and Counter EMP measures will be a pre-requisite.
(c) Ballistic Missile Defense (BMD) must be built up.
(d) Improvement of infrastructure in the North East.

The Road Ahead

Alongside operational preparedness, there are certain other improvements which need to be brought about in our national security apparatus; these have been pending for many decades:

(a) A greater degree of jointness in the functioning of the three Services, on the lines of the recommendations of the 'Group of Ministers', is *sine qua non*. Some of the patch-work solutions offered by Naresh Chandra Committee in this regard are like a cure which may be worse than the malady, and must be disregarded with the haste that it deserves.
(b) The Services must be made a part of the national strategic planning

structure of the Govt. The prevailing system of the Government of India and the Services working in isolated compartments needs to be shelved for the good of the country.

(c) The requisite fund allocations (155 billion US dollars in next 10 years exclusively for modernisation), and equally importantly, the ability to utilise these funds are an inescapable *must.*

(d) We must seriously move towards indigenous production by our Defence Research and Development Organisation (DRDO)–Industry combine and acquire at least 50-60 percent indigenous capability over next 10-15 years.

Conclusion

These are challenging times. The Armed Forces have been crying hoarse about the deficiencies to be covered. Our national leadership needs to take decisive steps and not bank upon the mirage of hope and possibilities of better relations developing between us and our adversaries. The history has proved that preparedness alone ensures security. Friendships develop strictly amongst the equals. Any weakness on our part can only provide temptations to our adversaries to be adventurous. Eternal optimistic that I am, I certainly believe that India has the sagacity and the requisite will power to rise up to the challenge.

*

July, 2013

15

India's Military Strategy vis-à-vis China

Lieutenant General Gautam Banerjee, PVSM, AVSM, YSM

A Legacy of Dispute

The territorial dispute in the Trans-Himalayan Region is a legacy of the eternal societal dispensation that prevailed over this vast swathe of high-altitude desert when this land provided for sustenance to the tribes living on its periphery by way of cattle grazing, mining and transit infrastructure for trans-Himalayan trade. That was the state till the mid-19th century, when commenced a 'game' of 'power-projection' to control the geographical properties of the regions of Tibet and East Turkmenistan, thus vitiating its pristine tranquility. British India and Russia were the ambitious participants in this power-play, with Tibet-China as the common denominator. It was therefore to be expected that given their cultural compulsions, there would be disputes amongst the contemporary regimes in Tibet, China and India.

The purpose of this chapter is to argue that Sino-Indian military confrontation has a hint of inevitability, unless the cost of armed conflict is rendered unacceptable to the revisionist party. Further, it is reiterated that it could be possible for India, the weaker party, to deter aggression across the Indo-Tibet Border by adopting a strategy that is ingenious and free of fixated encumbrances.

A Triumvirate of Trouble

The first of the triumvirate, China, is culturally assertive of her 'superior civilisation' and an instinctive hegemony. This culture must invariably manifest in *any* strong regime in Beijing considering as her property 'by right', *any* territory that at *any* point of time was under *any* form of control of *any* of the empires that reigned from Chang'an, Nanking or Peking. China's claim over Tibet, and by default over the Aksai Chin and the Tawang Tract, and by further extrapolation, over the entire Northern Ladakh and Arunachal Pradesh respectively, was, in hindsight, a foregone conclusion, which leaders of independent India may have failed to visualise.

Thus, with their institutional mastery over stratagems, the first step Communist China took within a year of seizing state-power was to annex Tibet. Next, in step with a steady military build-up, China contested the Indo-Tibet Border, then confronted India's so called 'Forward Policy' and finally in 1962, launched an offensive campaign across the McMahon Line and the Kun Lun Mountains. The following decades saw China continue with the build-up of strategic infrastructure in Tibet and modernisation of the People's Liberation Army (PLA). Confidence gained by progress of such ventures has, since past few years, caused Beijing, in a repeat of 1950's, to intensify its so far subdued claims over the territories of Arunachal Pradesh and Ladakh more and more assertively. Emboldened assertiveness is also evident in the unilateral promulgation of her 'sovereignty' over the Aksai Chin, annexation of the Shaksgam Valley and PLA's nonchalant march into Pakistan Occupied Kashmir. Expectedly, the charade of her protestations over the internal matters in Arunachal Pradesh continues, obviously with an intent to legitimise by incessant repetition, a claim which may be dismissed today but would become a *casus belli* some day. In some other politico-diplomatic issues too, China's assertiveness, bordering at arrogance, is palpable. Indeed, there are seeds of trouble in the Sino-Indian relationship.

The role of the central party of the contention, Tibet, is no less significant. Traditionally, Tibet has been as aggressive in conduct of her policies as her military power has permitted, and she has not failed to chastise Chinese as well as Indian intransigence whenever she could. Therefore, it may be expected that Tibet too, if and when the opportune moment comes, may raise territorial questions. That is but a lesson of history.

We may thus observe that a confrontationist situation along the Indo-Tibet Border is expected to continue in the foreseeable future. As a corollary, Indian strategists must look to foster a situation which motivates Beijing to seek solutions to her ambitions through political rather than military means.

The Military Equation

There is no way India can hope to match China's military power in the foreseeable future. Further, as evidenced by her past actions, China is unlikely to be dissuaded by the niceties of 'soft power' alone. The best India can hope to do therefore is to deter China from engaging in military aggression. And for that, the Indian armed forces have to conceive a strategy that would achieve that end within the means at hand, and organise accordingly.

The mandate is daunting. But taking cue from military history and teachings of great masters of military strategy, it might be possible for the Indian armed forces to devise effective measures to prevent China from achieving her objective of aggression. Indeed, history is replete with instances when the strong have given wide berth to the weaker adversary, and when yet engaged, the weak have triumphed over the strong.[1] Let us then see as to how can this mission might be accomplished in the Indian context.

We may begin with the most potent weapon of war-fighting: the 'mind' – that is a potent integration of intellect and ingenuity with strategic and tactical acumen which empowers military leaders to translate adversities into advantages.

Imposition of an Asymmetric War

We are aware that the concept of 'asymmetry' is as old as warfare itself. Military commanders down the ages have invested in manipulating the rules of armed engagement in a manner as to generate tactical advantages of their strengths while exploiting the adversary's limitations. Obviously, it is usual to impose *asymmetry* upon the opponent by fielding greater numbers of troops and weaponry. However, history teaches us that there are other ingenuous ways – some tangible (quantitative, technological, logistic) and others intangible (qualitative, tactical, psychological) – to achieve that end.[2] The PLA too, faced with prospects of conflict with the all-powerful US military forces on the Taiwan issue, has been propagating her version of asymmetric warfare – she illustrates the idea by a dramatic description: *"Assassin's Mace"*.

In view of the PLA's overwhelming military superiority, the recourse adopted by the Indian armed forces must aim at finding strategic and tactical ingenuity to negate the advantages of such superiority. The point to ponder here is that can such a recourse be in the realm of possibility? The answer is offered by what one of our finest generals had to state. Writing for the 'Seminar' in early 1962, General Thimmayya stated:

> I cannot ... envisage India taking on China in an open conflict on its own. China's present strength ... exceeds our resources a hundred fold, ... we could not hope to match China in the foreseeable future.... The country is a mass of

> mountains right up to the highest ridges of the Himalayas. The passes are practically impossible for over six months except for the men and animals, and that too with difficulty. China is, therefore, deprived of the use of its overwhelming superiority.... This is where we should make full use of our manpower and light equipment.... If the Chinese attack us with the intention of recovering territory which they believe to be theirs, we must meet them in those regions with commandos and highly equipped and fast moving infantry. If the Chinese penetrate the Himalayas..., we must be in a position to take advantage of our superior fire power and manoeuvrability to defeat them and at the same time continue to harass their lines of communications by the use of commandos and guerrillas....

Of course, the General was thinking of fighting a war that played mismatch to PLA's tactical strengths while permitting exposure of its vulnerabilities.[3]

Let us now examine certain core aspects of strategic asymmetry in the Sino-Indian context. We may begin with the fundamental factor of war: terrain.

Leveraging the Terrain

We are aware of the much lamented 'tactical advantages' enjoyed by the PLA on the open Tibetan Plateau. But we are also conscious of the fact that every item of PLA's war wherewithal on the Indo-Tibet frontline must be carted over 1500 kilometers from their logistic hubs at Lhasa and Kashgarh, which in turn must be stocked from central China, a further 2000 kilometers away. The entire logistic connectivity by road, rail, pipeline and air depends upon tenuous lines of communication and static staging yards, all situated over a terrain that is completely open, devoid of local resources and subject to such extreme conditions as it must obtain at 4300 meters of average altitude and sub-zero cold almost throughout the year. Even if China has engineered her transportation capacity to 24000 tons a day and therefore stated to be able to build up 30 divisions, including formations already in place, in 30 days, and sustain this force in war indefinitely, such theoretical calculations may be valid under 'test conditions', in practice this will invariably not be so. No doubt, the whole system of induction and sustenance for PLA's field forces in war would be ripe for interdiction by air power and special operations.

On the Indian side, the terrain south of the 4300 to 5400 meter high Himalayan passes, constricted and snow-bound most of the year, is characterised by razor-sharp ridgelines, steep slopes and narrow, gorge-like valleys generally running North to South. The Indian logistic installations are between 350 to 400 kilometers in depth, and therefore, in terms of turnaround time, comparable to that of the PLA in Tibet. Road axes connecting Indian foothills to the Indo-Tibet Border, being aligned more or less along the narrow valley floors, are extremely difficult to interdict by air or ground fire; these are targetable only in some stretches and even then require super-skills, high-technology and load of chance to score effective hits. Notably, scope exists to make such hits even more ineffective by means of modern methods of camouflage, deception and repair.

To undertake offensive operations in such terrain, PLA formations have to confine to constricted valleys that are hemmed in by successive ridge lines, thus limiting the scope for tactical level lateral manoeuvre. At the operational level, axes of offensive have to remain isolated from each other, while envelopment and turning movement; besides inviting risks of entrapment, it would entail such heavy logistic backup as to be prohibitive in terms of resources and time. Further, some distance down the Southern slopes into Indian territory, the terrain closes down to subsume the advantages that heavy weaponry and high-technology might bring to PLA's offensive. Indeed, the ground is heavily biased towards defensive operations – if conducted with aggressive intent.

We have reasons to believe that mother earth has not been overly supportive of aggression from Tibetan Plateau across the Himalayan Passes into India. Indeed, any PLA offensive across the Indo-Tibet Border has to contend with an adverse terrain anomaly: its build-up and spring-board areas straddle a ground that exposes its war machine to disruption by inhospitable elements as well as air and ground attack, while its offensive across the watershed passes would be beleaguered by a ground that favours classically conducted defensive operations. Indeed, PLA's offensive across the passes would have to fight '*friction of terrain*' and '*tension of logistics*' before engaging Indian forces – with "*General Snow*" ever ready to cut off its lifeline.

Therefore, even if the PLA commits overwhelming number of formations to its offensives, as to how many of these could actually be employable – along limited, narrow axes, and against successive lines of defences – remains a moot point to consider.

China's declaration of unilateral ceasefire in 1962 may be seen in this light. Only if Indian leadership had not lost its nerve and continued the state of war, matters would have been different.

PLA's Susceptibilities

With superior weaponry, missile arsenal, airborne forces, reconnaissance, communication, navigational and logistic capabilities, all of which are under continuous modernisation, we are well aware of PLA's overwhelming superiority over the Indian Armed Forces. Yet, the current state of Sino-India peace will be better fostered by factoring China's innate vulnerabilities in order to devise an affordable military deterrence.

Firstly, the 'hawks' in the Chinese establishment do not seem to be able to hide their hegemonic instincts till completion of the last phase of her 'four modernisations', as Deng Xioaping had advised. They have already started repudiating international norms on diplomatic, territorial, proliferation, economic and human rights issues. Reinforced with her past record of inciting trouble in the neighbourhood, this development has caused China to be seen as a predatory threat by most of her neighbours. In fact, the undercurrent of wariness of China's military buildup is already evident by signs of emergence of common-cause groupings among the Austro-Asian nations – with US participation. Possibly therefore, India's joint military exercises could gradually be elevated to the status of 'military co-operation' and bonded by a corresponding diplomatic understanding. The wise Chinaman certainly realises that in the contemporary international dispensation, such grouping among her target countries cannot be to her advantage. May be that consideration would curb her militaristic urge.

Secondly, buildup and war logistics of the PLA could be vulnerable to severe disruptions in Tibet. If they can be rebellious even when under the grip of a ruthless State, the discontented Uyghurs in the North-West and Tibetans in the South-East could also play a highly debilitating role on PLA's war-effort. Indian Army could leverage this vulnerability of the PLA by means of direct as well as indirect attacks on its rear echelons and thereby choking sustainability of its offensive across the watershed.

Thirdly, even as the modernisation programme imparts quantum empowerment to the PLA, there are intrinsic vulnerabilities too. Having propagated the doctrines of *"Informationalisation"* and *"War Zone Campaign"*, it has embarked upon adaptation of unfamiliar and complex concepts and practices of warfare. Therefore, its transition from a manpower intensive, low-technology 'people's army' to a modern army of high-technology, heavy weaponry and logistic-intensive formations cannot be free of complex glitches. The fact that its military leadership is relatively inexperienced and yet untested against spirited opposition adds to the PLA's burden. These vulnerabilities could afford opportunities to topple PLA's apple cart in the fog of war.

Fourthly, China is at a stage of 'wannabe superpower', when she is precariously open to losing her way by even stray developments, internal or external. Therefore, a conflict that fails to conclude with clear victory within a specified time frame will entail a serious setback to China's standing. Then there is the tactical vulnerability of the Chumbi Valley as well as across the passes in North Sikkim, Kailash Range and Aksai Chin, which present opportunities of potent riposte. Even if limited, such reverses can besmirch PLA's success elsewhere. Therefore, in a period when people's perceptions count, China may be wary of adopting military recourse against a resilient adversary. The complex concoction of time, terrain, counter-tactics and perceptions would not be easy for the PLA to tame in her adventure across the Indo-Tibet Border.

It may be noteworthy that the nuclear angle does not figure in the preceding discussion. This is deliberate. Firstly, because the nuclear doctrine espoused by both China and India – that of 'No First Use' – precludes any nuclear exchange. Secondly, should China circumvent her stated position, there is little India can do about it besides retaliation in kind to the extent of her arsenal, and then the script would be different. Lastly, beyond committing soldiers to conduct nuclear drills, Indian policy-makers have not mandated the military institution to nuclear warfare. Therefore, the Indian military hierarchy may not concern itself with what has been deliberately kept out of its orbit as a matter of higher policy of the government.

The preceding discussion leads to the observation that if not diverted from the verve of military preparations, it should be possible for India to build up credible deterrence against military attack by China to settle the contentious border issue. The question, however, is that how may that goal be secured?

The Burden of Indian Armed Forces

It needs no emphasis that China factors military power as a pillar of her politico-diplomatic goals. Accordingly, the PLA enjoys the blessings of China's visionary leadership and full range of support from the state, mandate in fact, to institute what restructuring and modernisation is necessary to maintain itself at the best state of operational and logistic efficiency. In contrast, in the Indian dispensation, the State apparatus arrogates military-specific policy making even if remaining innocent of what it takes to fight a war. It is under these conditions that the Indian armed forces are expected to deter the PLA, and in the event that China chooses to teach India another 'lesson' by recourse to military aggression, defeat that aggression. This is a popular mandate, even if the State may fail to find matching resources to gear up its military institution accordingly. Indian armed forces, therefore, have to devise appropriate strategies within the systemic limitations to strike at the PLA's vulnerabilities.

Certain indicators to such a possibility may be discussed next.

Taking up on *Sun Tzu's* Cue

It may be interesting to fall back upon teachings of the great masters of strategy, including the PLA's mentor, *Sun Tzu. "Being unconquerable lies with yourself"*, states Sun Tzu.

Therefore, we may resolve not to accept 'defeat' even if military engagements do not go our way. We could be prepared to remain in a state of hostility for months and years till PLA's great power is assailed, taking in our stride the death and destruction that might befall us. Taking heart from the historical fact that those who refuse to accept defeat, cannot really be defeated, the nation may refuse to conclude the struggle unless it is on its terms. Our expertise in cyber and psychological warfare strategy could add to the aggressor's misery, and India may thus refuse him the satisfaction of claiming 'victory'. That could suffice to bust her awe in the neighbourhood, strengthen internal dissent and affect her political and economic ambitions. Propagation of such a recourse may, in fact, deter military aggression; falling into a quagmire of never-ending military engagement is not an enticing prospect to any power in today's world. China is no exception.

Robert Greene prophesises, *"strategy is not a question of learning a series of moves and follow like a recipe, creative strategists stand out because they are able to drop preconceived notions and focus intensely on present".*

To 'turn the table' on a stronger adversary, Indian military leaders have to devise asymmetric strategies to garner advantages from blending of the terrain and tactics, mix of sophisticated and rudimentary technology and a venomous concoction of cunning, expediency and audacity. A potent combination of regular and irregular forces could be organised, equipped and trained to resist PLA's offensive from point elements to bases and beyond in depth, on the flanks, in simultaneity. Campaigning season being a limiting factor, India may continue the struggle in varying tempo and intensity to keep the aggressor bleeding till *"General Snow"* intervenes.

Indian armed forces may take cue from *England's motto* during the Anglo-Spanish War (1510): *"Aim at their weakness; make war expensive for them and cheap for you, outlast the most powerful foe. Hit their "Achilles' Heel"; size can be a weakness in the end".*

The tactics of resisting aggression may be devised in a manner as to cover India's military limitations while diluting the PLA's strengths. Indeed, if politically endorsed, resistance to PLA's presence at Lhasa and Xinjian may be built up, like it happened with the *'Mukti Bahini'*.[4] This would tie up the PLA in rear areas and has severe effects on its logistics. Logistic sustenance being the premier deciding factor in any war along the Indo-Tibet Border, an unstable Tibet would restrain PLA operations in a substantial manner; indeed, it could be a deciding factor in a long drawn war.

In *Sun Tsu's* words, *"To fight in a defensive manner is not a sign of weakness; it is the height of strategic wisdom, a powerful style of waging war, luring an aggressive enemy into imprudent attack and then waiting patiently for his moment of exhaustion to launch vicious counter-attacks, leveraging your weakness and limitations into power and victory".*

Indian forces could thus refuse to give classical battle till the PLA forces are stretched well south of the passes, canalised into narrow valleys and hemmed in by strongly held defensive features. All the while, the Army could deploy numerous 'strike teams' on man-pack, mule-pack, vehicle mounted or air-supported mode to strike at the flanks and rear of the advancing forces – skirmishing, hitting, feinting, retreating, baiting and overwhelming various elements of the attacking formations. Similarly, Air Force could bring devastation upon command and control centres, supply convoys, staging camps, logistic dumps and base areas that would invariably be sited all along the 2000 km stretch of the frontline and all the way back to the Sutlej Valley and the Western as well as the Eastern Highways – and thus impose strain and exhaustion upon the adversary.

Sun Tzu goes on to describe the idea of *"pre-eminent position" of a force that allows the defender the advantage of far-reaching tactical strength. He elaborates that these are positions that have intrinsic "energy" – like a stretched bow-string – rendering force-multiplying effects to own advantageous options while constraining that of the enemy's.*

In current military lexicon, we may consider these *positions* as the 'vital grounds' which would act as the fulcrum of own defensive operations that would be fought with ruthless aggression both in regular and irregular mode. Indian Army could master the vast high-altitude border belt like the back of its hands to identify access trails, gullies, catches, hides, crossings, tactical traps and dominating positions, and from these pivotal positions, attract PLA's repeated assaults, withdrawing, absorbing and recoiling as opportunities arise, and thus inducing the aggressor to commit more and more to gain less and less.

"By manoeuvring (the enemy) into precarious positions, by inducing feeling of

frustration and confusion, a strategist can get the other side to breakdown", goes on Sun Tzu.[5]

Indian armed forces could therefore operate according to a well-articulated tempo and varying intensity. It could potion offensive manoeuvre with positional resistance on the front, flanks and deep rear, and interspersed with periods of dormancy, keep the aggressor on the hop. The Indian Army could exploit its experience in high-altitude warfare, continuing resistance even during the non-campaigning seasons, without respite. Then, at an opportune moment, she could deliver a series of *coup de main* to decimate the aggression.

Following the *Napoleonic dictum* in the aftermath of the Battle of Austerlitz, that, *"if you hold back, waiting for the right moment to launch unexpected counter-attacks, weakness can become strength"*, Indian armed forces could strike back at a suitable juncture, holding the aggressor on ground of its own choosing and counter-attacking relentlessly his stretched forces. Then it might choose suitable sectors for offensive action across the border to balance out loss of ground elsewhere.

In the spirit of the *Churchillan* motto, Indians could proclaim to *"fight day and night, season after season, year after year; to fight in valleys, on peaks and passes, on land and in air, North and South of the watershed"*, and in their own terms – regardless – and deny victory to the mighty PLA.

India could thus dissuade the 'Great Dragon' from breathing fire and trying to teach her another lesson – by preparing for it; as Sun Tzu states, *"don't depend on the enemy not coming; depend rather on being ready for him"*.

Making Our Destiny

It will not be easy to convince a great power like China to desist from exercising her military strength in redeeming her aspirations of territorial expansion. Since most military disasters have resulted out of frigid strategies that proved to be irrelevant in the end, dealing with such an adversary would require the Indian armed forces to maximise its resources at hand by 'out-of-the-ordinary' recourses. We may also aver that limitations of tangible assets of war may, to good extent, be compensated by military intellect. The effort therefore has to be free of systemic inertia and deliberate.

Indian armed forces could group professionals who are unbound by mindsets and empower them to foster effective reorientation in the contemporary military thought and practice. Resources must be found by the nation to develop operational and logistic infrastructure, and breaking off from long drawn inertia, modernise field formations and strengthen air power. The recent raising of two divisions and positioning of some aircraft in the East would not be enough; more is needed to reap necessary operational advantages. Simultaneously, military diplomacy has to be promoted by means of joint training, logistic support and arms sales so that friendly neighbours may not have to look towards China. Of course, efficient intelligence setup has to be put in place to propagate deliberate deceptions by 'turning' the PLA's surveillance network. Above all, top class junior leadership has to be found to handle complex tactical challenges. And then, as *Xenophon* stated, *"for what leaders are; that as a rule, will the men below them be"*; the Indian armed forces would be prepared to take up the cudgel.

The trek is uphill. But given due political mandate, Indian military leaders have risen to the demands of the day before; they would do so again.

NOTES

1. Pyrrhus' war on Romans (279 BC), Anglo–Spanish War (1570), Shivaji's Deccan War (1650-1700), Anglo-Indian Wars of 18th Century, Austerlitz (1805), Afghan Wars of 19th Century, to quote just a few. More recently, Gallipoli (1915), Indo-China (1945-53), Vietnam (1965-74), Afghanistan (1980-89) – the list is endless. In a recent study, it was found that in the past century, as many as 50 percent wars have been won by forces inferior.
2. It was so that Babur created asymmetry in his favour by introducing field guns to rout the numerically much superior Lodi army in the First Battle of Panipat. Similarly, the Marathas adapted to the tactics of mobile warfare with light cavalry upon the vastly superior Mughal army in the Deccan; contrarily, they also invited disaster by adopting symmetrical tactics that suited the Afghan army in the Third Battle of Panipat.
3. Of course no one paid heed to General Thimmayya. Diverted from military sense by naïve politicians who propagated that the Chinese 'would never attack', 'it was not the job of the military commander to suggest as to who pose threat to the nation', and that all one had to do to stop the Chinese was to establish military 'posts' at locations decided by the Intelligence Bureau; the Army occupied defensive positions sans the paraphernalia of classical defensive battle, and when surrounded, cut off or assaulted according to a brilliant offensive plan devised by the Chinese General Staff, either got killed, maimed or captured, or broke up in flight.
4. Physically emancipated, psychologically devastated, tactically naïve and sparingly equipped, but mentally resilient, Mukti Bahini's "never say die" attitude was a major factor in Pakistan Army's defeat in Bangladesh War, 1971.
5. The strategy adopted by Czar Alexander I to defeat the overwhelmingly superior French Grande Armee during Napoleon's Russian Campaign (1812) comes close as an example. With his characteristic genius, Napoleon had prepared for a perfect campaign with his 4,50,000 strong Army and provided for every conceivable contingency, particularly logistic preparations down to the minutest details. Yet, continuously impeded by raiding Cossack Horsemen, undeveloped terrain and "General Winter", and in face of the Russia's refusal to give battle till the Grande Armee was stretched up to the village of Borodino – mere 150 km from Moscow – Napoleon had to resort to an ignominious retreat. Only 25,000 troops finally made it home!

*

April, 2015

16

Proxy War: 'Are We Fighting on Enemy's Terms?'

Colonel Karan Kharb

The Indian Army has a proud record of achievements – both in peace and war. Political leaders, government officialdom and people, all have absolute confidence in the Army as is evident from their eagerness to call for the military help in any eventuality too dangerous or difficult for others. Such absolute love and confidence should be a great source of happiness for the soldiers.

Having lost heavily in four wars, Pakistan has made bleeding India through state-sponsored terrorism more gainful. This strategy keeps the Kashmir in the news, keeps the Army on the run, causes public harassment, brings human rights into focus and turns public opinion against the Army. Far from reaching a final solution, the routine counter-terrorist operations undertaken by the Army in J&K have had a debilitating effect on the strength of the Army. A whole generation in the age group of 25 or less has grown up in a conflict-ridden environment. What more could Pakistan ask for? India must change its approach to the problem and seek an honourable final solution from a position of strength.

Bleeding India through Attrition

Proxy war is more sinister than conventional war in many ways. In a direct military-to-military confrontation, the enemy is clearly distinguishable from the civil population because in a conventional military scenario, capturing and holding of territory dictates manoeuvres. In the proxy war scenario, the terrorists merge with the population and have no interest in holding territory. They operate in small groups, carry out their terror tasks and easily melt away in the masses. Besides, the conventional enemy would be logistically organised and self-reliant whereas the terrorists depend on the local sympathisers and havens in towns, villages or *behaks* (shepherd huts in forests). Whereas the enemy supply lines would be discernible in the former case, there are no 'supply lines' in the latter case.

Pauses in infiltration and violence have been often assumed as defeat of terrorists and victory of the security forces. Such frequent assumptions have, however, always been proved wrong by fresh spurts in proxies sneaking in, reorganising and reviving their onslaught. Army units swing into action and carry out cordon and search operations, raids on suspected hideouts, lay ambush and establish checkpoints. The implication of such actions is that freedom of the local people is curtailed. Sometimes, innocent citizens get killed in the cross-fire between the army and the terrorists. There have also been a few cases where local informants have fed false information to the army units to get their rivals killed by planting credible evidence. This has been going on in J&K and Northeast for years. Two fallouts of this non-stop engagement are now having telling effects on the Army and the people: firstly, the Army's resilience is under strain; secondly, the local population is also becoming restive and anti-army. These shortcomings, though intangible, have far-reaching adverse consequences on the war-fighting capabilities of the Army and civil harmony.

The oft-quoted maxim, *'Laws are silent in times of war'* is no longer applicable in this war of wits. Military personnel are frequently taken to task for operations gone awry for want of workable intelligence or due to informer's deceit. There are many cases filed against military personnel in various courts of law for 'offences' during operations. J&K and North East lead in such allegations and court cases against military personnel. Imagine soldiers having to operate under constant apprehension of getting implicated for excesses on innocent civilians. These are inevitable operational hazards that mar soldiers' confidence in their leader who is either helpless or himself implicated as accused along with his men. Defence Minister Manohar Parrikar recently informed the Lok Sabha that as many as 108 military personnel committed suicide during 2014 as on November 21. "Reasons for such incidents", he said, "include long tenures of continuous deployment, domestic problems, perceived grievances, personal issues, mental built, financial problems and inability to withstand stress".

The Army has been fighting insurgency and terrorism for decades in Jammu and Kashmir (J&K) and Northeast. How long can it go on like this? Continuing counter-insurgency/counter-terrorist operations like this without seeing an end is surely not the way to deal with situations that are costing the nation dearly in every way – militarily, politically, socially and internationally. The number of soldiers sacrificed in J&K alone in the last 25 years is 7,443 (as in Feb 2014). This death toll is 1056 more than the combined total of 6387 Indian soldiers killed in the three Indo-Pak wars – 1965, 1971 and 1999 (Kargil). And while the Army's performance in the wars was spectacular thus earning the soldiers love and pride of the people, the attrition suffered by the Army during the last few decades has dismayed and disappointed both – people and the army. India has obviously fallen into the Pakistani trap and now continues to struggle there groping for a solution that is not visible.

'Offensive is the Best Defence'

One of the basic doctrines of war is that the side of the army that has the initiative and carries the war into enemy territory enjoys the advantage. In the given context, Pakistan has the initiative and all the fighting takes place on the Indian territory. The Pakistan Army selects, trains and pushes armed proxies not only into J&K but also to attack eminent targets in Delhi, Mumbai and elsewhere leaving India to *react* to devastations planned in Pakistan and enacted here from time to time. The effect is that India has been chasing these so-called 'non-state actors' raised and deployed by Pakistan for over 25 years now and the end of this dirty war is not in sight yet. India cannot win this war conclusively unless Pakistan is convinced that investing in such initiatives shall be retaliated most fiercely imposing costs that Pakistan cannot afford.

Professional modern armies like the western armies and the Israel Army have evolved decisive response systems to deter perpetration of state-sponsored terrorist acts. Israeli response to any provocation from any source has always been devastating. In its latest retaliation against Hamas kidnapping three Israeli teenagers in July 2014, the Israeli Defence Forces (IDF) launched an offensive into Gaza which left more than 2,000 Gazans killed and approximately 11,000 wounded. Israeli casualties were comparatively negligible: 66 Israeli soldiers and five Israeli civilians killed, 469 IDF soldiers and 261 Israeli civilians injured. After the 9/11 WTC disaster, the US Army invaded Afghanistan and continued man-hunt for the disaster's mastermind Osama bin Laden until the Navy Seals got him deep inside Pakistan in Abbotabad.

Quite on the contrary, India's response in the post-1971 scenario has all along been passively defensive rather than aggressive and punitive. In 1999 when India was already a nuclear power, Pakistan Army dared to intrude and occupy Indian territory in Kargil. Rather than reacting fiercely against this misadventure, the Indian Army fought with self-imposed restrictions and lost nearly 600 lives only to regain its lost territory and 'refrained' from crossing the LoC to avoid escalating the conflict. Again, responding to the December 2001 terrorist attack on its Parliament, the Indian Government ordered what is known to be the biggest military mobilisation since 1971 against Pakistan. The Army remained deployed for nearly a year without achieving anything. For years Pakistani and Chinese intrusions and cross-border mischief have been going on along the Line of Control (LC) and Line of Actual Control (LAC). Pakistani troops have frequently ambushed and even beheaded Indian soldiers on Indian soil in J&K. But retaliation even to such highly provocative acts has been no more than registering diplomatic protests and raising the volume of cross-border firing. Feeble response to these misadventures has established a pattern that has degraded the soldier's fighting potential and destroyed India's credibility as a military power in the region.

Expecting Pakistan to punish Zaki-ur-Rehman Lakhvi and six others charge sheeted for their role in Mumbai attack of 26/11 is like expecting Pakistan to prosecute its former President Parvez Musharraf for the Kargil intrusion in 1999. Army commando units and Special Forces in India are trained and equipped with capabilities to undertake special missions to strike at designated targets deep inside enemy territory. Special missions must, therefore, be considered and undertaken to pick up or liquidate criminals like Lakhvi and to destroy terrorist training camps in Pakistan. It is intriguingly self-defeating that instead of Nuclear India deterring Pakistan misadventures, Nuclear Pakistan has been deterring India unfairly but more effectively. Indian military authorities and Special Forces must work out a more effective response system that should compel Pakistan to negotiate peace with India. Most politicians and military generals in Pakistan have fair assessment of India's nuclear capabilities vis-à-vis Pakistan. It would, therefore, be unreasonable to perceive that any decision maker would be so insane there as to think of nuclear option to retaliate India's covert raids on precisely designated small targets like proclaimed offenders and terror breeding camps.

Pakistan Army's view notwithstanding, the pro-peace lobby in that country is growing with politicians, business community and intelligentsia favouring cordial relations with India. Fresh peace initiatives, therefore, should be India's first option but from a position of strength.

Factoring Military in the Emerging Scenario

Primary role of the Army is to defend the country from external aggression. Its secondary role includes internal security and relief operations in the wake of natural calamities or any other catastrophe considered beyond the capability of civil administration. The practice of deploying the Army in the interior civilian areas for protracted periods is a flawed concept which must change. Adverse effects of such deployments are serious and showing. The Army's war-fighting potential is degrading because in dealing with own civilians, the soldier's *'killing instincts'* are replaced by *'kinder restraint'*. The awe and respect for the Army in the civilian mind also diminishes gradually. Prolonged deployments and fighting with lots of restrictions imposed have had a telling effect on the morale of the troops. Therefore, dealing with security situations in the interior civilian areas should remain a police responsibility. Resources of local police could be reinforced by armed police forces like CRPF. In most of the affected States, police has its own 'special task force' (STF) squads who could be better trained and armed to carry out their counter-terrorist/counter-insurgency role more effectively. The Army should be left to concentrate on what is most expected of it – come into action only as a 'last resort' to deal with exceptionally grave situations by launching short and swift operations. Equally swiftly, the Army units must disengage and return to their primary role at the LAC, LoC or cantonments to train and prepare for bigger roles.

Although India's relations with China are apparently thawing, we still have claims and counter claims on territories across the 4,056 km LAC. Frequently, Chinese troops have intruded to stake claim on the Indian territory in Ladakh and Arunachal Pradesh. Development of rail-road network and military infrastructure in forward areas of the Tibet region has been a cause of concern for India. Despite fast-growing trade and economic cooperation between India and China, they have contentious issues spread from the South China Sea to the Indian Ocean besides the existing border issues.

Even more serious are the developments taking place further north where the Karakoram highway has been upgraded from 10 m to 33 m wide two-way road trebling its transport capacity and linking China to the warm water port of Gwadar. While Pakistan has already ceded Shaksgam Valley to China, there are also reports of Pakistan leasing the region of Gilgit-Baltistan to China for a period of 50 years. Since February 2013, the construction and operation of Gwadar Port has been assigned by Pakistan to the state-run Chinese firm – China Overseas Port Holding Company (COPHC). More recently, China has also sought to expand its economic footprint in Afghanistan. In February 2015, at an Afghanistan-Pakistan-China trilateral dialogue, Beijing announced that it would provide Afghanistan $300 million as grants over the next three years besides undertaking projects like rail-road development including development of the New Silk Road that connects South Asia to Central Asia. Besides the Uyghur insurgency in Xinjiang, China is also concerned about the rising menace of East Turkestan Islamic Movement (ETIM) who could continue regrouping along Af-Pak porous borders if Taliban is not kept under check.

Steadily, China is encircling India strategically from all directions. It is expanding its reach in Myanmar, Sri Lanka and other island nations in the Indian Ocean. Until now India had ignored the creepy Chinese advance that could result in India's 'continental isolation'. Thanks to the new assessment of security environment around India, the Modi Government appears to have woken up to the emerging geo-political scenario in the region as indicated by Prime Minister Narendra Modi's thrust in revitalising India's relationships with SAARC countries and island nations in the Indian Oceans.

A crucial fact that has been overlooked by strategists in India is that there is always a strategic military component woven into development projects China undertakes in the East and South Asian countries. China negotiates partnership and retains long-term control of the facilities created through joint projects ranging from mining to infrastructure development, ports and highways. Chinese military representation is inseparably integrated with the controlling management of such facilities. In the Indian context even today, it would be unthinkable to have a military say in foreign trade, commerce or matters relating to diplomacy and foreign relations. It is the flawed politico-bureaucratic perception of successive governments that has not allowed the military to disentangle from the environs of insurgency and proxy war to prepare and attend to larger national interests on and beyond land borders. Diplomacy, foreign trade and relations shall yield more if backed by credible military potential particularly when a number of India's neighbours look up to it for support. A visible military might will only buttress India's diplomatic initiatives at regional as well as global levels. As a component of foreign policy projection, Indian military should inspire confidence among our weaker neighbours and a caution among those who would otherwise browbeat India to have their way.

Conclusion

The speed at which the world is changing is unprecedented. Threat scenario in South Asia is also becoming more complex even as old problems among neighbours linger. While modernisation programme of our Armed Forces has remained neglected for over a decade, the Army has been virtually reduced to just another police force – only better armed, trained and led. In the coming future, keeping the Army so pinned down in the cobwebs of insurgency and proxy war could end up into a national disaster if and when the Army is faced with more complex military challenges and threats to national integrity and sovereignty. As the principal arm of the Armed Forces, the Army must visualise and prepare for the future roles that would lie far beyond India's land borders.

*

December, 2015

17

MILITARY MODERNISATION IN CHINA: ITS IMPLICATIONS

Jayadeva Ranade

Chinese President Xi Jinping's public announcement downsizing the People's Liberation Army (PLA) at the grand military parade on September 3, 2015, was a major event. It signaled that the final stages of reform and reorganisation of the PLA would begin now that internal consensus had been reached. Despite the transparently thin attempt to package the 300,000-personnel troop reduction as a move towards promoting peace, the troop reduction is actually part of a long-planned effort to streamline and strengthen the PLA and fashion it into a hi-tech, lethal, 'informationised' force capable of defending China's national interests at home and abroad while expanding China's strategic space.

These reforms have direct implications for India and countries in the region, with whom China has territorial disputes or who have borders with it. They will undoubtedly monitor the reforms closely.

Plans for military reforms and restructuring were finalised earlier and downsizing the PLA is part of the final phase. After the release for internal circulation of the 'PLA's Development Outline for Cultivating Armed Forces Talent before the Year 2020' (referred to only as the 'Outline'), which spelt out plans for restructuring the PLA, official documents described the five-year (2011-2015) period as "crucial" in the PLA's development. The plans received a substantive push when the Chinese Communist Party (CCP)'s Third Plenum, which was held in November 2013, approved proposals for major organisational restructuring and technological upgradation of the PLA. Within days after the

Third Plenum, CMC Vice Chairman and former PLA Air Force (PLAAF) Commander Xu Qiliang asserted that the reforms will be implemented, that non-combatant personnel would be "eliminated", and that the reforms will enable the PLA to "win wars".

On March 15, 2014, China's authoritative official news agency Xinhua announced the creation of a new 'Small Leading Group for Deepening Reform of National Defense and the Military'. It was set up as a subcommittee of the Central Military Commission (CMC) under the chairmanship of Xi Jinping assisted by two Deputy Chairmen who were also the Vice Chairmen of the CMC namely, General Fan Changlong and General Xu Qiliang. Names of the other members have not yet been disclosed, but outspoken General Liu Yuan, a high-ranking 'princeling' close to Xi Jinping and Political Commissar of the PLA's General Logistics Department (GLD), is probably one member.

Implementation of the reforms has been delayed by institutional resistance and the PLA's downsizing is now expected to be completed only by 2017. Among the factors prompting resistance were reports that consequent to the reorganisation of Military Regions (MRs) and PLA Headquarters in Beijing, a number of Generals and senior officers would be rendered redundant and transferred to Beijing. This meant loss of authority and perquisites, such as housing, which they currently enjoy. The different Services also resisted downsizing of their personnel strengths and reduction in their share of the budget.

At least two signed articles in the Liberation Army Daily (LAD) on September 9, 2015, publicised the existence of resistance to reforms inside the PLA. The first article cautioned that implementation of the reforms would be difficult and "would require an assault on fortified positions to change mindsets and root out vested interests, and that the difficulties would be unprecedented." Advocating their implementation, which it asserted were essential, the article observed that "if these reforms failed, measures still to come would be nothing more than an empty sheet of paper". Reiterating that implementing military reforms would be difficult, another article in the same paper said that as reforms begin to be implemented "there could be significant structural contradictions and an accumulation of institutional obstacles". Its author, Ma Depao, was associated with the Academy of Military Sciences (AMS) till 2006, but is now probably with the PLA Daily.

In this backdrop, the presence on the podium of Hu Jintao and Jiang Zemin, Chinese President and Chairman of the Central Military Commission (CMC) Xi Jinping's two immediate predecessors, was significant. Their presence next to

Xi Jinping was intended as assurance – to domestic and foreign audiences – of support for Xi Jinping and his plans to reform and restructure the PLA. Jiang Zemin's presence was particularly significant since a large number of the PLA Generals and senior officers under arrest, or under investigation, on charges of corruption are closely associated with Jiang Zemin or his protégés. Rumours were also circulating for some months in official circles in Beijing that Jiang Zemin was either already under house arrest, or likely to be detained soon.

A compromise regarding military reforms was undoubtedly reached before Xi Jinping announced the downsizing of the PLA on September 3, 2015. In addition to support for the reforms from his fellow 'princelings' and loyalists in senior echelons of the PLA, support would additionally have come from the younger more professional officers. Resistance would have been diluted by the vigorous campaign against corruption launched by the Central Discipline Inspection Commission (CDIC) in the PLA and efforts at 'education' by the PLA's General Political Department (GPD), with both efforts facilitated by the 40 percent hike in salaries and allowances awarded to PLA personnel last year.

The troop reduction of 300,000 announced on September 3, 2015, is far less than the 800,000 envisaged in 2011. In April 2011, the Beijing-owned Hong Kong-based Wen Wei Po publicised plans for reducing the PLA's size by 800,000 personnel. While the report was denied by China's Defence Ministry, Professor Han Xudong of China's National Defence University (NDU), commenting on the Wen Wei Po report to Global Times, a subsidiary of the authoritative CCP newspaper 'People's Daily', disclosed that Wen Wei Po's report was the personal opinion of a retired PLA General formerly in charge of downsizing. He added, though, that the Defence Ministry's denial did not mean there would be no reductions in the future. Hinting at the extent of personnel cuts, he elaborated that since the US has a 1.4 million army and India a 1.2 million army, a 1.5 million strength for the PLA would be adequate.

Separately, Chinese military officers commenting on the Wen Wei Po report on background to Jane's said the central authorities were working out targets for future downsizing, but big cuts are unlikely. Reductions, they said, could be expected in 2-3 years. However, they would not affect the PLA's capabilities as it would extensively use Information Technology and science and technology for advanced modern weaponry. PLA personnel would be better educated, better trained and more proficient. These comments as well as appearance of the report in the Wen Wei Po together with excerpts from the 'PLA's Development Outline for Cultivating Armed Forces Talent before the Year 2020' provided insights into the PLA's restructuring plans.

Commenting on the personnel cuts announced in September 2015, retired Major General Xu Guangyu, a Senior Consultant at the Chinese Military Disarmament Control Council and an expert of Chinese contemporary military affairs, justified the need for reforms and said, "these reductions are an effort to stay on this path and increase quality not numbers". Colonel Yang Yujun, spokesman for China's Ministry of National Defence (MND), clarified that troops to be disbanded are those "equipped with outdated armaments and office staff and personnel of non-combat organisations". Separately, the authoritative official news agency Xinhua said on September 3, 2015, that "Non-combat units and administrative staff will be cut, and units with older weapons and equipment will reportedly be targeted for demobilisation".

After a meeting of the CMC on September 10, 2015, the two Vice Chairmen of the CMC, General Fan Changlong and General Xu Qiliang, travelled to all seven MRs to explain the reform plans to middle and low-ranking military officers. Simultaneously, senior officers of the PLA's four principal general departments – General Staff Department (GSD), General Political Department (GPD), General Logistics Department (GLD) and General Armaments Department (GAD) – the PLA Air Force (PLAAF), PLA Navy (PLAN), Second Artillery Force (SAF) and People's Armed Police Force (PAPF) were instructed to express support for the reforms.

The proposed reforms, described as the most extensive and wide-ranging till now, are likely to introduce changes in the rank structure to bring them on par with international practice. Reports indicate that the new Theatre Commanders would be of lower rank than the present MR Commanders to reduce their political influence and Senior Colonels are to be designated as Brigadier General. The ranks of Second Lieutenant and Lieutenant will be readjusted with possible introduction of a rank of Lieutenant Commander.

Certain is that the PLA's four principal General Departments (GSD, GPD, GLD and GAD) and the Ministry of National Defence (MND) will be restructured. Equally certain is that non-combat units and administrative staff will be cut and units with older weapons and equipment will be targeted for demobilisation. This could result in the demobilisation of a number of Group Armies (GAs) whose inventories have a preponderance of older systems. The GAs being accorded lower priority by the PLA – evidenced by their not having Special

Forces and Army Aviation Brigades/Regiments – could similarly be earmarked for demobilisation.

Based on official reports, which state that Beijing perceives less external threat from the northern sector, analysts assess that three GAs from this area would be demobilised. These are likely to be 27th GA, Beijing MR; 40th GA, Shenyang MR; and 47th GA, Lanzhou MR. If the cuts are deeper, then possibly the 14th GA in the Chengdu MR and 20th GA in Jinan MR could be demobilised. Chinese media reports indicate that the PLA troop strength in the southern sector – southwest facing India and the southeast responsible for a Taiwan crisis, as well as the South China Sea and Vietnam – would not experience major cuts.

Reports suggest the restructuring will result in the establishment of four or five Theatre Joint Commands. There have been indications in China's official media since at least 2011 and in the official Defence White Papers issued since 2013 that the PLA is contemplating switching to Theatre Commands and discarding the present system of MRs. The increasing number of long-range, trans-MR Integrated Joint Operations (IJOs) being conducted by the PLA particularly since 2007 has been a pointer.

Based on Chinese media and other reports, the following outline of the proposed restructuring of the PLA emerges:

(i) The existing seven MRs will be replaced by four Theatre Joint Commands. These will be a Northeast Theatre Command created by merging the Shenyang and Beijing MRs; a Northwest Theatre Command centered on the Lanzhou MR; a Southwest Theatre Command consisting of Chengdu MR; and a Southeast Theatre Command formed by merging the Guangzhou, Nanjing and Jinan MRs; or

(ii) The seven MRs will be consolidated into five Theatre Joint Commands. In this case the Theatre Commands would be Northeast Theatre Command comprising Shenyang and Beijing MRs; Northwest Theatre Command consisting of Lanzhou MR; Southwest Theatre Command comprising Chengdu MR; and a Southeast Theatre Command that incorporates the Guangzhou and Nanjing MRs. This version claims that there will also be a Reserve Joint Command based on Jinan MR, which will provide forces to other Theaters as required and perform other allotted tasks. Yet another option being mentioned is that the Beijing and Shenyang MRs will be merged into a separate Joint Command with responsibility for defense of the capital and protection of the border with North Korea.

In such a case, the Southeast Theatre Command will include the Nanjing, Guangzhou and Jinan MRs. This version provides for one additional Command thereby implying that fewer troops/units would be demobilised.

(iii) Surprisingly, the reports claim that the Theater Joint Commands would not directly command troops, which will be under the individual PLAA, PLAN, PLAAF commands in each Theatre except in times of war. In times of war the troops will be placed under a Joint Command which is to be established in each Theatre.

(iv) The personnel strength of the PLA ground forces, for the past few years being officially referred to as PLAA, will be reduced to 360,000. China's Defence White Paper issued in 2013 had disclosed the PLAA's troop strength as 850,000.

(v) Both versions state that the personnel strengths of the PLAN and PLAAF will increase but make no mention of the secretive strategic force, viz. Second Artillery. This could be because the strength of the Second Artillery has increased by 10,000 personnel over the past year.

(vi) In the reorganisation of the PLA's four General Departments, the GSD will be upgraded and will include high-ranking officers from all service branches. It will be a higher echelon organisation than the other General Departments. It will be entrusted with planning functions and provide advice to the Chairman of the CMC and be modeled on the US Joint Chiefs of Staff. Also, the GLD and GAD will be merged into one GLD.

(vii) The PAPF will be transformed into a National Guard and will additionally absorb a considerable number of the demobilised PLA personnel.

(viii) The number of military academies will be reduced from the present 150 to 29.

Retired PLA Major General Xu Guangyu was quoted by the official state-run Global Times on September 6, 2015, as separately speculating that the ratio of ground, air and naval forces would finally be 2:1:1, a dramatic shift from the current estimate of about 4:2:1.

Meanwhile, the US-based Chinese news service Boxun reported that restructuring of the existing 150 military academies has already begun under the supervision of General Liu Yuan, Political Commissar of the PLA's General Logistics Department (GLD) and close associate of Xi Jinping. General Liu Yuan, who is the son of former Chinese President Liu Shaoqi and a ranking 'princeling', supports the military reforms pushed by Xi Jinping and has publicly spoken out against corruption in the PLA. Boxun said the 150 academies are to be reduced and merged into 29 academies, with the remaining being transferred to the local civilian administration. Only military academies catering solely to the PLA, like the Army Non-Commissioned Officer Academy, the Officer College, Staff and Command College, Logistics College, Military Engineering College, Armaments and Equipment College and Strategic Artillery Academy are to be retained.

Institutes like the National Defense University (NDU), the Defense University of Science and Technology, the Military Museum, PLA Archives, Military Academy of Medical Sciences, Engineering Design Institute, armaments research institutes affiliated with the general headquarters and military service branches, and science and technology and academic research organisations will all be incorporated into the national defense administrative system. A major reform measure is that officers of these establishments will be demobilised and no longer have military ranks, but be designated as civilian personnel. The National Defense University (NDU) will, however, continue to be responsible for training senior military cadres.

The reform and restructuring of the PLA essentially orients the Theatre Joint Commands as per their primary task. It is intended to concentrate firepower and troops trained for a specific type of warfare within a single Theatre for ease of rapid deployment. Land and sea warfare forces are to be grouped separately. For example, the Shenyang and Beijing MRs to be merged into the Northeast Theatre Command and the Jinan, Nanjing and Guangzhou MRs to be absorbed in the Southeast Theatre Command have a mainly maritime role. The primary objective of these Theatre Joint Commands will be to enable China to establish dominance over the East China Sea and South China Sea and stand up to a US-Japan alliance. Reports suggest that by 2020, the Theatres will be reinforced by three aircraft carrier combat groups with the existing aircraft carrier 'Liaoning' deployed in the East China Sea, and the other two aircraft carriers in the South China Sea. The time-frame for creation of the Theatre Joint Commands is five years.

The backdrop for these military reforms is the assessment of China's political and military leaders of the international situation and environment around China. Significant for India is the PLA spokesman's statement to the Beijing-owned Hong Kong-based newspaper Wen Wei Po on May 27, 2011. Stating that the strength of 2.3 million is appropriate for the PLA, he justified it because of the "vastness of Chinese territory, the difficulties of the tasks required for defending maritime interests and the endless number of national development interests which are putting new requirements on army building". The spokesman added that "China is currently facing an unsafe world and increasing uncertainty. The West is recovering while the East is anxious and the North is stable while the South is tense, dangerous situation on China's borders is increasing. There is also the possibility that the actions by outsiders will bring about complex changes."

The annual conference on the 'Global Military Situation' organised by the PLA's prestigious Academy of Military Sciences (AMS) on January 9, 2015, also discussed the regional security situation in the Asia-Pacific, Europe and the Middle East. It was attended by over 150 senior PLA officers and experts including from the CMC, the four General departments, NDU and the Commandant and Political Commissar of the AMS. The conference concluded that 'unprecedented changes are taking place in the global military situation; military force in international relations is more widely used; and the situation in the Asia-Pacific has worsened'.

Based on these and similar high-level official assessments, the reforms are intended to streamline the PLA and equip it to effectively defend China's claimed maritime domain and "fight and win wars". Chinese President Xi Jinping, who as secretary (Mishu) to Chinese Defence Minister Geng Biao in 1979 had a ringside view of how Deng Xiaoping thoroughly reformed the PLA, will guide implementation of these far-reaching reforms designed to make China strong and realise 'China's Dream'.

For India, it is pertinent that both versions of the restructuring proposals mention that Lanzhou and Chengdu MRs, which are oriented for military operations against India, will be retained as reinforced, independent Theatre Commands. While safeguarding Chinese investments in the northern areas of Pakistan could be a factor for the Lanzhou Theatre Command, the indication is clearly that China will maintain an 'offensive' posture towards India.

*

February, 2016

18

Indian Army: State of War Readiness – A Contemporary Perspective

Brigadier Rahul Bhonsle

Overview of State of Readiness

There has been much focus on capital procurements regarding artillery guns, fighter aircraft and submarines for fighting wars in the future. These are no doubt essential to ensure that the nation is ready to face a future challenge given the uncertain security environment in the neighbourhood and programme of rapid modernisation of the Chinese People's Liberation Army (PLA). At the same time, given the constant threat of proxy war waged by Pakistan – the Pathankot terrorist attack being a grim reminder – there is as much need to ensure readiness to fight wars today as in the future.

A series of exposures in the media in 2012-13 revealed a high state of hollowness in the Indian armed forces and more particularly in the Army. The state of ammunition, in particular, was considered critical while the level of holdings indicated to be adequate for fighting a 10-day war. The Ministry of Defence has reported in the Parliament that appropriate measures have been undertaken to redress this shortcoming. Indian Army's challenge of preparedness thus envisages being ready for battle today while preparing to deter a war tomorrow. Provision of budgeting for both these contingencies is a *sine qua non*. In the light of the above, some issues which need to be examined include the current state of ammunition, availability of funds for procurement and raising of the mountain strike corps.

Status of Ammunition Holdings – An Assessment

Ammunition is a critical warfighting requirement. Scales of holdings are laid down for this purpose at the national level regarding War Wastage Reserves (WWR), which are estimates of ammunition that will be expended in the case of an outbreak of hostilities. This is regarding 'Intense' (I) and 'Normal' (N) rates that are in the case of intense and normal battlefield activity.

In the recent past, the Comptroller Auditor General of India's (CAG) report had passed severe strictures on the Indian Army for shortages in ammunition. "While availability of authorised stock against WWR to meet the expected duration of operation formed the basic criteria for ensuring the operational readiness of the Army, we found during the review that against the WWR of 40 (I) days, the availability of ammunition was only in 10 per cent of the total types of ammunition held (March 2013)," the report said. "Further, in 50 per cent of the total types of ammunition, the holding was 'critical', i.e., less than 10 (I) days", it said. "To tide over the persistent acute shortages, the AHQ had set (1999) a minimum threshold of MARL (Minimum Acceptable Risk Level) 20 (I) days to be achieved first. We found that even after 15 years, the threshold of MARL could not be achieved. The acute shortage was a serious cause of concern directly impairing the operational readiness of the Army", it said.

The report is for the period 2008-2013. As of now, the shortage may not be 15-25 per cent of various types of ammunition as the Army has managed to make up deficiencies given the exposure of the issue in the public domain from time to time. The entire ammunition is likely to be made up in a couple of years.

The exposure of the deficiency and its persistence for one and a half decades from 1999 to 2013 indicates the need for a structured approach to effective management of ammunition as it affects operational readiness of the Army. With two primary sources of acquisition – Ordnance Factory Board and import – forecasting, follow-up and timely action in the case of shortfall rather than accepting the same as a matter, of course, is necessary. This was lacking from 2008 to 2013 but is now hopefully on stream. The roadmap for making up deficiencies of ammunition is planned to cost Rs. 19,250 crore to make up 50 percent war wastage reserves of ammunition by end of 2015 and 100 percent by 2019 at a cost of Rs. 19,250 crore.

As ammunition is procured from production agencies based on a five-year roll plan, streamlining the planning process, coordination and interaction with production agencies should be effectively managed to ensure that alarming deficiencies which are indicative of poor management do not recur. A holistic roll-on plan to include procurement ex-import and ex-trade to build up adequately targeted stocks in addition to training requirements will ensure adequate stocks are available at all times.

There are issues related to ammunition-manufacturing capacities. The Ordnance Factory Board (OFB) is reportedly capable of manufacturing all types of ammunition. Modern tank and artillery ammunition, however, have to be imported. Concerning indigenous production, there appears to be a lack of accountability in the OFB as even though there is a five-year roll-on indent by the Services, it has failed to meet the requirements with deficiencies of approximately 25 percent, which is inexcusable. Greater accountability of the OFB is necessary to ensure that indents placed as per the roll-on plan are provisioned and the requirements for the Services are met in full.

Funding Challenges

Ammunition is a part of the Stores Head of the Revenue Budget of the Army. As per the structured plan of the Army, deficiencies in the WWR of ammunition are projected to be completed by 2017-18. This was ensured by provision of an additional Rs. 700 crore in the Revised Budget Estimates in 2014-15, Rs. 1500 crore from the budget estimates of the same year, and an increase of Rs. 2500 crore from the 2013-14 expenditure. The approximate requirement under the Stores head for the Army is Rs. 20,000 crore per year as against the same the Army was allocated Rs. 15,990 crore in the Revised Estimates for 2014-15 and Rs. 16697.84 crores in the Budget Estimates for 2015-16. This would imply a shortfall in funding of Rs. 7300 crore in the past two years. This would have necessitated cutting quantities in procurements be it ammunition or other items. However, the reduction in allocations in the budget concerning demands made remains a perennial challenge.

The Parliamentary Committee on Defence has noted that while each year the Army got a major share of Defence Budget. However, it has been getting less than projections. Thus, while the Army projected a requirement of Rs. 93355.38 crore for the Revenue outlay, it was allocated only Rs. 81119.20 crore in the budget for 2013-14. This is almost a 15 percent shortfall. For the Capital outlay, as against Rs. 25528.08 crore projected, Rs. 17883.83 crore was allocated. Here, the shortfall in 2013-14 is likely to be as large as 25 percent. There is shortage of funds as generally projections by the Ministry of Defence (MoD) for the armed forces are reduced by the Ministry of Finance in the final budget by 25 percent or so. This is a vicious cycle – there is a problem of budget management wherein surrender from capital account and internal adjustments have led to the loss of credibility of the MoD financial management which in turn leads the Ministry of Finance to believe that the Services can do with lesser allocations.

However, the Army has streamlined budget management which was one of the shortcomings of the past. Thus, as per six monthly statements of expenditure for 2015-16 [April–September 2015], of the Rs. 104158.95 crore allocated under the Revenue Head to the Army, Rs. 50318.44 crore or 48 percent has been expended. The performance was even better in the previous budget year 2014-15 for the comparative period where expenditure was 53 percent up to September. Thus hopefully, the Budget allocations for 2016-17 which are being considered by the Finance Ministry will ensure that Services' projections are fully met.

Streamlining Procurement – Case of Bullet Proof Jacket

The necessity for streamlining procurement to ensure deficiencies do not accumulate is well established. A case in point is that of acquisition of bullet proof jackets (BPJs) by the Indian Army. A good BPJ is a life saver as well as it gives the requisite confidence to the soldier to engage in close quarter combat. The BPJ is also an essential protection for a soldier fighting in a counter-insurgency environment. While there is a long-standing requirement of 1,86,138 BPJs for the Indian Army as accepted by the Defence Acquisition Council (DAC) through Acceptance of Necessity (AoN) in October 2009 for capital procurement by 2012, these are yet to be acquired.

Defence Minister Manohar Parrikar, in a question in the Parliament recently, stated that the tender or the request for proposal (RFP) "was retracted on October 5 as the bullet-proof jackets fielded by the vendors failed in the trials". There are reports that the MoD is now carrying out "emergency revenue procurement" of 50,000 jackets. Two Indian firms (Tata Advanced Materials and MKU) have been shortlisted and trials are due shortly. It is pertinent to note that a critical warfighting aid for the soldier could not be procured for the past six years and is likely to be delayed for at least a couple of years, indicating the necessity for streamlining procurement of essential items. Such equipment has to be pre-trialed and inducted through the 'Buy (Indian)' or even 'Buy (Global)' route so that soldier safety and battlefield efficiency is not impacted.

Mountain Strike Corps

The aim of raising a mountain strike corps is to provide adequate capability to the armed forces to deter attempts by the adversary, China, to upset the *status quo* and grab land in its claimed areas of Arunachal Pradesh or other sectors. Reports indicate that the plan has been delayed given paucity of funds with competing requirements of the Services. There is an impression in some quarters that induction of technology will reduce the dependence on manpower. While technology has brought about revolutionary changes in conventional warfare in the plains and the desert sectors, the impact on wars in the mountains or in counter-insurgency militancy operations remains limited. The adage that 'mountains eat away troops' is true even in the 21st century as intervening terrain features in the mountains severely restrict visibility and fields of fire of direct firing weapons while restricting mobility to foot or light vehicles. This necessitates a greater number of troop deployment on the ground.

The delay in raising of the mountain strike corps comes even as China has undertaken major reforms of the People's Liberation Army (PLA). A united front has now been formed by combining the Lanzhou and Chengdu Military Area Commands into a West Zone with the aim of jointness, synergy and flexible application of forces in Xinjiang and Tibet. This development has increased the level of threat on our Northern borders as the PLA's West Zone commander would have at his disposal forces from Xinjiang for application in the Medog Sector opposite Arunachal Pradesh. This has effectively overcome our local force superiority that was created by raising of two new divisions in defensive role in the Eastern Command. There is, therefore, a necessity for prioritising the raising of 17 Mountain Strike Corps so that the formation is battle ready by 2020, thus deterring any designs for aggression by China in the Eastern Sector.

Conclusion

The necessity for enhancing efficiency in planning and provisioning of essential items of equipment for the armed forces procurements is well underlined. Systemic measures are necessary to ensure that requirements are anticipated well in advance and procurement process initiated, so that contemporary and state-of-the-art equipment is available to the defence forces. Deficiencies in WWR ammunition in no case can be acceptable. Budgeting for defence requirements has to be streamlined so that adequate funds are available for essential purchases. At the same time, creating long-term capacities such as the 17 Mountain Strike Corps cannot be relegated to the background just due to competing requirements.

*

June, 2016

19

The Ins and Outs of Infiltration: The Real Problem in J&K

Lieutenant General S A Hasnain, PVSM, UYSM, AVSM, SM (Bar), VSM (Bar)

Terrorist Infiltration in Kashmir

People often get into discussions on Jammu & Kashmir (J&K). One finds most of them have visited the State as tourists and have considerable interest in the security situation. Besides never being able to perceive why there is such large presence of the uniform all over the Valley, especially the tourist spots, the airport or even the Boulevard, the other most common question is something which astounds. They invariably feel that the Indian Army has failed in its job because we do not seem to be able to stop Pakistan-sponsored terrorists infiltrating into J&K, which is a valid point that the Army's PR machinery has never been able to explain with any degree of credibility. It needs a detailed commentary to allow the right perception to sink in. For that we need to go back to 1988-89 and progressively see how the J&K theatre's threats panned out, with a focus on the role of infiltration.

The Situation: 1987-89

It is not necessary to describe the triggers which sent the Valley in flames. The apparent strategy Pakistan followed was to seize the moment when all parameters of India's security were almost rock bottom. In 1988-89, four of our frontline army formations (about 20,000 men each) were deployed in Sri Lanka; Punjab had an ongoing major internal security problem and Operation Blue Star had made handling the situation even more tentative. The Bofors case took away attention from what was building up in Kashmir and the political front was in turmoil after Rajiv Gandhi's exit. All Pakistan needed was the induction of enough young Kashmiris trained in fighting the guerilla way led by a few foreign terrorists and Special Service Group (SSG) men from their own army. The diabolic 'Zia Plan', conceived in 1977, would then be underway in execution.

The Indian Army's Line of Control (LC) posture had a 'conventional military deployment' just barely sufficient to ensure the 'sanctity' of the LC. These terms need brief explanation. The Army's role and task was to prevent any encroachment on the LC. It did then and does that even today by holding static piquet's and posts; the gaps between them are patrolled regularly. This ensures the sanctity of the LC. Surveillance existed for conventional war when the adversary could make attempts to infiltrate large columns to attack from the rear. In conventional operations, the adversary can at maximum attempt one or maximum two such operations all along the LC if it has to have any success at all. Small-scale infiltration (strength of 6-8) could hardly be catered for.

Commencement of Infiltration

What the Army's conventional posture on the LoC came up against in 1988-90, and thereafter, was first the infiltration of some Pakistani servicemen in small numbers making use of multiple routes much as they did in 'Operation Gibraltar' in 1965. These formed the core teams for recruitment who motivated and selected the volunteer youth for jihad and sent them across the LC through exfiltration along different routes, into the Pakistan Occupied Kashmir (PoK). The ease of infiltration and exfiltration of cadres and recruits was thus established. In fact, these were commonly referred to as 'highways' denoting the relative absence of capability of the Army to stop this movement. The Pakistani sponsors used the services of guides from the LC belt who knew the terrain blindfolded having spent all their lives there. They could always outwit our troops who usually spent two-year tenures in their areas of deployment. Ground knowledge of troops could never compare with local guides.

To many this may sound extremely critical of the Indian Army. It actually isn't when you realise that an Army is not trained, equipped or psychologically conditioned to prevent irregular movement across a linear alignment on a 24×7 basis. That it has mastered it since then is a measure of its extreme flexibility.

Perceptions among our countrymen and specifically among the media have been largely based upon visits to the traditional tourist spots and the Valley floor of Kashmir; they have never been enabled a perception of the difficulties of the actual terrain where the LC exists. Most media persons get a faraway glimpse while driving along the 'media route' to Uri's popular Kaman 'Aman Setu' or when they are taken on a structured tour by helicopter to the famous 'Shararat Post' in Tangdhar. None ever visits the very famous landmarks along the Northern Gullies or the Pir Panjal because they don't know enough about them. They can go only where the Army wishes to take them.

Getting back to the progressive increase of infiltration and its reduction in subsequent years, it is important to know that in 1989 a single formation (division) of the Army had the responsibility of the LC in the Valley Sector. There were insufficient troops to increase the density of deployment on the LC to cater against small-scale infiltration. During 1988-91, the trend of exfiltration of recruits and infiltration of trained cadres, leadership and military wherewithal continued. Switching from sanctity of LC to effective counter-infiltration role was a near impossible military task. In 1991, it may be recalled by some, how an Indian Army post was attacked by Pakistani regulars in the Keran sector. That commenced a series of such threats forcing the Army to take measures to strengthen the defensive posture which opened gaps for infiltration, even as it retaliated in kind. Not before the arrival of the first Rashtriya Rifles (RR) units did some semblance of balance start returning. Redeployment from Ladakh reinforced the LC to a great strength and the reserve units could then start deployment in the second tier.

Important to remember that through the 1990s and even later, the Valley had infiltration from every direction – even over the Pir Panjal. Since the training camps (ultimately 42 of them) were spread all over the PoK, even well south of the Pir Panjal in the Kotli, Nikial and Mangla areas on the PoK side, infiltration took place into the Jammu division too. Here staging areas and bases were established. Once inducted there, terrorists could infiltrate further over the Pir Panjal into the Valley. They made use of its high passes where there was almost no Army or police deployment. The arrival of the RR made a major difference as it deployed into South Kashmir and took charge of the Pir Panjal. For many years, terrorist firm base for infiltration into the Valley using the Pir Panjal routes was at *Hilkaka* (destroyed subsequently in 2002).

Infiltration: The Concept Adopted by Pakistan

Principally, the concept from the Pakistan side was to employ trained local Kashmiri youth to foist a supposed home grown militancy. They were first recruited, then exfiltrated, trained and then infiltrated back across the LC. This proved counter-productive as the chances of being interdicted during the two moves over the LC started increasing. As the energy levels among local militants started to wane, more foreign terrorists were inducted for fixed tenures, with handsome remuneration on return or guaranteed funds to their survivors if killed. The idea was that certain threshold strength of terrorists would be built inside the Valley to undertake hit and run operations against the Security Forces (SF), keep the flag of resistance flying all over the Valley and intimidate the fence sitters.

Much as the Army would achieve in terms of operations in the hinterland, at the end of each year the sum total was always against it. That is because even if an average of 1100-1200 terrorists were neutralised in a single year, Pakistan could quite successfully induct 1500 or more through infiltration. The lofty jagged peaks rising to 14,000 feet, broken ground, and jungle which abounds the terrain along the LC was dominated by the Army night and day but small numbers (6-8) could slip past silently even at a 10-15 feet distance from ambushes – there were very limited number of night vision devices. The nooks and crannies in this terrain always work for the infiltrator. In the cusp between winter and summer, terrorists took risk to infiltrate when snow levels were still high.

Yes, in theory any infiltration can be stopped a hundred percent, but only in theory. That is by having one Indian Army soldier at every 1 meter along the 750-km LC, something which can remain only in the figment of imagination. The task remained split between the protection of posts and piquet's, sanctity of the LC (no encroachments or intrusions) and counter-infiltration. The three ways tasking always created a dilemma which was further accentuated by exchanges of artillery fire. Terrorist attrition was reasonably high but for every terrorist killed on or near the LC, it was estimated that at least three got through.

In spite of the successes that the Army achieved, the counter-infiltration grid till as late as 2000-2001 (post-Kargil) could not be optimised. Ambushes were randomly deployed based on appreciation of ground and previous knowledge but there was no uniformity of pattern or concept to defeat infiltration.

Infiltration is usually a well-planned process but often terrorists continue repeating the very same routes on which their colleagues have been killed in droves. This is because of the compulsion they perceive of getting to the 'reception area' at the earliest. The reception area is a point to which a group of terrorists already inside the Valley move with basic logistics to receive and guide infiltrators to the nearby villages and subsequently to the safe houses in the urban areas. Routes which involve longer marches are generally avoided due to the feasibility of interception by surveillance of different kinds.

The LC Fence: Concept and Execution

In 2003, under the stewardship of General Nirmal Vij, then Army Chief, the concept of counter-infiltration finally changed with a landmark decision based on the experience of almost 15 years. For the first time, a clear-cut mission was given to commanders and troops in the Valley: 'To reduce the strength of terrorists in the Valley and Jammu to sub 1000'; there could not have been a more specific mission. When such missions are given, it is usually left to senior field commanders to evolve the concept of operations with resources being provided to match the concept as much as is feasible. General Vij, in conjunction with his senior commanders, conceptualised the LC Fence as the 'limit of infiltration', demanding from field functionaries that it be continuous, overcoming terrain constraints.

The LC Fence did not become a Maginot Line as many claim but rather a system with the marrying of physical obstacles, electronic surveillance devices, weapons and human resources in varying ratios. Units and formations took ownership of their segments and focused counter-infiltration efforts began in July 2004. The one item of equipment which acted as a force multiplier was the Hand Held Thermal Imager (HHTI) and its connected surveillance devices (LORROS), procured on fast track after Kargil 1999. Surveillance and Sub Surveillance Centers were set up integrating all the inputs. Improvisation also became the norm and 'Gaddi dogs' (robust Gujjar owned dogs) became the eyes and ears on many posts. Units took the trouble of setting up training nodes for these dogs.

As the LC Fence matured the quantum of successful operations increased exponentially. Some segments became virtually 'no go' areas for infiltration. Terrorists developed techniques to defeat the Fence but nothing really worked. The only lacuna was that the wire obstacle would get compressed by the huge volumes of soft snow in winter and the iron pickets would bend needing various high-altitude segments to be reconstructed against time in April-May each year. This took away much time and energy from conventional preparedness.

Effect of the LC Fence

The combination of enhanced and focused counter-infiltration employing the LC Fence led to much improved intelligence, better coordination and sharing, and far better dissemination from all agencies – that helped in reducing infiltration. By 2007, more terrorists were being neutralised at the LC and the hinterland by the SF than the number which could infiltrate. In 2008, a bold decision was taken to reinforce counter-infiltration deployment by induction of troops from the Pir Panjal South to the Valley Sector. The effect was enhanced control over infiltration with some very large contact battles in the Kupwara Sector. This had a dampening effect on the situation in the hinterland which continued to improve. However, an indirect effect was the resort to street protests and small scale acts of terror in the hinterland.

Focused elimination of terrorist leaders from 2007 onwards further diluted terrorist capability. The progressive success of counter-infiltration which reduced the numbers of terrorists from PoK reaching the urban and semi urban areas in the Valley had the following effect:

- Large-scale terrorist actions reduced drastically.
- Resort to gun snatching increased.
- IED incidents reduced and in fact almost completely vanished.
- New militancy characterised by presence of local Kashmiri youth progressively increased in South Kashmir with the hold of Pakistani terrorist leaders having reduced.
- Street protests on the slightest pretext found preference as a way of keeping alive the issue of Separatism.
- New methods of mass mobilisation of street power to unnerve SF during encounters also found favour.

For the layman, it is important to appreciate that at no point has infiltration ever reduced to zero. The Army always maintains that a zero figure is never possible to achieve. That is the experience of handling counter-infiltration at various levels from the lowest to the highest.

Is the surge in terrorist activity in recent weeks due to enhanced infiltration? The Army would hotly contest that, and rightly so, because there have been a good number of successful operations in the vicinity of the LC right through 2015-16. The indicators appear to show that infiltration is well under control. However, leakages do continue. North Kashmir, where the presence and hold of foreign (Pakistani) terrorists is higher, is relatively free of terror acts. Sopore, Bandipura, Pattan and Baramula are unusually quiet. There has been activity around Uri, Tangdhar and Lolab (all nearer the LC) indicating successful and some unsuccessful counter-infiltration operations. If terrorists have successfully reached their destinations, there will be a spurt in violence just around early July when the tourists start returning home and the Sri Amarnath Yatra gathers more steam.

The Anantnag (South Kashmir) Situation

The events in Anantnag do not thus far seem related to any surge in infiltration. In yester years, concentration of terrorists at Anantnag would also be from the Jammu division infiltrating over the Pir Panjal. That may be possible even currently while the by-election is underway till 19 June. However, the strength in the Jammu division itself is extremely low and does not support that analogy.

The Army has to remain on alert at the LC as there are areas which have not been exploited for some years. The routes over the Shamshabari in Uri sector, Naugam, Tangdhar, Pharkian and Zamindar Gali have been frequented far too often. Mostly the terrorists using these routes end up at the forest tracts – Rafiabad, Rajwar and Hafruda – which are under SF domination. Gurez and Gulmarg need some additional focus. Helicopter-borne response teams are necessary for these areas along with unmanned aerial vehicle (UAV) surveillance and observation.

Link with Situation in Pakistan

Infiltration efforts are also indirectly proportional to the internal situation in Pakistan. Now that the internal security environment is under better control and the closing months of General Raheel Sharif's tenure are on a countdown, perhaps a surge is what the Inter-Services Intelligence (ISI) could be planning for.

The Lashkar-e Taiba (LeT) and Jaish-e-Muhammad (JeM) are rabid outfits and in their strategy major attrition of jihadis is acceptable as long as a few prominent leaders can be inducted along with some logistics, military wherewithal and lower-end cadres. For an attempt by 100 terrorists, they are willing to lose up to 60 percent if not more. That means the Army's success in neutralising terrorists on the Counter Infiltration Grid may not necessarily mean reduced strength of terrorists in the hinterland, especially if the 'Deep State' in Pakistan decides that a surge is what it wishes. The only deduction from this is that the counter-infiltration machinery has to be fully geared up, and reinforced if necessary with intelligence being generated and disseminated in near real time. None of that 'put up on file' business, which some warriors not used to the grid, may be wont to follow.

The lesson from this essay is that the focus of operations may be on new militancy in South Kashmir and on the mobs obstructing operations. That is all fine – operational and tactical. The real strategic level decision making is on bolstering the counter-infiltration grid so that the progress of the last 13 years is not allowed to languish. The Army is up against a reinvigorated ISI which will look for innovative ways and areas to attempt to execute its aim of increasing the footprint of the sponsored terrorists in the Valley. There is no rest for the Army. Its 24×7 posture everywhere has to remain activated. That is most so on the LC and the reception areas of North Kashmir. Rafiabad, Hafruda, Rajwar, Lolab and Tehgam, all household names in the lexicon of the Army in Kashmir's vocabulary, must remain dominated and free of terrorists. The flanks will also feel the pressure and the old traditional routes will need all the attention as focus shifts to those.

The Indian Army has to succeed; given its professionalism, it will.

*

January, 2019

20

PAKISTAN'S NUCLEAR AND MISSILE PROGRAMME: AN ASSESSMENT

Rana Banerji

Introduction

The closest formulation of Pakistan's Nuclear Security doctrine, if any, was enunciated in an article appearing in *The News*, in October 1999, written by former Foreign Minister Agha Shahi, former Foreign Secretary Abdus Sattar and Air Chief Air Marshal (retired) Zulfiqar Khan. It was India-specific and spoke of credible, minimum deterrence – it would be flexible in response in a dynamic threat environment. India's offer of 'No First use' was rejected – instead, Pakistan offered a 'No War Pact', which was not acceptable to India.[1]

The primary rationale for the Pakistani bomb was security. Islamabad's loss of East Pakistan in the 1971 War was a key motivation; Pakistan needed the Bomb to ensure its survival. This rationale was bolstered by the perceived inevitability of the Indian bomb after the 1974 test, and the lack of a credible security guarantee. Always worried about Indian conventional superiority, Pakistan considered nuclear weapons as a means to avoid a defeat on the battlefield. An added benefit of the program was the ability to protect Pakistani support for the Kashmir insurgency by neutralising the risk of major conventional war. This may have been a misguided belief but it has periodically helped Pakistan to internationalise the Kashmir dispute, playing upon Western Powers' fear of an avoidable nuclear conflagration in South Asia.

There was also a political component in Pakistan's nuclear policy. Zulfiqar

Ali Bhutto wanted Pakistan to "walk tall". Though maintaining equality with India was a primary motivation, being the first Muslim nation to be endowed with the 'Bomb' was also a matter of pride, and to this day the program remains popular in Islamist circles. This rationale has continued to exist after the 1977 coup that toppled Bhutto. In the late 1970s, Pakistan's nuclear weapons program became synonymous with national sovereignty and national prestige, even when it was run by the very military that had eliminated Pakistan's best-known populist politician. In the context of its nuclear policy, Islamabad did not believe that China would be ready to risk war to support Pakistan in case of hostilities in South Asia. The rocky history of US-Pakistan relations also made it impossible for Islamabad to count on Washington.

KEY ELEMENTS OF PAKISTAN'S NUCLEAR DOCTRINE

In practice, Minimum Credible Deterrence translates into four objectives: (1) deterrence of all forms of external aggression; (2) building to this effect an effective combination of conventional and strategic forces; (3) avoiding a pre-emptive strike through protection and the threat of nuclear retaliation; (4) stabilising strategic deterrence in South Asia. The theory of deterrence of the strong by the weak envisaged the possibility of a smaller country to deter a larger one through the threat of damage incommensurate with stakes of the conflict. It aims at being able to inflict "unacceptable" or "unbearable" damage to India. As it would be difficult to define unacceptable damage, overkill would by necessarily be built into the response. From an initial capability to deliver a few weapons on Indian cities with some guarantee of success, the level of minimum deterrence could change over time, eliciting flexible response, not quantifiable in static numbers. Guaranteed unacceptable damage implied survivability even after a first strike by the adversary.

Though Pakistan has consistently stated that its nuclear weapons are solely intended to deter military aggression, in view of its assessment that "in view of the fact that India produces significant quantities of fissile materials and nuclear weapons from un-safeguarded nuclear reactors", Pakistan Strategic Planning Division (SPD) held earlier that the country may need 68-70 warheads to hit at least 10 identified enemy targets at a time, before a pre-emptive strike by India. Pakistan reached the nuclear threshold somewhere between 1984 and 1987. The exact date is unclear and depends on whether one refers to the year enough Highly Enriched Uranium (HEU) was produced, or the year when weaponisation was achieved.[2]

Conventional wisdom now accepts that China helped first test out Pakistan's nuclear bomb at Lop Nor, sometime after 1987 and before 1989 but this was kept secret till Dr. A.Q. Khan deliberately leaked the information through Mushahid Hussain to Indian journalists Kuldip Nayyar and Shekhar Gupta. Initially, Pakistan clandestinely followed the Enrichment Route under the guidance of Dr. A.Q. Khan. Centrifuges were installed at Kahuta. At peak capacity, the Kahuta Research Laboratories (KRL) was capable of producing 60-80 kg of enriched Uranium annually. KRL remains outside International Atomic Energy Agency (IAEA) safeguards, though enrichment is not being done there anymore.

Facilities at KRL and Gadwal have in later years been used for developing ancillaries for Pakistan's missile program. Uranium waste from KRL is now diverted to Khushab for use under the Plutonium route. Pakistan has nuclear reactors at the Pakistan Institute of Nuclear Science and Technology (PINSTECH), Nilore (near Rawalpindi) and Karachi Nuclear Power Plant (KANUPP), Karachi, which along with a later nuclear plant at Chashma, are under IAEA safeguards. These follow the Plutonium Route – as do reactors at Khushab–4, all built with Chinese assistance – which are not under IAEA safeguards. Present assessment of capacity at Khushab is around 45-50 kg of nuclear grade Plutonium annually.

Pakistan's nuclear history has been marked by the rivalry between the Pakistani Atomic Energy Commission (PAEC), the initial organisation created to deal with the nuclear program (both civilian and military), and the Khan Research Laboratories (KRL), originally created solely for uranium enrichment but which became in the 1980s a true competitor to PAEC, as both became involved in weaponisation and missile acquisition. Fed initially by intense personal rivalry between Dr. Munir Khan, Chairman, PAEC and Dr. A.Q. Khan at KRL, this competition was probably deliberately encouraged by the Pakistani civilian and military leadership.

In the years 1999-2001, after the expose by USA of Dr. A.Q. Khan's clandestine sales of nuclear equipment to North Korea, Libya and Iran, a reorganisation of the program took place. All military or dual use nuclear activities are now controlled by the National Command Authority (NCA), and the SPD. A division of labour among laboratories has been defined. The National Engineering and Scientific Commission (NESCOM, created in 2001) oversees weapons systems development. It has authority on the National Development Complex (NDC, created in 1990 as an offshoot of PAEC), which is in charge of weaponisation.[3]

The circumstances that might warrant nuclear use were described (for international audiences) by Lt Gen (Retd) Khalid Kidwai in late 2012, as shown below:

(1) **The Spatial Threshold**. Penetration of Indian forces on a large scale would elicit a nuclear response. The threshold could be low (some 50-100 km perhaps) in Kashmir and in Punjab.

(2) **The Military Threshold.** Destruction of a large part of Pakistani land or air forces could lead to a nuclear response if Islamabad believed that it was losing the cohesiveness of its defence and feared imminent defeat.

(3) **The Economic Threshold.** Economic strangulation refers primarily to a blockade of Karachi, but could also concern the stopping of the Indus water flow, or the capture of vital arteries such as the Indus and the Karakoram highway.

(4) **The Political Threshold.** Destabilisation of the country fermented by India could also be a nuclear threshold if Islamabad believed that the integrity of the country was at stake.

Pakistani planners insist that these thresholds are indicative and should not be viewed in isolation one from another. This policy statement, it was averred in official handouts, was intended to deter Pakistan's adversaries from attempting a counter-force strategy against its strategic assets by effectively securing the strategic assets and threatening nuclear retaliation should such an attempt be made.[4]

Fissile Material Cut-off Treaty (FMCT)

Pakistan has opposed start of talks on FMCT at the Conference on Disarmament since 2009. Its position has been that it would sign Fissile Material Treaty if the countries with fissile material reduce their stocks to a proportional level before setting the cut-off date, instead of agreeing on existing stock levels which put the country in a disadvantageous position. Concomitantly, Pakistan claims to possess all credentials for qualifying for access to civilian nuclear technology and becoming a member of the multilateral export control regimes including Nuclear Suppliers Group (NSG) on non-discriminatory basis. As such, it remains opposed to any arms control arrangement that is detrimental to its security and strategic interests.

Missile Development Program

Pakistan undertook a full-scale missile development program with Chinese and North Korean help in the mid-1990s. Starting from the 'Hatf' series, it moved to 'Ghazni' and 'Shaheen' variants, using both liquid and solid fuel propellants.

Pakistan's initial experience with space and missile technology began in the

1960s when the Space and Upper Atmospheric Commission (SUPARCO) blossomed under the guidance and stewardship of Abdus Salam and I.H. Usmani. Collaboration between the US National Aeronautics and Space Agency (NASA) and SUPARCO resulted in the 'Rehbar' series of sounding rockets. But this series remained very basic, at best. The wars of 1965 and 1971 took a toll on both the PAEC and SUPARCO – two premier organisations – when nearly half of their work forces, consisting of Bengali talent, left when Pakistan was dismembered and Bangladesh was created. In the 1970s and 1980s, Pakistan's focus was on development of the nuclear fuel cycle, fissile material production, and the development of nuclear weapons in the face of obstacles from the non-proliferation regime. Lack of funding compounded these problems.

In the 1990s, Pakistan's focus shifted toward acquiring ballistic missiles, especially after receiving a shock when its then-principal delivery means – F-16 aircraft – was withheld by the United States as a consequence of the Pressler amendment. Over the past quarter-century, Pakistan's strategic thinking has been based on three key premises. The first is that the reliance on Western technology and arms sales was a risky strategy. The demise of the Soviet Union reduced Pakistan's strategic significance, while Pakistan's pursuit of nuclear deterrent capabilities ran counter to Western non-proliferation objectives. The second premise is that Pakistan must become self-reliant in matching India's missile threat. The third premise is that ballistic missiles would become the premier delivery means of Pakistan's strategic arsenal. Pakistan's deterrence strategy involved buying technology off the shelf to fulfill immediate requirements; the transfer of technology from China and North Korea were necessary steps toward long-term self-reliance.

Pakistan's missile quest began with the development and testing of the 80-km range Hatf-I in 1989. In the 1990s, the focus shifted to Intermediate Range Ballistic Missiles (IRBM) with the acquisition of the Ghauri (Hatf-V) from North Korea by the KRL, and development of the Ghaznavi (Hatf-III) and Shaheen-I (Hatf-IV) by a subsidiary of the PAEC, the NDC. These missiles were earmarked for counter-value strikes inside India. Pakistan's acquisition of solid fuel technology eventually led to solid propellant baselines and the foundation of future missiles. Flight test of the Ghauri (liquid propellant), conducted on April 6, 1998, was a failure, with the missile burning up on re-entry. Another Ghauri test a year later also ended in failure.

Pakistan's missile arsenal currently includes 11 different types of ballistic and cruise missiles:

Table 1

Name	*Range (in km)*
Hatf-1A	100
Abdale	180
Ghaznavi	290
Shaheen-I	750–900
Shaheen-1A	1,100
Ghauri	1,150-1,300
Shaheen-II	1,500–2,500
Shaheen-III	2,750
Nasr	60 (two types of cruise missiles are deployed)
Subsonic Babur Land Attack Cruise Missile (LACM)	500-700
Subsonic Raad Air-Launched Cruise Missile (ALCM)	350

A version of the 'Babur' (Hatf-X) is believed to be under development and might have been tested by the Pakistan Navy from naval platforms along with other Land Attack Cruise Missiles (LACM) following the creation of the Naval Strategic Force Command in May 2012. Among ballistic missiles, the Ghauri is Pakistan's only liquid fueled system; all others use solid propellants. Several flight tests of each of these systems have been conducted over the past 15 years to achieve improved performance, targeting, and accuracy parameters.[5]

Recent Shifts

In September 2013, in a meeting of its NCA, Pakistan formally moved from a position of minimum credible deterrence to 'full spectrum deterrence', committing itself to second strike capability and parity with India through pursuit of land, air and naval nuclear capacity (nuclear triad), including new delivery systems such as short-range missiles (Nasr), air-launched (Raad) and naval (Babur) cruise missiles as well as miniaturisation of war heads. Of the nine ballistic missile systems in Pakistan's arsenal, five are short-range – the Hatf-1A, Abdali, Ghaznavi, Shaheen-I, and Nasr. Three cruise missile systems – the Babur, Raad, and the prospective naval variant of the Babur – are also only suitable for short-range counter-force targeting. Only four ballistic missile types have been tested with enhanced guidance and penetration capabilities – these four are intermediate-range systems – the Shaheen-1A, Ghauri, Shaheen-II, and Shaheen-III – which possess ranges suitable for deep strikes inside India. These missiles could be utilised for counter-value or counter-force targeting. Given their payload capacity, at least two of these – the Shaheen-II and Shaheen-III – are likely to have the potential to carry Multiple Independent Re-entry Vehicles (MIRVs).

A serious pursuit of MIRVs and counter-force capabilities requires the availability of large stocks of fissile material and the engineering potential to weaponise these stockpiles for a variety of warheads of different yields and designs. Currently, Pakistan's fissile material stockpiles are assessed to have gone up to over 145 warheads. No precise information exists about storage sites of these warheads, which are in de-mated status. These could be in underground facilities in general area of Kirana Hills, near the NDC complex at Fatehjung. A recent report leaked by Pakistani sources suggested that nuclear capable missiles are already deployed with the Strategic Forces Command field installations and that the time to install de-mated warheads on to operationally capable carriers (missiles) has been reduced to two hours.

Taking a cue from perceived developments in India, indicative of a palpable shift toward more counter-force targeting along with counter-value targeting, current concern of Pakistan's nuclear practitioners has focused on Ballistic Missile Defense (BMD) and MIRV. To proceed towards MIRV capability, it was assessed that Pakistan would need to design guidance mechanisms, compact warheads, and a 'bus' that could carry and release multiple warheads. Pakistan's nuclear policy strategists may be considering three options in this regard.

The 'Ignore' Option

In a major departure from past practice, Pakistan could simply decide to rely on its existing mix of counter-value and counter-force targeting capacities. This would involve accelerated production of single-warhead ballistic and cruise missiles while taking additional steps to increase the survivability of its deterrent, such as the multiplication of missile storage sites. Mixing real with dummy sites would complicate India's targeting ability. Pakistan could also add to its stockpiles of Tactical Nuclear Weapons (TNWs). Given the domination of the military-bureaucratic-scientific enclave in Pakistan, and Pakistan's history of competing with India in nuclear capabilities, an 'ignore' option is unlikely.

The 'Tortoise' Option

This option presumes that Pakistan will try to match India if it flight tests and inducts missiles carrying multiple warheads, but at a measured pace. This choice of a middle course would be dictated by resource constraints, including available stockpiles and production rates of fissile material. In this quest, Pakistan might face natural uranium constraints (e.g. depleting reserves in Bagalchur) in the absence of foreign supplies and fresh discoveries at home. By 2020, Pakistan can be estimated to have accumulated about 450 kg of weapons-grade plutonium from the four production reactors at the Khushab Complex. This would be sufficient for perhaps 90 warheads, which would have to be distributed on a priority basis among delivery vehicles. If a projected Pakistani nuclear arsenal includes perhaps 200 miniaturised warheads, this might require at least 800 kg of weapons-grade plutonium. By choosing the 'tortoise' option, Pakistan could still employ counter-vailing strategies to defeat the twin threat of Indian MIRVs and missile defenses.

Under this option, Pakistan's strategic deterrent would still pose a threat to India if, first, it were to employ increased dispersal and a higher state of readiness. Second, Pakistan could increase production of missiles carrying single warheads. Third, Pakistan could undertake less costly counter-measures to assure penetration and destruction of Indian targets. Pakistan's strategic forces could employ depressed trajectories for ballistic missiles; rely increasingly on cruise missiles; resort to simultaneous launches; develop maneuvering re-entry vehicles that are not MIRVs; increase electronic warfare capabilities; and acquire rudimentary stealth technologies. Pakistan will most certainly undertake counter-measures such as decoys and chaff. All of these steps could be taken while the technological maturation of MIRVs occurs at a measured pace.

The 'Hare' Option

For the 'hare' option, it would necessarily entail increased production of fissile material. Under this option, Islamabad would spend and have to do what it takes to deploy MIRVs as quickly as possible. In responding to India's capability in MIRVs and to counter prospective Indian BMD deployments, Pakistan has unfurled plans to test a new missile, the 'Ababeel'. Pakistan conducted a "test launch" of the Ababeel on 24 January 2017 (Urdu: أبابيل ; lit. Swallow), a surface-to-surface medium-range ballistic missile, with a claimed maximum range of 2,200 km (1,400 mi). The missile can reportedly carry both conventional and nuclear warheads, and is claimed to use MIRVs, a first for Pakistan's arsenal. Ababeel is claimed to be a development of the Shaheen-III airframe and solid-fuel motors, but with a payload fairing of enlarged diameter, "to house the MIRV carrier bus".[6] The second stage is also lengthened. Independent Indian assessments suggest partial success in use of a single warhead missile for re-entry purposes but work is proceeding apace for perfecting multiple warhead re-entries. In addition to MIRV-ing, Pakistan is likely to marginally, but not significantly, increase the number of its delivery vehicles and transporter-erector launchers.

The 'hare' option is fraught with obstacles and risks for Pakistan at a time when it wants to be recognised as a legitimate, normal, *de facto* nuclear power like India. Islamabad is struggling to counter India's efforts to prevent Pakistan's entry into the NSG. It is trying to project an image as a responsible nuclear power, making significant efforts on nuclear security and safety while tightening export and custodial controls. Pakistan's utmost desire is to be treated on par with India. Islamabad would rather avoid spending additional sums for Pakistan's nuclear program in addition to avoiding additional challenges to its nuclear legitimacy. Further, this option requires significant help from China that is not assured – especially during periods of crisis – given China's evolving strategic outlook and priorities in the world.

Conversely, if Pakistan seems unlikely to gain legitimacy via NSG membership, and if it is unlikely to secure equal treatment to India as a 'mainstreamed' nuclear State, then there would be no incentive for self-restraint if India were to embrace MIRVs and BMD. Pakistan's strategy would also be contingent on other variables, such as budget constraints, technological challenges, and the willingness of friends (China) to extend financial or technical cooperation.[7]

A third test of Shaheen-III missile carried out on Jan 28, 2018 was a total failure. The earlier two tests had been successful, with full range of 2,750 km being achieved and the circular error probability was also okay. This time, at the Windar testing range near Sonmiani, Baluchistan, the missile exploded into fireballs soon after the launch – the then Prime Minister, Shahid Khaqan Abbassi had to be escorted to safety from the VIP visitors' camp which had been set up to witness the launch at the testing range. The technical reasons for the failure could not be known – it is possible they were testing the liquid propellant aspect for the engine to be used in the final stage of launch, or for the dummy warhead mating. The Inter-Services Public Relations (ISPR) maintained complete silence afterwards. A meeting of experts was held at Karachi under supervision of SPD afterwards to determine the cause of failure. The Windar Range has been closed down for repairs at site till May 2018. Despite this failure, Pakistan has not given up preparations for launch of Shaheen IV missile, which will have a range of 3,500 km using solid propellant fuel.

Civil Military Dissonance in Nuclear Context

Though Pakistan's nuclear scientists have been lionised in the past, disclosures regarding Dr. A.Q. Khan's clandestine nuclear component sales through Scomi Precision Factories of Syed Abu Tahir Bukhari in Malaysia and UAE created a major blot on their reputation. The military leadership under President Musharraf tried to distance itself from any foreknowledge of these dealings. This strained credulity of the Pakistani nuclear scientists' community, especially after nine of Dr A.Q. Khan's top team of scientists and personal staff working at the KRL were arrested in November 2003 and January 2004 – Dr. Mohammad Farooq (uncle of Syed Abu Taher Bukhari), Brig Sajawal (retd), Maj Islamul Haq (retd), Dr. Badar Habib, Dr. Yasin Chohan, Dr. Saeed Ahmed, Dr. Abdul Majid, Dr. Zubair Khan and technician Shameem. Their families were placed under surveillance of the Inter-Services Intelligence (ISI) even as they sought legal remedies (*habeus corpus*). The scientists categorically let Western newsmen and Human Rights NGOs know, through some Pakistani intermediaries, that the attempt of the Pakistani military leadership to pose ignorance of these sales to North Korea, Libya and Iran was palpably untrue. They contended that Gen Aslam Beg and even Musharraf definitely had prior knowledge or may have given concurrence.[8]

Though Gen Kidwai introduced Personal Reliability Programs in all nuclear-related establishments afterwards, this intense dislike of the military within Pakistan's Nuclear Scientists community is unlikely to have diminished, especially as the SPD leadership at its top echelons is almost entirely headed by army generals. This distrust permeated families of the arrested scientists. Some Western journalists tried to exploit this resentment in quest of hard inputs, but their efforts were scuttled by effective deterrent counter-measures by the ISI.

NOTES

1. Agha Shahi, Zulfiqar Khan and Abdul Sattar, 'Securing Nuclear Peace,' *The News International*, Karachi, October 5, 1999; also cited by Brig(retired) Naeem Salik : The Evolution of Pakistan's Nuclear Doctrine: Carnegie Endowment for International peace, June, 2016.
2. Bruno Tertrais, Pakistan's Nuclear Program: A net assessment; No 04/2012, recherches & documents; June 13, 2012, https://www.files.ethz.ch/isn/151278/RD_201204.pdf
3. Feroz H. Khan, *Eating Grass: The Making of the Pakistani Bomb*, Stanford University Press, California, 2012.
4. Peter Lavoy, Carnegie Endowment for International Peace: A conversation with Gen Khalid Kidwai, March 23, 2015.
5. Tertrais, op. cit., paras 2-5.
6. Maj Gen Asif Ghafoor, 'Pak successfully conducted first flight test of SSM ABABEEL, Rg 2200 Km.' Twitter Post (@OfficialDGISPR), January 24, 2017.
7. Feroz H. Khan and Mansoor Ahmed, 'Pakistan, MIRVs, and Counterforce Targeting' in Michael Krepon, Travis Wheeler and Shane Mason (eds.), 'The Lure & Pitfalls of MIRV, Stimson Center, Washington DC, 2016. https://www.stimson.org/sites/default/files/file-attachments/Lure_and_Pitfalls_of_MIRVs.pdf
8. Adrian Levy and Catherine Scott-Clark, Nuclear Deception, New York: Walker Books, 2008.

August, 2019

21

Is Indian Airpower Preparing for Tomorrow's War?

Air Vice Marshal Rajesh Isser

ABSTRACT

Technology is moving ahead in leaps and bounds, and in the years to come, it will be a prime driver of doctrinal changes in how conflicts are started, managed and won. Technologies such as big data analytics, hyper-connectivity, robust and ubiquitous sensors, internet of things, lasers, hypersonic and 3D printing allow endless scope for battle concepts such as swarming, unmanned warfare in high-risk environment, non-contact warfare from stand-off ranges and militarisation of space. Multi-domain war fighting seeks cross-domain synergy by close synchronisation. And a true whole-of-nation approach. Most evolved armed forces are fully on board the race to develop asymmetric capabilities, such as China's A2AD. These have implications for India.

At the same time, India has to be prepared for conflict handling in the present that is characterised by increasing uncertainty and complexity. A spectrum of counter-insurgency, hybrid and compound wars need adaptive capabilities of a very high order which incorporate multi-agency synergy and fast learning curves, among others. Some pertinent questions are posed that are relevant to Indian airpower capability building.

Introduction: An Uncertain Future

This article essentially poses questions that must be asked, and which never are. Technology is moving ahead in leaps and bounds, more so after the explosive and exponential advances in Information and Communications Technology (ICT) such as Artificial Intelligence (AI). Truly, in the years to come, technology will be a prime driver of doctrinal changes in how conflicts are started, managed and won. The article does not give any definitive answers but the writing on the wall is clear. Old agendas of turf under a cloak of core competencies need to be looked at with a microscope for relevance in the coming decades. It touches on certain core sectors that impinge directly on employment of air power in the future. It takes stock of how current conflicts using multi-domain concepts are acting as test-beds, and how countries like China are bridging the divide in combat capabilities. The proper questions the premise of continuing to do the same in a dogmatic fashion.

The 4th Industrial Revolution: Technology Driving Doctrine?

Trans-disciplinary approaches in research and academia have resulted in convergence of ideas, and brought in a new creativity to science. For example, the marriage of neuroscience and engineering has revolutionised fields such as machine deep learning, human-machine collaboration and teaming, and machine-assisted human performance (exoskeletons). Similarly, a nexus of nano-technology and biology has resulted in ability to produce material with specific properties such as avoiding or causing rusting in large structures. High-density energetic properties have increased the potency of explosives by ten times, with great spinoffs in rocket and missile technology. But the downsides include ability to manufacture deadly pathogens even in a garage.

While electromagnetic pulse (EMP), through a calibrated nuclear blast in the atmosphere to burn out integrated circuits and chips, has been around for some time, its employment was debateable. Currently, convergence of natural science, computer-aided design (CAD) etc. has allowed pulsed power generation that can be directed to burn out computer chips which are at the heart of any weapon system. Technologies such as big data analytics, hyper-connectivity, robust and ubiquitous sensors, internet of things, lasers, hypersonic and 3D printing allow endless scope for battle concepts such as swarming, unmanned warfare in high-risk environment, non-contact warfare from stand-off ranges and militarisation of space.[1] This requires huge investment in pure and applied research, nurturing innovation and creating ecosystems and a solid manufacturing base. Israel is a good example of such visionary planning. Most nations are heavily investing in AI, additive manufacturing (3D printing) and a range of human-machine partnerships. It promises to not only change the character of war but even its very nature with man out-of-the loop and action.[2] Propensity for risk-taking and effective deniability may change strategic decision-making too in the future.

The age of massed armour, fleets and aircrafts with human beings in them may be going away faster than currently thought possible. Already, surveillance and precision have revised fire and manoeuvre concepts at land, sea, air. These developments necessitate doctrinal rethink especially since it may even lead to less expenditure in capital and revenue. Prime Minister Modi in his address to commanders of all armed forces in 2015 clearly underlined transformation as a preparation for the future and not doing more of the same or preparing perspective plans based on outdated doctrines. He also highlighted the point that the services had good field commanders but now the need was for thought-leaders who can drive change in the national security system.

Leaping Technology

Considering developments in the field of science and technology related to military-oriented applications, the future of warfare will be characterised by short-duration, high-intensity and information-centric warfare, with greater emphasis on a light or medium-size tactical force capable of rapidly escalating capabilities in its region of influence.[3] Some of these emerging fields are truly disruptive and capable of making existing counter-missile technologies redundant, enable stand-off and no-contact actions, hit targets difficult to hit by subsonic weapon, compress shooter-to-target window, and in effect, change many defence and offence concepts.

Additive Manufacturing

3D printing technology has tremendous potential, with new uses being demonstrated almost continuously. The US Navy printed a carbon fibre submersible as a proof of the concept.[4] With potential positive results such as cost avoidance, reduced inventories, delivery time, acquisition and sustainment programs can be truly responsive.[5] Efforts are on in many countries to actively shorten supply chains by additive and just-in-time manufacturing as part of the overall acquisition strategy. By avoiding conventional processes that are subtractive, removing excess material and creating waste especially in the aviation sector where expensive materials are used, huge cost savings hold promise.

Another advantage is the micron-thin width of successive layers that allow newer geometries, designer strengths and reliability. In conjunction with (CAD) techniques, it is capable of producing prototypes and subsequent scaling up at a faster pace and at lower costs. If spare parts can be produced locally, rather than waiting for non-stocked items to be ordered and delivered, down times can be eliminated. In addition to the ability to deliver parts without warehousing, it can actively support legacy equipment and weapon systems. Diminishing manufacturing sources and obsolescence lead to lack of spares which is a significant force degrader in extending the service life of weapon systems.

Hypersonic Technology

For at least two decades, US' the Defence Advanced Research Projects Agency (DARPA) has been engaged in work on the concept of Hypersonic Cruise Vehicle that promises to carry a 12,000-pound payload consisting of common aero vehicles, cruise missiles, small diameter bombs or other munitions. The Falcon Hypersonic Technology Vehicle 2 and 'HyperSoar' are designed to fly at Mach 10 (3 kilometres per second) and carry approximately twice the payload of subsonic aircraft of the same take-off weight.[6] The Hypersonic Boost Glide Vehicle is used for extending the range of ballistic missiles. There is a DARPA-USAF Tactical Boost Glide (TBG) programme meant for developing and demonstrating technologies to enable future air-launched tactical-range hypersonic boost glide systems. The hypersonic air-breathing weapon concept is another joint programme to develop and demonstrate critical technologies of advanced air vehicle configurations capable of efficient hypersonic flight, hydrocarbon scramjet-powered propulsion, management of thermal and affordability.

Russia, China and India too are investing in this technology. China's re-designating of the PLA Rocket Force (PLARF) and elevating it to a fourth military service, alongside the PLA, PLAN, and PLAAF, indicates its intent. It has made major investments in hypersonic gliders or Hypersonic Glide Vehicles reaching speeds of Mach 10. These are ideal attack munitions which could be used against a variety of hard targets—like warships, command and control facilities, communications links, hangars, and intelligence facilities. This will be crucial to its Anti Access Area Denial (A2AD) campaign against the US. In India, Brahmos II, a hypersonic cruise missile, is currently under development. This will have extended ranges of about 600 km and speeds of 7 Mach.

Nano-technology

In general terms, nano-technology manipulates matter at the atomic, molecular or macro-molecular levels. High speed, functionality and weight penalties demand smaller and miniaturised designs. Newer properties such as high density, conductivity, efficiency and focussed strengths are possible to be created, which affect critical components in aviation technologies. Molecular nano-technology (MNT) is one such process in which nano-robots will be used to create objects and will also be capable of assembling themselves, just like the cells in the organic world.[7]

In 2006, Chinese sources listed seven military fields for nano-technology, including potential nano-discs with a million times more storage than current computers, nano-structures, a hundred times stronger than steel, produce generic weapons, super thin radar-absorbing coatings for stealth, micro-weapons, nano-satelites, and soldier equipment including armour and laser-protected headgear.[8] Similar and varied programs are being pursued by many nations including Russia, EU and India. A convergence of 3D printing, nano-tech and other newer disciplines could revolutionise fields in aviation such as radars, communication, weapons, unmanned vehicles, and more importantly, integration of all these game-changers. Many countries have demonstrated these capabilities, and due scaling up will only optimise costs and allow operationalising.

Multi-Domain Operations

This classification is not really a revolutionary concept. Many current weapon and legacy systems possess reach, accuracy and networking to allow a multi-domain (MD) approach. Joint operation concepts and architecture are in place to enable effective synchronisation and deliver winning 'effects'. Multi-domain is actually higher in the evolutionary ladder enabled by technology that is developing and changing at paces defying the Moore's Law. More importantly, it is difficult to radically change mindsets emerging from strict hierarchical organisations to a domain-less or domain-free environment. For example, control or partial control of the air may not be dictated by only air force assets, both manned and unmanned. It may be dictated by capabilities in other domains, i.e. land, sea, cyber, information and space. This is decidedly more potent than joint operations or 'fires'. This synergistic approach, that generates much more than sum of joint capabilities, poses a number of questions and challenges:

- With profound and fast-paced changes around the world, do we completely revamp our joint structures to cope or is tweaking enough?
- Is it possible to respect core competencies and yet demand a cultural and cognitive shift in military leaders to take up the multi-domain challenge?

Multi-Domain war fighting seeks cross-domain synergy by close synchronisation which is enabled by high degrees of situational awareness and freedom of decision across all sensors and shooters connected to the combat cloud.[9]

This allows distributed effects that not only fox an adversary but also cover up vulnerabilities in any domain. It even enables local and temporal superiority in any domain through cross-domain support.

Since networking and connectivity are the foundations of a multi-domain battle, it obviously becomes a prime target for any adversary. Data linking is underlined by a need for accuracy and addressing vulnerabilities that can lead to degradation.[10] Besides built-in redundancy against soft and hard kill effects, an important point is recognising the degree of degradation which allows reconfiguration or other measures to allow the battle-tempo to continue. With shorter OODA loops enabled by technology and AI, it is imperative that this happens equally fast. Protecting a network's reliability is possibly a more important issue than acquisition of large expensive platforms. Most networks are robust enough to avoid any single-point failure architecture; however, ingenuity of the human mind assisted by machine algorithms will continue to throw up new challenges. There will always be a need for constant human-machine interface for innovation and adaptability to counter this.

So does this combat-cloud enabled warfare remove the usual characteristics of war such as the fog of war? In fact, uncertainty and unpredictability will persist without fail – albeit in newer and quicker forms. Network-centric combat allows larger and mixed forces across the six domains to be dispersed, and allows distributed escalation, attrition, pre-emption or surprise – all aided by degrading the other side's information grid. This targeting of an adversary's grid could be for short or long-term, aimed at different levels of degradation, soft or hard kills, or outmanoeuvring the network's resilience. Therefore, battle-network analysis is more important to optimally get the right effects in the overall target analysis. This would necessarily cover deciphering of capabilities, vulnerabilities and adaptability of the grid or cloud. It would flow out of specifics such as a network's design, robustness, main functional objectives, nodes, redundancy paths etc.

One character of war that technology has surely changed is the blurring of offence and defence in and around the battle space. This is a result of the hi-tech networking grid of shooters and sensors, deeper reach of ground-based weapons, precision and accuracy. The Russians demonstrated it quite effectively by decimating two Ukrainian mechanised battalions in a matter of three minutes. It was an example of convergence of networking, lethality, reach and true multi-domain strategy. A similar effect was put in place in Syria led by Russian air power against Islamic State and Syrian rebels. Information and perception shaping formed the core of both these successes. And quite obviously, cyber and Electronic

Warfare domains extended on both sides of actual combat. In Ukraine, the partnership of recce Unmanned Aerial Vehicles (UAV) with long-reach ground weapons in producing quick-time response was so effective that just the sound of UAVs would make troops dive for cover. This fear effect was used to the hilt by the Russians. All this is exactly how Gen Gerasimov had conjured up the concept of a 'Hybrid War'.

Robotic Swarms

Scenarios of unmanned, autonomous, high AI-based, cheap and expendable swarms of drones to support fire or manoeuvre have been painted for a long time. With exponential leaps in AI, nanotech, cloud-networked system-of-systems, hypersonic technology and other such advances, this is quickly becoming a reality.[11] Initial forays such as US Navy's airborne LOCUST and the European ADDER ground vehicle have shown great promise that threaten to revolutionise concepts and character of war fighting. Even today, such swarms can easily overload and overwhelm air defence systems. Ground forces now can vision every soldier being a sensor with his mini and micro-UAVs feeding the common information grid or cloud. Future swarms could have individual as well as group OODA (Observe, Orient, Decide, Act) loops that beat human coping capacities. Air-launched swarms increase possibilities of redefining air power in terms of risk-taking, cost-effectiveness and innovative ways to paralyse an adversary.[12] DARPA is even experimenting a recoverable system based on a large fixed-wing platform that will open up unlimited possibilities in terms of reach and response (programs such as GREMLIN, CODE and ALIAS). A critical enabler is secure communications with adequate redundancy. Advances in quantum computation are revolutionising the field of secure data communication.

In light of a 4th Industrial Revolution and a looming 7th Military Revolution,[13] the following questions are posed:

- Is the Indian Air Force's (IAF) insistence on 42 plus squadron strength of manned fighters relevant or does it close windows to adapt for future change in war's character or do we need to put our money into integrating multi-domain capabilities. Is this even possible without implementation of CDS and theatre commands?
- Will technology outpace doctrines and concepts based on large and expensive platforms, and are our current assessment based on flawed vision and turf bias?

- How far into the future can we plan our capability build-up in light of changing character of war and pace of technological advancements, and, is it possible to plan on some unique and niche capabilities that will be suitable to India in terms of cost, effective deterrence and future adaptability?

5th Generation Air Warfare

The Royal Australian Air Force (RAAF) views a 'combat cloud' as essentially four grids layered and intermeshed by hi-tech networking. These are information, sense, effects and control. Superimposed over the operation theatre, this cloud offers quick and accurate situational awareness (SA), caters for redundancy and resilience, offers inter-domain complementarity, and allows a commander full-spectrum flexibility that is limited only by imagination. The concept of fusion warfare directly flows out of this grid in terms of command and control of this whole disaggregated potency. This is real centralised command, distributed control and decentralised execution.[14]

The RAAF recognises six domains, i.e. land, air, maritime, space, information (cyber and electromagnetic or EM) and human (physical and cognitive). The last three of them offer the chances of covert belligerence which allows strategic surprise of sorts. This can easily be followed by short-duration high-intensity multi-domain localised conflict. Any reacting force would have to cater for quick adaptability to this surprise and promise effective response as a deterrent. This brings us to some principal questions:

- Is the Multi-Domain concept a force-design initiative or a force-employment model?
- Should core competencies such as plans for acquisition, manning and training remain a services domain or an integrated approach is more suitable to multi-domain?

The most suitable approach would be to allow core competencies to be developed by single service under an overarching integrated capability build-up plan that looks through a multi-domain lens from the earliest stage. Since all commanders and leaders at the strategic, operational and tactical levels would have to deeply understand synergy and multi-domain concepts, it is important to incorporate these in professional training, exercises, simulations and other validation programs. It is critical for a central strategic core to ensure that multiple agencies, services and their programs are aligned. The tension of managing present issues and ensuring that these do not close future adaptations and windows of opportunity must be guided and managed. Capability building should allow strategic leaders to design and rapidly reconfigure a fit-for-purpose multi-domain task force in the shortest time. These task-forces would inevitably face four challenges: first, limited quantum of capability in each domain will demand prioritisation; second, professional mastery and delivery in each domain is taken for granted; third, robust and reliable networks all across; and fourth, encouraging bottom-up innovation that allows quick adaptability.

Defence vs Offence Spiral

Is it cheaper, in terms of overall costs and manning, to have highly effective air defence systems to deny high-performance and prohibitively expensive platforms (manned aircraft)? The exponential increase in competency of detection and single-shot kill probability (SSKP), and the lowering of costs will finally decide this debate. Long ranges of detection, ubiquity of a variety of sensors, high and improving SSKPs, and newer technology such as AI enabled autonomy, hypersonic flight and directed energy (DE) might just tilt the balance towards defence.

Current Al technology is highly specialised, restricted within a framework of software limited to learning, reasoning and problem-solving within a specific context. What is not currently possible is for these to adapt to new contexts or dynamically changing situations that human cognitive capacities are accustomed to. However, this is now changing at a break-neck speed despite the active debate on how much autonomy to be granted to non-humans. For example, the X-47B program of the US Navy that is working on an Unmanned Combat Aerial Vehicle (UCAV) for ship-based operations. It already is competent for catapult take-offs, arrested landings and aerial refuelling. The ALPHA program of USAF and its research laboratories has an Al agent that has beaten all experienced combat pilots in simulated combat through fuzzy logic. It holds great promise for human-machine teaming. An example is the US Army's program of teaming Apache helicopter pilots with unmanned MQ-1C towards winning in a multi-domain battle.

In the USAF's 'Loyal Wingman' program, an unmanned F-16 formatted with a manned one broke off to do some air-to-ground firing at multiple targets, modified its flight responding to mock dynamic threats, and rejoined the formation. This opens future avenues of large formations doing 'flocking' and 'swarming'. Conceptually, the risky part would be done by these unmanned components of the swarm. In another experiment, a fighter ejected a swarm of nearly a hundred autonomous micro-drones that demonstrated collective decision-making, adaptability in the air and self-healing capacity.

AI in Decision-Support

As every sensor and shooter gets networked into the 'combat cloud', the volume and velocity of data flows become impossible to be effectively handled by human decision makers. However, human ingenuity, creativity and adaptability cannot be yet replaced by anything else. But what AI can do is handle this data in terms of monitoring, triage, scoping etc. at a basic level, and have manageable information for decision makers to handle. Machines could also provide decision-support on suggested actions to be taken. Decision-support tasks would include data-mining from all forms of inputs and fusion into a standard form; applying big-data analytics and suitable presentation; providing courses of actions and their consequences; and provide means to validate the reliability of all these functions.

Assessing China's Capabilities

China's A2AD strategy is primarily aimed at keeping far superior US naval and joint capabilities far away from where it can be devastatingly effective. This is tailored to its eastern seaboard where all the maritime claims would inevitably cause friction and conflicts. Rarely has a medium power achieved a super-power status without conflict. China is getting ready for that, albeit planning to fight a war that it can through asymmetric approaches and not the one that the US wants it to fight.

A2AD is essentially multi-domain with an integrated mix of sensors and shooters based on land, air and maritime platforms.[15] Weaponry includes long- and medium-range artillery, rocket regiments, surface-to-surface missiles, air launched munitions, a variety of anti-ship and anti-aircraft missiles, long-range cruise and ballistic missiles etc. More importantly, these are all networked to align and respond quickly as per a larger strategic intent.[16] Space-based prowess and anti-satellite weapons add by improving own situational awareness while degrading the adversary's. The final picture is completed with capabilities in the cyber and information realms. Primary targets for hard-kill would be large platforms in the carrier–fleet, airborne command and control aircraft, airborne refuellers and such others that would effectively curtail full-spectrum freedom in the designated zone. All this would be done along with a core effort to degrade US' superior network-centric setup.

The war in the domains of space and information (cyber and EM) would start in right earnest well before the deployment in other domains. PLA reforms implemented since 2015 show a distinct trend towards 'informationisation'.[17] In addition to theatre commands to allow multi-domain operations, China established a Strategic Support Force (SSF) under the Central Military Commission (CMC), with a mandate to directly integrate and function with theatre commands.[18] Besides joint and integrated operations with theatre commands, the mandate includes full-spectrum Intelligence, Surveillance, Reconnaissance (ISR), management of satellite operations, defence of the electro-magnetic spectrum and cyber space tasks, and providing all these services to users.[19] This architecture clearly recognises the validity of multi-domain operations. The Chinese believe that a potent mix of space, cyber and EW are key to the overall information campaign.[20] The SSF integrates these quite tightly.

China's main focus is on East China Sea and South China Sea. It is clear that Taiwan, island claims and future geo-economic issues here would define its trajectory to usurping the USA. Indian and related Line of Actual Control (LAC) issues are a subsidiary of this content as the West would want India as countervail to China. By no stretch of imagination can it afford to redeploy most of its capabilities for an all-out war on the LAC. It would leave a crippling void for USA to exploit. As is well known and analysed by many, using Pakistan as proxy and adequate pressures on the LAC would cater for the period till its rise to top. In this analysis, the questions that are forefront are:

- Is a 2-front war even remotely possible and is a capability build-up towards this needed in light of the huge costs?
- Should India prepare for limited but intense localised spats after assessing some of the A2AD capacities and a likely plan for attrition by multi-domain operations by the PLA to effectively neutralise Indian airpower?

A COMPLEX PRESENT

Preparing for Uncertainty and Complexity

All participants in modern armed conflict will attempt information warfare, cyber-attacks, irregular war, disruptive technology employment, and other unexpected initiatives before a force-on-force engagement. In the book 'Unrestricted Warfare', two PLA colonels strategise that "the new and old terrorists who consistently uphold the principle of resorting to every conceivable means are still the best teachers of each nation's government."[21] They emphasise that the heart of unrestricted warfare is breaking down the traditional ways of looking at war to a newer perspective. It means overcoming of boundaries, restrictions and even taboos that separate the military from the non-military, the weapon from the non-weapon, and combatant from non-combatant.

Yet unrestricted warfare does not mean that unlimited methods are always suitable. While the focus has been on conflicts such as Israel-Hezbollah (2006), and Crimea-Ukraine currently, closer home, Kargil (1999) was a classic hybrid mode adopted by Pakistan against India. It combined regular army troops (Northern Light Infantry) disguised as Mujahidin, occupation and holding of key locations, use of portable missiles, and even support of Pakistan Army artillery and counter-battery units.

Compound wars are conceptualised and directed at a strategic level, where regular and irregular forces operating independently are coordinated towards a strategic objective – for example, the Vietcong and North Vietnamese Army operations in the debacle faced by the US in the Vietnam War. The Indo-Pak War of 1965 is another example where 'Razakars' in Operation Gibraltar were coordinated with subsequent operations of the Pakistan Army. Hybrid wars differ in terms of more detailed involvement, fusion and integration at the operational level, e.g. the Israeli-Hezbollah Conflict in 2006.

Hybrid warfare is an emerging mix of tactics, techniques, and technology that combines some of insurgency's key advantages with some conventional strategies such as control and hold of territory. It combines highly decentralised Command and Control (C2), loose leadership, light footprint, and population support with tactics to hold areas and cause attrition using man-portable anti-tank and anti-aircraft missiles, rockets, and mortars. A true hybrid campaign will encompass an entire spectrum of capability that can only be countered by a whole-of-nation approach, including nuances of combined-arms, manoeuvre and counter-insurgency. This 'gray zone' campaign, that nibbles away without a big bite that may invite all-out reactions, will surely surprise forces that are trained only in classic conflict management.

United States Air Force doctrine defines Irregular Warfare (IrW) as a violent struggle among state and non-state actors for legitimacy and influence over a population, with the non-state entity favouring asymmetric approaches. The nature and characteristics of such a conflict are significantly different from traditional war. Conventional and unconventional refer to the weapons and forces conducting operations.[22] IrW includes insurgency, counter-insurgency (COIN), terrorism, and counterterrorism, but is not limited to just these. A hybrid war is a blend of lethality of state conflict with asymmetric characteristics of irregular war, such as the Israeli-Hezbollah conflict of 2006.

The future holds conflicts that would be a battle of narratives and multiple truths, besides the 'real fighting'. By its very attributes of flexibility, adaptability and availability, airpower can play a critical role in shaping such narratives by causing effects on its own or supporting other agencies of the government. Airpower leadership has to be keenly aware of the context, understand the strengths and limitations of partner agencies, and be innovative and adaptive in the joint campaign. At the same time, they need to be aware of costs or affordability of airpower, and its vulnerability on ground and air. Optimum solutions can only follow if the bigger picture is not lost sight of.

Complexity and Adaptability

The term "wicked" for problems is reserved for complex issues that are not fully understood till solution formulation; have a no-stopping rule or do not go away; there are no right or wrongs, as well as no given alternative solutions; and the issue is unique and novel. The approach to such issues involves collaborative participation of all stakeholders, and plans on taming the problem and focussing on the unsolved part. An integrated approach to managing such complex problems requires coordination with objectives of acting on learned lessons and not just pre-planned targets.

Adaptability has two facets, as in the two faces of a coin: the ability to sense a change in situation demanding a change in response, and the ability to commit to that requirement. There can be no better teacher of adaptability than biology and the subject of evolution. Mutations and selections of the fittest are lessons that can be applied when dealing with CAS or wicked problems. The Australian Army replaced the famous OODA loop with an Act, Sense, Decide, Adapt (ASDA) loop that deals better with non-linear, complex and unpredictable states. What does complexity leadership entail? The natural instinct for a managerial leader to a developing complexity is to respond with orders, directives and even more control. However, this effectively reduces diversity of thought, crowd-sourced ideas and bottoms-up innovative solutions. A leader needs to balance administration control and generative impetus for better solutions. The control part regulates the generation of adaptability and newer ideas from going into a chaotic status. The environment thus created will do both, explore and exploit emergence at lower levels.

In the ASDA cycle, action is first because in uncertainty one needs to prod to elicit a requisite response for assessments to be made. Decisions are made based on these assessments followed by deeper reflection and adaptation. An example from 1971 War is illustrative. Dacca was never an objective even in the final operational instruction by Army HQ to Eastern Command.[23] However, the famous prods by special heliborne operations (Mi-4s) ordered by Gen Sagat Singh (Indian IV Corps) caused disequilibrium and a wrong decision by Pakistani Gen Qazi to defend Sylhet by two brigades rather than defending River Meghna crossings towards Dacca. This allowed IV Corps to reach the doorsteps of Dacca almost 8 days earlier than possible. Deeper reflection allowed the Indian Army to quickly go for the jugular and reach the doorsteps of Dacca. There, for some inexplicable reason, it was made to wait for II Corps to fetch up from the west and claim the honours.

Avoiding Decision Paralysis

Complexity cannot be countered by paralysis or adopting a fundamentally reactive wait-watch-adapt actions. A faulty premise is that wicked problems do not allow for 'good enough' approaches or preclude right or wrong solutions. Overstating complexity may muddle thinking and also delay and degrade imperative actions. Three approaches can help avoiding this state. First is prioritisation by revising key assumptions and allowing for tactical flexibility in unintended consequences. This does account for non-linear phenomena, butterfly effects, self-organising systems – all hallmarks of complexity. Secondly, effective delegation of power and authority encourages and enables empowered players at different levels. And finally, understanding what empowers an adversary, in terms of effect of technological advances and speed of changes, is important.

Adopting a COIN Culture

Irregular warfare will force conventional forces to be able to respond across the spectrum of conflict and contingencies. Air warriors will have to learn to be adaptive and responsive to the demands of unconventional and irregular warfare. An aviation-combat unit must be capable of executing both the hard and soft elements of COIN in differing environments. The main focus must be on creation and training of strong capable leaders who can operate in environments of great uncertainty. Next, it must develop low-cost and quick-result training methodology that allows multiple iterations of basic skills common to all leaders. This is then followed by special skills such as terrain-specific flying or maintaining aviation assets under combat and rugged conditions.

MULTI-AGENCY FRAMEWORK: MAKING IT WORK

Inter-Agency Trust

A shared vision and a synchronised plan of action can force relationships to develop that will allow objectives to be achieved in a whole-of-government campaign. The main four obstacles to inter-agency cooperation, collaboration and effective integration are a lack of personal and institutional trust; absence of networks for information-sharing; stove-piped plans and strategies in silos; and competition for resources.[24]

Institutional trust is dependent on beliefs about institutional behaviour and perceptions of competency.[25] It grows when an agency is perceived to be value-based, and demonstrates integrity, credibility, reliability, openness and consistency. While elements of personal trust will always be present, it must add on to the edifice of inter-agency trust. For example, ministries of home, defence, diplomacy, and other development agencies needed to synergise plans and execution in a COIN campaign at strategic, operational and tactical levels institutionally. However, the Indian Peace Keeping Force (IPKF) experience showed a dominance of personal rapport and inconsistent networking.

Differences in doctrine, guidelines, practices and agency cultures need to be explained and discussed to avoid misunderstandings, especially between civilians and military. Education and integration can be effectively assisted by liaison cells which allow horizontal integration. Liaison officers and staff, and overall coordinators are necessary when a situation is highly dynamic and constantly in flux. It follows that such personnel must be of quality, perhaps even more competent than those in the field. However, the opposite is the reality, where mediocre or even unmotivated people are cast in such assignments. Liaison officers need to be recognised in their core competencies by 'own and others', as well as possess high skills of negotiation, integration and understanding of other agencies capabilities. Another important issue is the levels of authority and decision-making such officers possess that in turn affects trust and confidence levels in others. Conflict resolution and de-conflicting of agendas can be effectively addressed by empowerment at delegated levels. It is also important to acknowledge that people-skills, that are mostly individualised, are critical to this communication-based endeavour.

Planning Processes

The complexity of operational planning in irregular war or less-than-war situations is further accentuated by dynamism of threats and challenges. The process per se needs to be flexible, adaptive and collaborative. The key to shared goals and understanding is effective communications. It can be disabled by silo-mentalities and bureaucratic approach.[26] The requirement is of a dynamic model where multiple procedures are performed simultaneously at different levels enabled by real-time data through a net-centric environment. Constant iterations of the OODA loop allow cyclical collaborative exchange to cater for tempo variations. For example, in response to an emergent contingency, leaders can respond rapidly rather than schedule meetings.

Multi–Agency Decision Making

Extensive research in the USA post-9/11 World Trade Centre (WTC) disaster and Hurricane Katrina has pointed fingers at hierarchical command and control setups for major crises, and advocates a more collaboration-based emergent model for effective emergency handling. Main factors that contribute to this thread are complexity of multiple and diverse organisation converging; uncertainty due to inadequate information and analysis; time constraints and life-and-death criticalities; physical and mental stresses on participants and affected communities; risks involved and high-stakes; and experiences of actors in a previous disaster.[27]

Collaborative Leader

While a complicated environment or problem can be dissected by domain-experts for proposing solutions, a complex one cannot be so addressed because of its inherent adaptability, uncertainty and unpredictability. Subject-matter specialists in silos may be of little help in never-ending complexities. These need creativity, an experimenting approach and fast-learning curves to be addressed adequately. In this context, the OODA loop's decide and act steps become synonymous with experimenting or testing the waters, with repeated iterations of the loop serving as feedback and learning facilitators. In such settings, collaborative dialogue means individual inputs add to a greater amount than the mathematical sum of all – almost like a building-block of ideas. Senior leaders must, in the first instance, discern in which zone the problem lies, i.e., complicated, complex or chaos. Thereafter, they must adopt an appropriate form and style of working, along with the hierarchical structure, i.e., flat or conventional. A flat structure promotes creative debate, dialogue, diversity and dissent (loyal). Here a follower is as, if not more, important as the leader in terms of cognitive contributions.

The potential solution, if that is a plausible proposition, to a wicked problem facing a nation will be beyond the domain, scope and capacity of any single organisation, agency or ministry. Collaboration in an inter-ministerial endeavour will require leadership to look at multiple stakes and competition, and nurture the grouping towards shared understanding and goals. Leadership must be focused on making things happen and acting decisively with rectitude. While there will be formal leaders and authority flowing out of task-force structuring and hierarchy, considerable work gets done by champions who are passionate on the task in hand and entirely committed to larger objectives.

Multi-Domain Capabilities

The Clausewitzian theory was focused solely on physical force and attrition. But with great advances in technology and morphing of asymmetric threats, pure physical capabilities of air, land and naval forces are no longer enough to manage conflict. National comprehensive power will include elements of diplomacy, information, military, and economic, and their synergy. At the strategic, operational, and tactical levels, these elements operate on land, in the air, at sea, and through informational, cyber, and electronic means – in other words, a multi-domain endeavour. Synergised national capabilities should look to create zones of dominance to enable successful pursuit of national objectives and end-states. A corollary is that mental and physical dislocation of an adversary capable of multi-domain operations is an imperative. Armed forces with multiple capabilities working as part of joint, inter-organisational and multi-national teams will provide national leaders multiple options across all domains needed to deter and defeat highly potent adversaries.

Airpower and Special Action

Special Forces have unique and innate adaptive ability, and are employed to respond with agility to uncertainty from unpredictable enemies. They are masters in asymmetric approaches to problem-solving. Achievement of tactical surprise, a key in such campaigns, is enabled by speed, stealth, and agility, along with superior technology. The ability to appear at an unexpected place and time of own choosing, with an offensive mindset, enables retaining initiative and surprise. This is an effective asymmetric counter to the advantages of experienced insurgents, i.e., local tacit support, early warning networks and local terrain knowledge. A paradox is that the characteristics that render Special Forces an ideal choice for dispersed and geographically isolated insurgency is premised upon mobility, responsiveness, and firepower provided by air power. In a Special Forces environment of hyper-competence and sense of purpose, operations are characterised by clear mission orders and appropriate technology that allows dispersed command, control, and execution. Employment of air power must reflect complementary response structures of command and control.

Advances in technology and tactics allow acute target discrimination and weapon effectiveness of air-delivered weapons. Precision weapons can achieve unthinkable accurate and overwhelming firepower in support of light and agile Special Forces; additionally, it greatly reduces fratricide and collateral damage. Persistent ISR can provide appropriate flank protection and early warning. Mobility and effective firepower can allow even 'lighter and more lethal' Special Forces. Terrain following radar, varied flight profiles, all-weather abilities, standoff ISR for threat and detection avoidance, and offset landing zones allow stealth in a true sense. This force structure requires deeper reflection in terms of acquisition plans, training and interoperability.

Conclusion

It is clear that technology is moving ahead at a pace that was unbelievable even a few years back. More importantly, convergence of different fields such as AI, additive manufacturing and autonomous weapons threaten to even change the nature of warfare, at least to some degree. At the same time, multi-domain and hybrid warfare concepts, among others, promise to bring further synergy that cannot be countered by theories and force structures based on lessons from the last war.

The first step in looking at future threat scenarios is posing some uncomfortable but right questions. This paper has put forth nine pertinent questions flowing out of a quick look at some issues that are staring at all armed forces. While the title of the paper and thrust is on airpower in general (and the IAF in particular), these affect all agencies that contribute in a whole-of-nation approach to conflict management. The bottomline is that an over-investment in current doctrines, concepts and platforms today may close the windows to adapt to future revolutionary changes in the coming decades. Complexity and uncertainty are a given in the future. It demands agile, curious, creative and questioning minds to gauze ahead and build adaptive capabilities. Asking difficult questions and posing disruptive thoughts is a good start to face such a future.

NOTES

1. Jeffrey L. Caton, Autonomous Weapons Systems: A Brief Survey of Development, Operational, Legal and Ethical Issues, Letort Papers, Carlisle, PA: Strategic Studies Institute, 2015.

2. F.G. Hoffman, 2017, "Will War's Nature Change in the Seventh Military Revolution?" *Parameters* 47(4), Winter 2017–18, p. 27.
3. Development, Concepts and Doctrine Command, Strategic Trends Programme: Global Strategic Trends—Out to 2045, 5th ed., Shrivenham, UK: Ministry of Defence, 2016, p. 67.
4. Andrew Liptak, "Navy 3D Printed a Concept Submersible in Four Weeks," *Real Clear Defense*, July 30, 2017, available at www.realcleardefense.com; Meredith Rutland Bauer, "Weaponizing 3-D Printers: Cyber attacks Could Turn Battlefield Tech into Threats," *FifthDomain.com*, November 13, 2017, available at www.fifthdomain.com/dod.
5. T. Russell, 2014, "Themed Competition: Additive Manufacturing for Future Military Equipment", Centre for Defence Enterprise, Army Technology, 2(4), p. 4. www.technologyreview.com
6. Ajay Lele, 2017, "Hypersonic Weapons", Institute for Defence Studies and Analyses, IDSA Occasional Paper No. 46. www.idsa.in (accessed on 27 May 2019).
7. Sanjiv Tomar, 2015, 'Nanotechnology: The Emerging Field for Future Military Applications', Institute for Defence Studies And Analyses, IDSA Monograph Series No. 48, p. 18. https://idsa.in/system/files/jds/ (accessed on 05 Mar 2019).
8. Ibid.
9. Robert O. Work, Foreword to DoD Artificial Intelligence, Big Data and Cloud Taxonomy, Washington, DC: Govini, 2017, p. 2.
10. Nathan P. Freier, 2017, "Strategic Insights: Speed Kills, Enter an Age of Unbridled Hyperconnectivity," Strategic Studies Institute. http://ssi.armywarcollege.edu (accessed on 23 May 2019).
11. Ajey Lele, 2019, "Debating Lethal Autonomous Weapon Systems", Journal of Defence Studies, Vol. 13, No. 1, January-March 2019, pp. 33-49. https://idsa.in/jds/jds-13-1-2019-debating-lethal-autonomous-weapon.
12. Peter Layton, 2016, "A New Direction for Australian Air Power: Armed Unmanned Aircraft", Chief of Air Force Occasional Papers, Paper No 5, Air Power Development Centre. www.airforce.gov.au/airpower (accessed on 20 May 2019).
13. MacGregor Knox and Williamson Murray (eds.), *The Dynamics of Military Revolution, 1300–2050*, New York: Cambridge University Press, 2001, pp. 6–7.
14. Kainikara, Sanu, 2016, "What Does Multi-Domain Integration Mean for the ADF?" Proceedings of the 2016 RAAF Air Power Conference, Multi-Domain Integration – Enabling Future Joint Success, National Convention Centre, Canberra, 15–16 March 2016. Squadron Leader David Burns (ed.), pp. 40-51.
15. T.M. Bonds et al, 2017, "Land-Based, Multi-Domain Anti-Access/Area Denial Forces." Santa Monica, CA: RAND Corporation.
16. R. Cliff, 2017, *Shaking the Heavens and Splitting the Earth: Chinese Air Force Employment Concepts in the 21st Century*. Santa Monica, CA: RAND Corporation. Document no. MG-915-AF; www.rand.org/pubs/monographs.
17. Elsa B. Kania, China's Artificial Intelligence Revolution," *Diplomat*, July 27, 2017.
18. P.C. Saunders andJ. Wuthnow, 2016, "China's Goldwater-Nichols? Assessing PLA's Organizational Reforms", *Joint Force Quarterly* (JFQ), No. 82, p. 70. www.ndupress.ndu.edu (accessed on 15 May 2019).
19. Kevin L. Pollpeter et al., 2017, "The Creation of the PLA Strategic Support: Support Force and Its Implications for Chinese Military Space Operations", RAND Corporation, p. 7. www.rand.org (accessed on 20 May 2019).

20. Amrita Jash, 2018, PLA's Strategic Support Force: A New Art of Modern War. Scholar Warrior, Spring 2018, CLAWS. www.claws.org (accessed on 10 may 2019).
21. Qiao Liang and Wang Xiangsui (PLA Colonels), 1999, Unrestricted Warfare: China's Master Plan to Destroy America. PLA Literature and Arts Publishing House.
22. John Nagl, Counterinsurgency Lessons from Malaya and Vietnam: Learning to Eat Soup with a Knife, New York: Praeger, 2002.
23. P.C. Lal, 1986, My years with the IAF. New Delhi: Lancer Publishers, pp. 207-216. ISBN 81-7062-008-2.
24. N. Alexander and C. Thibodeau, 2016, Trust and Networks in the Interagency, *InterAgency Journal*, Vol. 7, Issue 3, Fall 2016. Arthur D. Simons Center for Interagency Cooperation, Fort Leavenworth, KS, USA.
25. S. Mussoni, G-J. de Vreede and A. Buckles, 2016, The Criticality of Collaborative Planning, *Joint Force Quarterly* (JFQ), 80, 1st Quarter 2016. Available at http://ndupress.ndu.edu
26. R.M. Klein, 2007, Adaptive Planning: Not Your Great-Grandfather's Schlieffen Plan, *Joint Force Quarterly*, 45 (2nd Quarter), pp. 84–88. Available at http://ndupress.ndu.edu
27. N. Kapucu and V. Garayev, 2011, Collaborative Decision-Making in Emergency and Disaster Management. *International Journal of Public Administration*, 34, pp. 366-375. DOI: 10.1080/01900692.2011.561477.

*

PART 3

DEFENCE MODERNISATION

June, 2011

22

MODERNISING THE MOTIVATIONAL CONTEXT OF THE INDIAN ARMED FORCES

Major General G. D. Bakshi

The Basis of Regimentation

Dietmar Rothermund and Harman Kulke state that the non-revolutionary transfer of power from the British Empire to the Indian Republic enabled it to inherit intact the instrumentalities of governance like the armed forces and the civil and police bureaucracies. The newborn republic was beset with the trauma of partition and the first war in Jammu & Kashmir (J&K), and thus forced to focus on immediate consolidation. It had little time or energy to transform the colonial instruments to the needs of an Independent Republic. Hence, the basic structure and motivational ethos of the armed forces in general and the Indian Army, in particular, has remained rooted in the colonial context.

The British had organised the Indian Army on the basis of ethnicity/sub-nationality-based regiments. The trauma of the First War of Independence had led them to discontinue all recruitment from the present day States of Bengal, Bihar and most of UP. These native troops (who had once formed the backbone of the Mauryan Army that had first unified India politically in third-century BCE era) were declared 'non-martial' and excluded from further recruitment. Also dispensed were the troops from the South that had formed the backbone of the Madras Presidency Army.

Lord Roberts of Kandahar propagated his 'martial race' theory and the entire recruitment bias of the British Indian Army was switched to North and North

West India. The Sikhs, Punjabi Musalmans and the Gurkhas (who had largely stayed out of the 1857 struggle) formed the bulk of this new colonial Army. We thus saw the formation of ethnicity-based regiments like the Sikhs, Jats, Marathas, Dogras, Rajputs, Kumaonis, Garhwalis and Gurkhas who were deemed martial classes. The primary concern of the British Indian Army was to sanitise this force and ensure that no nationalist sentiments would ever arise in this colonial instrument, that there would be no repetition of 1857 and this colonial army would faithfully obey orders to shoot at its own citizenry whenever necessary. To that extent, the very idea of India as a unified entity was anathema to the British.

Nationalism was a dangerous word in the ranks of the colonial military. The entire basis of military motivation was therefore focused around the *Izzat* (honour) and martial traditions of the sub-nationality-based regiments. The pride in the '*quam*' (sub-nationality) was the primary basis of the military motivational ideology. The history and achievements of the *quam* were used to inspire the soldiery. Such a motivational ideology by itself would obstruct the emergence of nationalist sentiments based on fashioning a pan-Indian identity. The critical question is that six decades after Independence, why are we still fixated on a colonial model of military motivation designed to curb nationalism and encourage a plethora of regional, ethnic and sub-national identities?

In practical terms, the British colonial, martial race-based recruitment model proved too narrow to support a large army. It broke down in the First World War when the colonial army had to be rapidly expanded from 350,000 to 1.1 million men. A large number of non-martial classes like the Mahzbi Sikhs, Mahars and allied scheduled caste ethnicities had to be per force recruited. In the Second World War, the British Indian Army had to be expanded to an all-time record size of 2.5 million men to fight the Japanese and also contribute troops for Europe and North Africa theatres. The martial class recruitment base completely broke down and a very large number of 'non-martial' class soldiers had to be recruited. The Bihar Regiment was once more a part of the British Indian Army along with a host of castes and communities that had earlier been labeled as non-martial. The martial class narrative as a basis of military motivation had, in practice, failed to meet the needs of a very large army even before the Independence.

Post-Independence Developments

In theory, the martial race concept was debunked after Independence but it continued in practice to form the basis of regimental motivation. Recruitment was thrown open on all-India all-class basis. However, the legacy regiments were retained to prevent organisational turbulence and the simple fact was that the martial race-oriented model had become deeply engrained in the psyche of the Army. No need was felt to disturb functional organisations that had performed well in the war. Three types of Units were now retained:

- Single Class Regiments, e.g. the Sikhs, Dogras, Jats, Marathas etc.
- Fixed Class Regiments, e.g. the Grenadiers, the Punjab Regiment etc. with fixed class composition (like two Company Dogras, two Companies Jats, Dogra-Sikhs combinations and so on).
- All-India All-Class Regiments: these had a heterogeneous mix of all Indian castes/classes; all new regiments, e.g. Paratroopers, the Guards, Mechanised Infantry etc., that were raised post-independence, were on this mixed model and have performed very well.

General Rodrigues Era Reforms

Post-Operation Blue Star, mutinies in some battalions of the Sikh and Punjab Regiments sharply underlined the perils of overreliance on sub-nationality or ethnicity-based regiments and systems of motivation in the present day context when insurgencies are largely focused on ethnic identities. However, Gen Rodrigue's attempts to breakdown the existing 'Fixed Class' Infantry regiments into heterogeneous compositions, by deliberately mixing sub-units of different regiments, were deeply resented as they disrupted the historic continuity of organisational entities with long histories of corporate existence and collective memories of inspiring battle performances.

This experimental reform process was deeply resented in the Army and was revoked a few years down the line. Its basic flaw was in trying to mix sub-units of existing regiments rather than trying to organically grow new units of mixed compositions. It missed the essential point altogether. The Basic problem was not with the composition but the emphasis on ethnicity for motivation. Units can be formed on regional basis to ease administrative/functional problems. However, what is of essence is their basic motivational philosophy. Is it based on regional chauvinism or on a larger theme of Nationalism and Patriotism – the aggressive promotion of a pan-Indian identity? The honest fact is that the colonial culture that was deeply suspicious of any Nationalist sentiment in the Army unfortunately persists as a historical anachronism. Some officers at the highest levels still claim that the Indian Army fights not for the country or any patriotic fervor but for the 'Izzat of the Paltan' – the ethnicity-based regiment. Such an attitude is a clear hangover of the Raj period and its colonial narrative that emphasised regional identities to prevent the emergence of nationalism in a colonial Army. There is a need to understand and transform this cultural context and outgrow the anachronisms of a colonial Past.

Nationalism as Basis of Combat Motivation

The British had superimposed their own regimental model based on regional/ ethnic identities (Scots, Irish Guards etc.) on the British Indian Armies. Most Western Armies base their regiments on such regional basis and limit motivational narratives to the unit/regimental level. However, the Germans and the Japanese, and to an extent the Russians, based their motivational themes on a highly aggressive promotion of militant nationalism. The motivational focus was placed on the highest organisational entity – the Nation State itself and not anything lower. All else was secondary. The highest loyalty, the highest cause was the Nation State. This served as a common theme for motivation across organisational boundaries – the Army, Navy, Air force and Marines all subscribed to a common motivational ideology that stressed not regional but a pan-national identity. This facilitated inter-services coordination and synergy.

Militant nationalism served as a highly effective basis of combat motivation in World War II. Post-War evaluation of Allied and German/Japanese military unit performances indicated that the German Wehrmacht and the Imperial Japanese Armies (even though they lost the War due to overall asymmetry of industrial resources that the United States' entry into the war generated) proved to be the more efficient and effective armies. American studies have indicated that German units decimated to the extent of 80 percent still retained their combat cohesion in World War II. Field Marshal Slim had lamented that "We all talk of fighting to the last man and last round – the Japanese are the only ones who do it". The Kamikaze suicide pilots bear testimony to the very high levels of combat motivation in the Japanese Armed Forces.

Thus, 'militant nationalism' as a basis for combat motivation has worked in a most effective way in past wars. It generates tremendous organisational coherence and a high degree of motivation. It creates the inspirational climate that fosters extremes of sacrifice. It is a well tried and tested model with proven battlefield validity. We could not adopt it in the past – because we were a colonial Army, but 60 years after Independence, what is it that prevents us from adopting this combat-validated model?

In March 2006, a Vietnamese Army delegation had visited Headquarters Eastern Command of the Indian Army. One of the Vietnamese Generals was keen to know what the Indian Army did for patriotism training. The look of astonishment on his face, when he was told that we do nothing of this kind but rely on the regimental system to motivate our men, will long haunt those present. The Vietnamese General's insight deserves to be reflected upon. The organisational need is to outgrow the cultural context of colonialism and find own moorings as a Nation State and future power to reckon with.

An Alternative Indian Model: Learning From the Indian National Army

Gen Shankar Roychowdhury, when he was the Chief, highlighted the need to transform the Indian Army's motivational methodology to a militant nationalism model that emphasises patriotism and aggressive championing of a pan-Indian identity. He suggested that the Indian National Army (INA) of Subash Chandra Bose provided a readymade model for the Indian context. The INA had tried to apply the German and Japanese techniques of military motivation to the Indian context with considerable success.

The simple fact is that most of our post-Independence efforts to Indianise the Indian Army are borrowed from the INA. "Jai Hind" our salutation comes from the INA. Gen Roychowdhury had decreed that the INA Marching Song of 'Kadam Kadam Barhaye Ja' be played at the Passing Out Parades (POPs) of the Indian Military Academy (IMA) and the Officers' Training Academy (OTA), and at all the POPs of the recruits at the Regimental Centers. This was a step in the right direction and the practice is still in vogue. The INA is a very vibrant and extant model that needs much greater study and analysis. Anton Pelinka writes, "Bose was certainly always a nationalist. For him the Indian nation was an idea, the anti-thesis of the princely State and the caste system, the religious struggle and linguistic conflicts, and above all, the anti-thesis of Jinnah's theory of 'two nations'."

The INA had strength of 1500 officers and 60,000 men. It was organised into three divisions, command troops (to include special forces, armored, anti-aircraft, transport and logistics troops). It had an Officers Training School and a Women's Regiment (Rani of Jhansi Regiment). The First and Second Division saw action in Burma and the Third was deployed in Malaya. In Burma, the INA Division fought along with the Japanese 15th, 31st, and 33rd Divisions in Manipur, Kohima and Imphal, respectively, and then took part in the difficult retreat across Burma (especially the Battles of Meiktila and Irrawaddy crossing). Morale and motivation across formations and units was not uniform and some units formed from surrendered Indian Army prisoners of war (POWs) did not do as well as those raised *de novo* and trained by the Japanese.

The best performance of the INA perhaps was at Mount Popa where an INA company fought bravely with petrol bombs against a British Tank assault. The astounding fact is that overall the INA took 26,000 casualties in World War II. This accounts for almost 43 percent casualties. Yet, most INA units had retained their combat cohesion till the end of the War. Sustaining morale in retreat is a very difficult proposition. INA's motivational philosophy clearly enabled it to do so. The INA had come too late when the tide of war had already turned. Nevertheless, its overall impact on the Indian freedom movement was far greater than is realised; it is deemed by many as instrumental in shaping the British decision to leave India. Even in defeat, the INA inspired victory.

The INA Indianised many German and Japanese techniques of military motivation and emphasised on militant nationalism. Though both German and Japanese models do have a negative resonance and may appear somewhat anachronistic, yet some of their concepts could be modified to suit modern Indian conditions. Today, there is a need to emulate the INA model with perhaps some modifications. In this respect, we need the following:

- Heavy emphasis on nationalism at the entry levels of the National Defence Academy (NDA), IMA and OTA, which are foundational in their impact. The courses must commence with a Motivational Capsule of a week before main training commences. It must rely on a capsule of Indian History, Indian Military Traditions and post-Independence achievements. It must rely upon motivational films and inspiring war movies to provide role models and include talks by gallantry award winners.
- There is a motivation training capsule in the current Recruit Training Syllabus. It comes in the middle of the training regime at the Regimental Centers. This needs to be made the start point of recruit training. Heavy emphasis must be laid on emphasising the Indian ethos, the Regimental History and Films on regimental military Heroes and award winners who can act as role models for the young soldiers. Heavy emphasis must be laid on community singing of patriotic songs, marching songs and singing with military bands. European armies have traditionally used community singing as a powerful motivational tool.
- Middle and Senior Officers must be encouraged to study Indian History (especially Indian Military History). Capsules on the organisational

culture, ethos and motivational philosophy must be run at the basic courses at the Army War College and College of Defense Management.

A Consideration

There is a need to outgrow the colonial context in our organisational culture and transit to a 'nationalism' model that emphasises loyalty to the highest organisational entity of the Nation State. Such a similarity of motivational context across organisational boundaries will promote inter-services synergy and coordination. Different Services will then place national interest above parochial Service loyalties as a deeply ingrained habit of thought. This is a combat validated model that worked brilliantly in the Second World War and is still practiced by the Vietnamese and Israeli Armed Forces. In the INA, we have a readymade model of motivation customised for the Indian context.

*

September, 2014

23

Strategic Defence and a Mountain Strike Corps

Lieutenant General Gautam Banerjee, PVSM, AVSM, YSM

"Begin, be bold and venture to be wise"

– **Horace**

Cause for a Mountain Strike Corps

Right from the days when the People's Republic of China (PRC) decided to use military power to address its border issues with India, the Indian Army suffers from a serious operational debility. This debility arises from an absence of counter-offensive capability across the watershed of the Indo-Tibet Border or the Line of Actual Control (LAC). Indeed, India's defense-oriented military strategy remains inconclusive unless it has within its ambit a viable component of *autonomous counter-offensive* or *riposte* capability to confront the aggressor with counter-threat(s) that forces him to divert or recoil from his venture.

The decade past has found that Beijing, perhaps buoyed by fruition of her military modernisation, is no more able to restrain from exercising her tactic of *forcing gradual migration* into claimed territories. Having already firmed up her possession of the Aksai Chin and Shaksgam Valley, she is engaged in preparing grounds for her next phase of expansionism through outlandish claims over the Arunachal Pradesh and many other bits. Accordingly, the LAC is subject to increasing intrusions at Hayuliang-Fish Tail, Asaphila-Longju and Lungma-Kerang areas in the Eastern Sector, Thag La–Barahoti areas in the Central Sector and Chumar, Demchok, Pangong Tso, Depsang Plains and Daulat Beg Oldi areas in the Western Sector of the Indo-Tibet Border. In the process, the PRC has advanced its notional claim-lines well into the Indian territory.

Offensive-in-Defence

Captain B H Liddell-Hart had argued, with substance of historical proof, that though neither flamboyant nor spectacular as the offensive, it was the defensive strategy in most cases that brought assured victory in the end. However, there is a *caveat.* According to the universal 'Principles of War', for a defensive strategy to come successful, an effective offensive content must be intrinsic to each level of its prosecution. It is so that the various stages of defensive operations to harass, delay, resist, limit and cause attrition to the enemy's attacking forces have to be infused with offensive characteristics. At the tactical level, this principle manifests in the form of the defender's raids, spoiling attacks, reinforcing manoeuvres and local as well as deliberately planned counter-attacks, the last named being an exclusive operation for which contingency plans are made and forces earmarked.

Further, as the history of warfare teaches, to trigger final collapse of the enemy's aggression, a capability to undertake *autonomous counter-offensive* – as distinct from the aforementioned 'counter-attack' phase of a defensive battle – at a place and time of the defender's choosing must be but imperative to what may essentially be an ambit of defensive strategy.

Beyond the Line of Defence

Navies perform their mandate of defending national waters and coastlines by engaging in operations beyond the nation's maritime boundaries. The Air Forces too target the enemy beyond the national air space; only in case of hostile ingress would they direct their attack into own territory. In similar vein, in order just to maintain the sanctity of a given line of defence but no more, ground forces have to resort to offensive action across that line. To be really effective, these offensive operations – call it *counter-offensive* or *riposte* – have to be launched from distinct firm base(s) and at timing(s) that are well clear from the tumult of defensive engagements; needless to state, in the contemporary context, all of these would be *joint service* operations. The purpose here is to exploit those sectors where the aggressor prefers to remain in relative dormancy, and so upset his strategic designs by disrupting his force-matrix, terrain-orientation and 'task-to-time' equation. The United Nations Forces' offensive on Inchon in the Korea War of 1951-53, India's counter-offensive in the Lahore Sector during the 1965 Indo-Pakistan War and Israel's encirclement of the 3rd Egyptian Army in the 1973 Yom Kippur War are apt demonstrations of this principle.

The Idea of 17 Corps

By the Year 2007 or so, the extent of build-up of the PRC's military infrastructure along the Indo-Tibet Border had at last stirred the Indian Government's conscience. Thus, it raised two army divisions and beefed up air power to round off India's defence capability in the Eastern Sector. However, the void of that element of *autonomous offensive action*, which must be intrinsic to any defensive strategy, remained unaddressed. That is the deficiency which is sought to be filled by the raising of a 'Mountain Strike Corps', the proposal for which had been pending with the Government since some years past; the Depsang La incident in April 2013 may have been the last straw. That was when the Chinese troops set up camp well behind India's LAC and refused to budge, just as it had done earlier in the Zimithang, Asaphila and Hayuliang areas in Arunachal Pradesh and Demchok area in Ladakh, thus highlighting – for the nth time – the helpless situation that could confront India should Beijing decides to spurn India's entreaties to vacate intrusion.

According to the official version and its implications, the 17 Corps is under raising at Ranchi, where during the Second World War, General William Slim's 14th Army had geared up to win back Burma from the Japanese, and where the Eastern Command Headquarters was located till 1953. Once fully raised, the Corps Headquarters would move to establish itself at Panagarh in West Bengal, another World War II logistic base from where the wars in Burma and China were sustained. The Corps would have two specially structured mountain divisions – 59 & 72 Divisions – headquartered at Panagarh and Pathankot, respectively. Besides, there would be two each of independent armoured and infantry brigades, one of each being located in Ladakh in the West and the other two stationed in Sikkim and Arunachal Pradesh in the East. A Corps being a very large formation of nearly 70,000 troops and vast paraphernalia of weapons, equipment, transport etc., the brigades and units, numbering above 200 odd, would be located variously from Ladakh to Arunachal Pradesh. Another division is reportedly being considered to be orbatted to this Corps in which case the strength would be around 90,000 troops. Of course, there would be many changes affected in the force-structure and their locations as the Corps shapes up in step with its evolving concepts of operations.

The idea of 17 Corps is unique in military history. No field formation has ever been assigned to operational contingencies so fluid, across so distinctly separated frontages and axes spread over 4000 odd kilometres, over freezing deserts of 4300 to 5300 metres altitude where living itself is no less a battle, to prosecute offensive operations as a corollary to strategic defence. These challenges are sought to be tackled over the next seven odd years, to which end elaborate surface and air transportation, communications and base infrastructure are to be created along the border belt. Formations and units are to be located close to air bases and surface communication hubs, expansion of the Air Force transportation, railways and border roads being a step complementary. Even then, it would have to be a formation that is structured to operate at the far ends of tenuous lines of communications, build up and deploy astride rudimentary axes after acclimatising the troops over one to two weeks, and prosecute offensive operations in confrontation with a great military power.

The charter is mind boggling. It is doable of course, but there are complexities and concerns to be dissected in all seriousness and addressed with strategic sagacity. Therefore, a discussion on the core considerations would be in order.

Role and Objectives

The likely role of 17 Corps, within the overall ambit of the nation's defensive strategy, may be envisaged in light of the preceding discussion. Foremost, it would be to launch in *counter-offensive* – autonomous or conjoined with other formations – to unhinge any military aggression. Next, it would be to *balance out territorial loss* in one sector by sallying out in sector(s) of choice, to secure, in part or whole, the Indian version of the boundary alignment. Other roles could be to deploy to limit and *destroy the attacking forces*, or to *invest the adversary's ingress* and to evict it if necessary. In other words, besides its classical counter-offensive role in war, even in 'no-war' scenarios when the option of forcible eviction of the intrusion may not be exercised in order to avoid escalation, it would be possible to, firstly, contain the intrusion, and secondly, to counter it by advancing the LAC in some other location – a sort of tit-for-tat.

Proceeding further, the first question to arise in the context of any worthwhile 'strike' relates to the possible *objectives* of significance. Obviously, the objectives would be such as to unhinge PRC's military aggression, and that purpose would be indicative of the optimum *depth* of operations. Starting from the Indo-Tibet-Myanmar Tri-junction and ending at the Aksai Chin, the Western periphery of Gongrigabu Qu (River)-Chayu, the Southern periphery of Yarlung Zangbu (Brahmaputra River)-Langquen Zangbu (Sutluj River) and the Eastern periphery of Lingzi Tang-Kailash Range – inclusive of the Western Tibet Highway or its subsidiaries – could be that reckonable depth.

Within the aforementioned belt, one class of objectives could be *territorial* in nature. Considering the historical legacy, these territorial objectives may be broadly identified as one, in the North-East, the areas West of Chaya (Rima) and South of Nyngchi, Tsona Dzong, the Chumbi Valley, Khamba Dzong and the Brahmaputra River; two, the Mansarovar (Mapam Yumco)-Sutluj River Belt in the Central Sector; and three, in the Western Sector, the Pangong-Indus (Senge Zangbu) Valleys and the Depsang-Soda Plains. Herein, any of the tactically feasible axes of operations, single or multiple, leading to territories across the LAC or up to and beyond the Indo-Tibet Border may be activated. Indeed, there are many possible areas which may be logistically upgraded within a decade or two to support offensive operations of battle formations ranging in composition from brigade group size to two divisions plus; some of these axes may even be upgraded in just a few years' time. Notably, while the desolate terrain may not offer classical military objectives, the very act of pulling off territorial riposte would be sufficient to lever India's cause. Besides, targeting logistic hubs at Nyngchi, Gyangze, Ngari, Rudog and some more, denial of bridges over Yarlung Zangbu and Langquen Zangbu, and breach of the Western Highway or its subsidiaries would definitely tell upon the People's Liberation Army's (PLA) aggression.

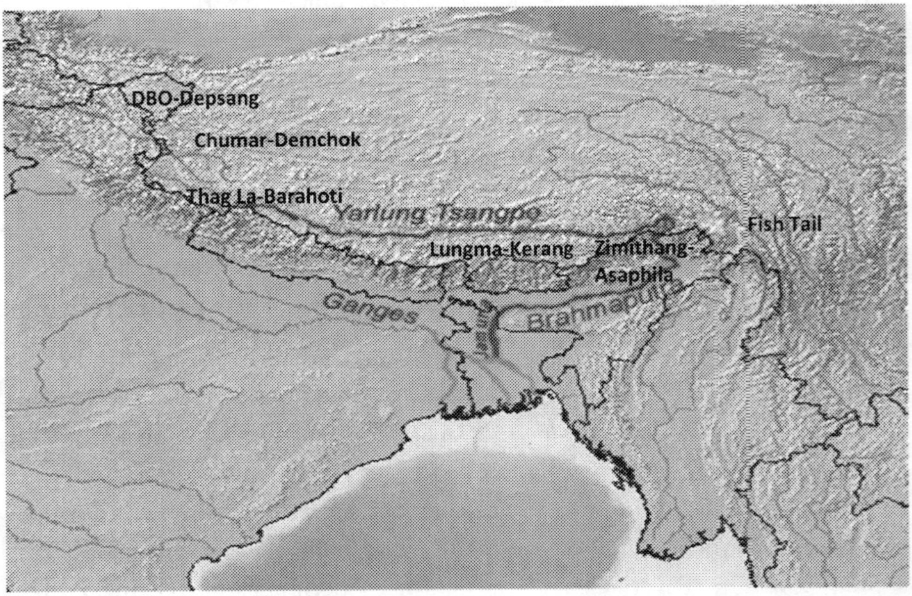

The other class of objectives could aim at *force-destruction*, in which the attacker would be contained in hostile terrain, weakened and then destroyed. Notably, the modest scale of India's retaliatory strike in comparison to China's doctrine of massive offensive may not be an issue – just penalising and holding up a giant would dampen his blustery, and therefore could be seen as a politico-military redemption.

Organisational Structure

By far the biggest challenge in raising the 17 Corps would be to structure a potent and cost-efficient force and equipping it for the kind of terrain – and as a corollary the kind of warfare – it would be called upon to master. In that context, recourse to replication of orthodox tactics, structures and equipment profile would offer strong attractions. However, having seen that the force, terrain and mission, all three are unparalleled, adoption of templates would be a grave mistake. For the right organisation to be devised therefore, it would be appropriate to evaluate the functions of the terrain and conceptualise appropriate battle tactics to harness its nuances.

From India's view point, the terrain is like a funnel, its narrow stem widening into an expanse as the watershed is approached and the Tibetan Plateau unfolds. Resultantly, for nearly three-fourth of the 300-450 kilometres to the watershed, deployment of forces would have to be along relatively narrow, steep, winding and rugged valleys, mostly over single axes, with availability of shunts and laterals few and far between. Obviously, forces would have to move and deploy in echelons over restricted axes till they cross over to the plateau-land whence they would have the option of either diverging or converging combat power to reduce selected objective(s). Indeed, in that remote and desolate expanse of cold high-altitude desert, the quantum of force-application would be decided by the logistic capability to field and sustain battle formations. As a corollary, the Corps may need to divide itself to operate astride multiple axes, even across multiple sectors – North-East, Central and West – in varying combinations of divisions and independent brigades to sally out into the plateau-land.

The *severe dictates of the terrain attributes may be turned into tactical advantages provided organisation, tactics, equipment and logistics are customised in exclusivity.* For example, induction, establishment of logistic bases and movements through the rugged mountains on Indian side of the watershed may well be rendered much safer from air and missile attacks as compared to the enemy on the plateau-land who would be open to detection and interdiction from air-ground operations. Even from the consideration of time and space, the factors would not be adverse towards India when the traversing distances, communications and altitudes are weighed in comparison. Lastly, when well reconnoitred and adapted to, the plateau-land would offer to the Indian forces good scope for 'behind the line' operations.

Factoring analogies from past campaigns as well as concurrent tactical concepts, *the tactics would hinge upon manoeuvre of multiple combat elements to shape the battle-matrix and followed up with sharp engagements, rather than a replay of mass assaults of the kind propagated before the advent of Revolution in Military Affairs*. The objectives could either be communication and logistic hubs, or opponent forces. Indeed, the campaign would follow the eternal practice of what is currently described as 'Hybrid Warfare', in which 4th Generation battles would shoot-off from field formations engaged in deliberate offensive campaigns. Of course, dominance in air power would play a singular role in reconnaissance, information war, destruction, interdiction, support to ground operations, troop mobility and logistic sustenance of the war effort.

In the overall context therefore, *organisation and equipment for the 17 Corps have to be exclusive*. For example, the Corps may be composed of integral scout, reconnaissance and special service units and brigade groups integrated into flexible mix of light and heavy combat arms. It may also have to be structured for transportable, manoeuvrable and higher volume of fire-power and enhanced grouping of support arm elements. Similarly, provision of in-built force-multiplication elements of information warfare – like command and control warfare, reconnaissance, intelligence preparation and deception – and geo-spatial survey teams would be mandatory for the Corps to fulfil its role. Above all, the Corps operations must be tuned to true articulation of air power for manoeuvre, air assault and operational logistics.

Equipment

Needless to emphasise, it would be wise to equip 17 Corps with transportable and manoeuvrable war-like equipment, the loss of mass being compensated by higher scales of holdings and brisk operational momentum. The problem is that the global arms industry has not found it profitable to invest in development of weapons and equipment that answer to the characteristics of high-altitude mountain warfare, and therefore most such equipment do not form part of importable inventory. Most of its theatres of war being mountainous, India's defence planners could have turned this dearth into self-advantageous force-superiority through indigenous research and development. Regrettably, they failed to adapt to that rather obvious need, confined as they were with dated notions about ponderous characteristics of mountain warfare. *Equipping the 17 Corps in a manner operationally desired would therefore require specific design modifications, field trials and mix of import and customised production under an overarch of economical viability*. Given India's system of functioning, the officially promulgated time-line of seven to eight years to acquire the right range of weapons and equipment may therefore turn out to be rather tight.

But more than that, optimal equipping of the 17 Corps would be an exercise advantageous only if the Indian military fraternity sets out to assimilate what weapons and equipment that may be readily acquired, and subsume the qualitative shortcomings into specifically devised battle-tactics and operational procedures. In other words, to begin with, *it would be wise to foster tactical ingenuity to customise orthodox tactical concepts, and accept redundancies in scales to overcome lesser performance from what military hardware is available at hand.* Great armies are known to do so; Indian Army has done so before.

Logistic Springboard

The *quantum of force that can be committed to offensive operations through a given sector would be dictated by the extent of sectoral logistic capacity, existence of operational axes therein, and the robustness of these.* Besides, final outcome of trans-Himalaya operations would be decided by logistic survivability of that force in a terrain so unliveable. By implication, therefore, based on the intended counter-offensive tasks of the 17 Corps, logistic infrastructure would have to be developed, both in terms of sectors and axes of possible operations as well as the quantum of likely force-application along those sectors and axes. This capability would have to be built up in the form of static installations – such as roads, air-heads, administrative bases, dumps, services, survivable-habitat, etc. – as well as expendables like ammunition, rations and fuel. Besides, once across the watershed, the burden of logistic sustenance would require to be extended, insulation, portability and mobility being the key determinants in this case. Further, logistic capacity-building would have to be maximised to conform to foreseeable operational contingencies. No doubt, planning and build-up of logistic infrastructure calls for intelligent forethought and deliberate time-and-cost intensive undertaking at the national level.

Even if well within India's engineering capabilities, infrastructure development projects would necessitate deployment of additional construction agencies and enormous funding; these two factors would determine whether the projects would take a decade or double that to be in place. As for the turnover or replacement of expendables, the challenge would be even more complex. Life-cycle stocking and turnover of ammunition in itself would be a tedious and costly commitment. Lastly, in environs so excruciatingly hostile, air-power would have to play a lead role in forward provisioning to the forces for them to survive and fight. The period of seven or eight years for the Corps to be fully operational must have been decided based on such considerations. But as to the implementation, there must be alacrity – India's traditional elephantine pace would not deliver.

In adopting the above-mentioned measures, logistic services to be integrated at unit, formation and theatre levels would have to be freed from the standard templates and reconstructed according to the unique conditions of Himalayan warfare, grouping of detachments, manpower, load handling equipment, mobility and communications being the thrust areas. The *orthodox advocates of the 'teeth-versus-tail' issue may have to reconcile to larger complements of logistic services if they set their hearts to winning a war in the High-Himalayas.*

Notably, not just the raising of a Mountain Strike Corps, it would be the *build-up of commensurate military infrastructure that would signal to the adversary, the scope and options of India's military deterrence.* To forestall military adventurism from PRC therefore, Indian defence planners would be wise to break out of the festering stagnation that grips infrastructural development in border areas.

A Larger Strategic Dividend

If there is one matter to which the Indian psyche would never reconcile, the military debacle and political drubbing India got in 1962 from Mao's China would be that one. No wonder therefore that even when conscious of the PLA's overwhelming combat power, making China pay heavily for any future aggression remains a matter of faith for all Indians, indeed the Indian Armed Forces. So far, this aspiration had been stifled by the void of autonomous offensive capability that, to reiterate, must form part of any worthwhile defensive strategy. *Raising of a Mountain Strike Corps will therefore round off the Indian strategy for the defence of its territories.* No doubt, the cabal of India baiters cannot be enthused by the advent of the 17 Corps.

Raising of the 17 Corps is one of the landmark events of India's military strategy. However, to make the best of this unique military formation, the Indian defence fraternity must prepare to prosecute wars that are exclusively 'Indian' in nature – exclusive in terms of tactical concepts, force-composition, and balance in deployment.

Finally, as military history tells us, when marshalled with tactical innovation, a strategic force of the nature of the 17 Corps will invariably offer a range of strategic options which may go beyond its role initially mandated. *Articulated with free flow of strategic acumen, this military asset therefore may offer exponential peace dividends.*

*

July, 2015

24

The Indian Navy: Trendsetter in Indigenisation

Vice Admiral Pradeep Chauhan, AVSM & Bar, VSM

Preceding Prime Minister *Modi's* contemporary clarion call of *'Make-in-India'* by half a century, the indigenisation drive first launched by the Indian Navy in the 1960s has, over time, matured into a success story worthy of both adulation and emulation. Often ploughing a lonely furrow as it seemingly marched to the beat of a different drummer, the Navy alone amongst our three defence Services has been a true trendsetter of comprehensive indigenisation. The results are impressive across a range of capabilities – from a staggering 119 combat-platforms themselves to their propulsion-cum-generation systems and the state-of-the-art weapon-sensor suites that have made our ships, submarines and aircraft both feared and revered.

This remarkable feat is really the revival of a far older tradition, for India was well-known for its ship-building skills some two-centuries ago. In 1817, Mumbai Docks (today the Naval Dockyard) built the *Trincomalee* – the oldest British warship afloat, which is currently berthed in Hartlepool, UK – and HMS Minden – on which Francis Scott Key composed America's national anthem, "The Star Spangled Banner" – as also HMS Cornwallis, on which China signed the Treaty of Nanking in 1942, ceding Hong Kong to the British!

The Directorate of Naval Design (DND) has produced as many as 19 different warship-designs – from modest patrol vessels in the 1960s to the formidable destroyers of Projects 15-A and 15-B (the *Kolkata* Class and the *Visakhapatnam* Class, respectively), right up to our first indigenous aircraft carrier, the *Vikrant,* which is currently under construction in Cochin Shipyard. It is a telling fact that even today, neither the Army nor the Air Force has an equivalent design-agency of its own. 2014, which was the DND's golden jubilee year, saw new 'Commissioning Pendants' being flown aboard three different 'Types' and 'Classes' of the Indian Navy – the *Kolkata* (the first of a new class of guided-missile destroyers), the *Kamorta* (the first of a new class of anti-submarine corvettes), and, the *Sumitra* (the fourth of a new class of Naval Offshore Patrol Vessels). The maturity of indigenised design continues to be strikingly visible, as witness this April's launch of the stealth-enhanced guided-missile destroyer, the *Visakhapatnam* – the first of its Class.

As things currently stand, Indian shipyards have as many as 41 indigenously designed warships in various stages of construction. These stand testimony to the Indian Navy's consistent view that indigenisation is a fundamental tenet of its planning and growth. Apart from supporting and encouraging the resurgence of Indian industry, indigenisation also cut costs or dependence levels, both of which translate to significant vulnerability since one has to depend upon imports throughout the life-cycle of the platform and its equipment.

The Navy certainly seems to be acutely aware of the urgent need to incorporate private shipyards into warship-construction and to actively support and, wherever possible, contribute to the modernisation of existing shipyards by adopting modular construction-practices and the preparation of very large pre-fabricated sections. Even with all this, there is a necessity for the country to proactively encourage the creation of 'green-field' shipyards, with latest technologies and ship-building techniques/practices.

Between 2005 and 2009, the Navy was in the throes of a process of particularly focused transformation. In 2006, acutely conscious of the need to stay abreast the gallop of technology and the need to emulate the DND success through matching indigenous capability in terms of ship-borne and shore-based equipment, the Indian Navy set-up the 'Directorate of Indigenisation' (DOI), in New Delhi, as the nodal directorate for navy-wide indigenisation activities. In so doing, it sent out the unambiguous message that it intends to continue to take advantage of the technological revolution in both, software and production, increasingly establishing itself as a 'Builder's Navy', with attendant spin-offs that would build capacity and enhance capability amongst India's regional friends and partners.

These indigenisation efforts are guided by an ongoing '15-year Indigenisation Plan', covering the period up to 2022, which has been shared with the Confederation of Indian Industry (CII) so as to ensure wide publicity among industry leaders and greater participation from industry. The Navy has also prepared a 'Science and Technology Roadmap-2025', aimed at the development of indigenous technology in respect of naval applications. Indian industry is increasingly entering into a number of new and exciting partnerships with global players on the one hand and the Indian Navy, on the other. Top-end examples would include major systems required for aircraft carrier operations, such as Electro-Magnetic Launch Systems, arrestor-wires and aircraft-lifts.

Contrary to the pervasive pessimism that all too often seems to be the staple diet of some segments of the media, the truth is that the Navy's relentless drive for indigenisation has already yielded impressive and encouraging results in a number of critical war-fighting areas. A number of illustrative examples exist. The DRDO has frequently received adverse media-attention, but it has many success stories as well – at least insofar as the Navy is concerned – and it would be churlish not to acknowledge this. The range of Electronic Warfare Suites such as the revamped 'AJANTA', as also the 'ELLORA', 'KITE', 'HOMI' and 'PORPOISE', all of which are fitted on the Navy's latest frontline surface, airborne and subsurface combatants, and which are designed to detect the presence of enemy combatants without disclosing one's position or identity, are certainly success stories of which we ought to be proud – and these have all been designed by the Defence Electronics Research Laboratory (DLRL), Hyderabad, and are manufactured by Bharat Electronics Limited (BEL).

The same is true of the Navy's advanced underwater-sensors such as the APSOH, HUMSA NG and USHUS family of sonars. These have been developed by the Naval Physical and Oceanographic Laboratory (NPOL), Kochi. Likewise, an indigenous state-of-the-art electro-optical Fire Control System (FCS) the 'EON 51 Mk II', designed by IRDE, Dehradun, and productionised by BEL, is now a standard fit. Pitching-in directly with its own formidable developmental expertise, the Navy's WESEE (Weapons and Electronics Systems Establishment), along with the Centre for Development of Telematics, has rendered yeoman service to the overall indigenisation effort through its series of world-class 'Combat Management Systems' (CMS) and data-link systems (LINK-II Mod 3), now being manufactured by Bharat Electronics Limited (BEL). These form the heart of the entire C4I2SR (command, control, communications, information, intelligence, surveillance & reconnaissance) set-up on board most classes of the Navy's frontline warships.

Likewise, the indigenously designed and developed 'REVATHI' three-dimensional 'Central Acquisition Radar' (CAR), which is installed aboard the *Kamorta* Class Anti-Submarine Warfare (ASW) is not only a success story, but is also a good example of the growing 'Public-Private Partnership' (PPP) in defence production. The design and production of this radar has been undertaken through a collaborative effort between the Navy, the DRDO and M/s L&T, Mumbai. Similarly, the Indian Navy has partnered GTRE, Bangalore, in 'marinising' the 'KAVERI' Gas Turbine and will induct at least four units. Deserving of special mention are four indigenously developed system-management suites, namely, the 'Integrated Machinery Control System (IMCS), the 'Integrated Bridge Management System' (IBMS), the 'Integrated Propulsion Management System' (IPMS) and the 'Battle Damage Control System' (BDCS) that now equip the *Shivalik, Kamorta, Kolkata and Visakhapatnam* classes of warships, as also the *Vikrant.* The successful leveraging of Navy-designed IT networks and IT-security platforms stands in sharp contrast to the grave concerns often expressed in respect of the country's remaining critical infrastructure.

Even outside of 'equipment', there is much to cheer about. The Defence Metallurgical Research Laboratory (DMRL), Hyderabad, in collaboration with M/s Steel Authority of India Ltd (SAIL), and with active participation from the Indian Navy, has successfully undertaken the indigenous development and production of warship-grade 'DMR249A' steel plates and bulb structural sections for ship and submarine applications. This represents an enormous step in freeing ourselves from the yoke of pressures and prices associated with the import of steel, as was the norm until very recently. The results are evident in the construction of the Navy's big-ticket platforms such as the Vikrant and the future submarines being constructed under 'Project 75-India'.

In recognition of the criticality of the PPP-model and guided by the recommendations of the 'Dr Vijay Kelkar Committee' that had been set up to look into the issue of private sector participation in the defence industry, the Navy has taken a number of measures to optimise the potential created by the growing capability of Indian Industry coupled with the shift in Government policy to allow for private partnership in the defence sector. Regular buyer-seller meets and vendor-development programmes are being conducted by nodal organisations within the Navy. The procedures involved in registering as defence vendors are being tweaked to make them both simple and transparent, and if the industry is able to adhere to the specifications that are needed and deliver the desired products at competitive prices, there is immense scope for collaboration for mutual benefit.

And yet, although the Indian Navy is an acknowledged pioneer in terms of promoting private participation and private-public partnerships for the induction of equipment, there is much that remains to be done. Where manned and unmanned aircraft are concerned, for instance, the state continues to be grim. While the efforts of Hindustan Aeronautics Limited (HAL) can hardly be downplayed, there is a widening gap between the requirement and capability. It is true that the Navy – like its sister Services – needs to freeze specifications at a reasonable point in time. It is, however, equally true that the gallop of technology and the telescoping of the point of obsolescence cannot be ignored. What is at stake here is not merely the somewhat esoteric, long-term development of capability, but of real lives that an enemy is actively engaged in attempting to snuff out. Armed combat is brutal, real, and terminal in nature. We cannot afford the luxury of a media-debate when precious lives are at stake. This may sound a trifle dramatic, but it is, nevertheless, a fact that needs to be recognised. As a consequence, there is certainly a need to encourage far greater synergy between the uniformed and civilian segments of the Ministry of Defence and continuously refine the Defence Procurement Procedures.

The current aim of the Navy is to achieve 85 percent indigenisation through extensive interaction with the Confederation of Indian Industries (CII) and the Organisation of Small Scale Industries (OSSI) to identify the right sources for our equipment. All this notwithstanding, there is no gainsaying the fact that howsoever impressive the advances that have made, the way ahead is still a long and challenging one. The MSME sector is yet to weigh in with its much vaunted effervescence and this needs to be the Navy's next focus-area. But that's a story for another day.

*

July 2016

25

Strategic Gaps in India's Net Centricity

Lt General (Retd) Davinder Kumar, PVSM, VSM Bar, ADC

The Power of Net Centricity

In the digital battlefield of 21st century, Technology and Information are the new currencies of power. Exploitation of both of these to create efficiencies, economy of effort and facilitate full-spectrum operations (nuclear to asymmetric and strategic to tactical) is the essence of Net Centricity. Synergy through sharing of information in all its stages, namely collection, storage, processing and dissemination, is at the heart of net-centric capability. It also encompasses Information denial, perception management through exploitation of electronic and print media, social networking and warrants involvement of all organs of the nation from the very beginning.

Net Centricity is technology intensive, with Information and Communication Technology (ICT), communication networks and media as the nucleus. The primary aim of net centricity is to bring about informed decision making, synergy, maximum effects and higher speed in execution while ensuring extensive battlefield transparency. Paradoxically, net centricity demands synergy to create synergy. While the principles of war and the need for net centricity have not changed, the parameters have changed drastically. The battlespace has enlarged disproportionately making the physical borders irrelevant and changing the concept of national sovereignty. When combined with the accuracy, range and lethality of present day weapons and munitions, it has given rise to a new concept of Effect Based Operations. Ubiquitous application of ICT has resulted in a Digital Battlefield with tremendous increase in the speed of operations, diffusion of power, associated vulnerabilities and Information Warfare emerging as a new dimension of warfare.

The Indian Government, defence forces, other security forces, intelligence agencies, industry and all security-related organisations need to prepare to operate and fight in this evolving battlefield environment where the 'bits' may cause more damage than the 'bullets' and in all probability would precede the bullets. Central to this preparation would be our national security doctrine supported by enhancement of our Net Centricity through advanced technological, organisational, training and related capabilities in all dimensions of land, air, sea, outer space and cyberspace across full spectrum of warfare. This is an inescapable requirement for binding the nation's comprehensive combat power into a viable and coherent force. It would be economical, enhance our kinetic effectiveness, command and control and provide various options, through situational awareness, for both protecting our own assets and addressing the weaknesses of our adversaries in offensive operations.

Unfortunately, our efforts towards net centricity, particularly during the last decade or so, have been tardy at best. Consequently, while we have islands of excellence in each Service and in the Government, they lack effectiveness and synergy. Our Commanders and policymakers largely continue to be technology shy and prefer to operate in their comfort zone of industrial era warfare of tanks and guns. They still seem to be fighting the last war as is quite evident from the literature available in the open. There is an urgent need for the Government to intervene at the highest level to ensure development of Comprehensive National Power relevant to the emerging contours of warfare across the full spectrum. This is a strategic requirement in the light of threats faced by India as also her projected role in the Asian region.

WHAT INDIA MUST DO

National Security Doctrine and a Vision

To start with, we need to promulgate the National Security Doctrine and the related comprehensive vision document, policy and the road map for capacity building in the contemporary and futuristic battlefield scenarios. These should be formulated together by all the stakeholders, duly approved by the Parliament, backed by necessary finance and an empowered implementing organisation accountable to the Government. Based on this document, we should work out the technologies, organisation, training and human resource requirements. We should take the existing assets in account, and transform and integrate those with the new system.

Technology

Availability of requisite technology by way of hardware, software, and semi-conductor chips fabrication facilities, electronic manufacturing eco-system, research and development (R&D) infrastructure, system integration capabilities, and an enabling policy framework for involvement of the private sector and academia and skilled human resource are some of the challenges India faces to harness technology and implement relevant net-centric solutions. While, in some cases, policies have been promulgated but their implementation is completely lacking. We hope that these would receive due attention from the present Government. We need an urgent and innovative drive to build these capabilities and achieve "Technological Sovereignty" preferably by 2020 but by 2025, the latest. Time is certainly at a premium.

Organisation

An extremely significant aspect of 21st century warfare is the fact that when threatened, it is not only the Armed Forces but the entire nation, the Government and all its organs, the media and the people, who will have to respond in an integrated and unified manner. Herein, therefore, lies the absolute importance of organisation transformation for net centricity.

The single point politico-military dialogue, which is required to establish a coherent national strategy and quick decision making is lacking in the present security setup. We needed the Chief of Defence Staff yesterday! The inescapable doctrinal implication of this post is the integration of conventional (including cyber, outer space and special forces) and nuclear doctrines. This is also required to negate the glaring anomaly in our security decision making structure by way of the absence of a military high command in decisions of war and peace. Present security environment necessitates joint threat assessment, planning and execution within the Armed Forces and with the Ministries. There is an urgent and definite requirement of greater integration of the three Service Headquarters with the Ministry of Defence. Further, an institutionalised policy framework is required for Service headquarters and Integrated Defence Staff to interact with other Ministries and Government institutions. A cohesive, practical and responsive civil-military framework is absolutely essential for comprehensive capacity building for 21st century warfare, economy of effort and as a foundation for advanced net centricity in our national security set up.

In the current security scenario, nuclear, space, cyber security and special forces capabilities are at the heart of a nation's comprehensive combat power.

Decisions regarding formulation of cyber, outer space and special forces organisations need to be expedited as indeed the formulation of Integrated/Joint Theatre Commands. At least two of these, one for the plains sector and the other for the mountains must be cleared immediately. It may be noted that operationalisation of these commands is likely to take anything between five to seven years. The recent statement of the Raksha Mantri in this regard is quite encouraging.

Concurrent exercise to streamline the existing organisations and provide resources for raising of new units/formations is badly overdue. The announcement of Lt Gen DB Shekatkar Committee is welcome. Similar studies, by eminent people, have been carried out before but their recommendations were either not carried forward due to vested interests or implemented partially creating confusion and uncertainty. The political leadership has to demonstrate the will and the ability to take hard decisions with risk management strategies in place, for an effective and quick organisation transformation. India needs highly synergised, integrated, mobile, lean and mean, joint organisations, relevant to 21st century warfare, supported by efficient logistics and infrastructure. Organisation transformation is likely to take 3 to 5 years to become effective and operational from the day it is started.

Communication Networks

Communication Networks are at the heart of net centricity. These form the nervous system for the management of a nation's comprehensive power and would be the primary targets of the adversary, most likely in the very start of hostilities. Hence, their survival and availability are of utmost importance. There is an urgent need to upgrade and integrate existing networks of the three Services with the national networks, and place them under a single authority. Indian standards for communication and data networks must be propagated without any further delay.

In view of the threat of cyber warfare, India must develop indigenous capabilities in the design and manufacture of network products based on indigenous chips and carry out own system integration. This is a strategic deficiency which very seriously impacts on the survivability and availability of our Defence and National Networks and hence the net centricity of India. In the interim, other requisite measures must be taken to protect our networks. This will require innovation as also the ability of our forces to operate without/restricted communications for limited periods.

For true and secure net centricity, operationalisation of National Policy on Electronics, 2012, and establishment of viable Defence Industrial Base are strategic imperatives and pre-requisites.

Command, Control, Computers, Communications, Intelligence, Surveillance and Target Acquisition (C4ISTAR)

C4ISTAR, in essence, is about co-evolution of technology, organisation (i.e., architecture and processes) and people, and about control and disruption of information and quick decision making. It is the vehicle to promote expeditious 'synergy of effects' through effective integration of sensors, decision makers and shooters.

Indian Armed Forces, individually, have done well and have developed rudimentary capabilities, particularly at the operational and tactical levels. We need Joint C4ISTAR capabilities duly supported by technology, highly skilled human resource, innovation and training. Joint C4ISTAR enables ability to mass effects without massing forces, protects against asymmetric threats, and provides joint force flexibility, analysis, interpretation, and efficiency. It calls for interoperability of systems and subsystems, standards and protocols for interconnection, integration and information management, and policies, procedures and formats for Information assurance, data storage, data retrieval and data security and so on.

In a digital battlefield, while C4ISTAR is an inescapable requirement, we must have systems, drills and capabilities to interfere and negate the adversary's C4ISTAR assets through electronics, optical, cyber and physical means. Concurrently, we must protect our assets and ensure that they operate successfully in the hostile environment.

Electronic Combat

Preparation for Electronic Combat (EC) in association with or independent of kinetic warfare is at the heart of executing operations in the present day digital battlefield. EC is an ideal tool for carrying out asymmetric operations. Unfortunately, this aspect has not got the attention it deserves. India needs to develop her potential for EC and that would demand creation of indigenous capabilities in each of the components of EC. EC would require capacity building in Electro-Magnetic (EM) Space Management, creation and negating the Electro-magnetic Environment Effects (E3), Electronic Warfare (EW) to include generation of and protection from Electro-Magnetic Pulse (EMP) and Electronic Deception.

EM Space

The EM Space is extremely complex, crowded, contested and needs to be managed and regulated dynamically in real time. The situation is much more challenging in a digitised battlespace environment where practically every system starting from a diesel generator to a missile system requires spectrum to operate or else contributes 'Noise' which restricts the availability of the EM space. Add to this the high power of various radars, communication systems and electronic warfare systems and the fact that the same resource is being used by the adversary and the civilian networks. Security and Availability of EM Space would be critical factors in the execution of war in the digital battlefield. Denial of EM Space as also ensuring its availability to own forces is the essence of 'Spectrum Warfare' which in near future would include cyber warfare along with EW.

The development of high-energy beam weapons, LASER weapons and designators, and other aviation resources, missiles and Ballistic Missile Defence (BMD) systems, and satellite constellations have further added to the challenge of management and regulation of EM space. We would need a system and an organisation that would ensure the availability of the navigation and position locating systems, bandwidth, communication ranges and connectivity in an intense and hostile EM space environment, including EMP, in real time. This would require electronic intelligence, modeling and simulation of the battlespace EM environment and highly skilled man power drawn from the nation and abroad. It would be a national effort with dedicated organisation within the defence and security forces.

Electro-magnetic Environment Effects or E3

The increasing EM density of users and high power in weapon radar systems and communications have an impact on electronic control and devices that may malfunction, and cause desensitisation and random undesired effects called the E3.

Electronic Warfare (EW)

Electronic Warfare (EW) is one of the sword arms of Information Warfare (IW). This includes optical warfare and E-Bombs for generation of non-nuclear EMP. As a corollary, we need to develop operation rooms, communication centres and command posts suitably protected from effects of EMP in particular and EW in general. India needs multi-platform and multi-frequency, light weight, high power and adaptable EW systems suitably integrated across the three Services for maximum effects. This requires a common EW policy, joint training, appropriate equipment and a central management organisation preferably under the Integrated Defence Staff. Indigenous development of EW systems is a strategic requirement. While India has done well in this field, she needs to develop systems for platforms like satellites, Unmanned Aerial Vehicles (UAV), drones and pods. There is an urgent need for coordination of R&D and all procurements to ensure economy and quick capacity building.

Electronic Deception

The term 'electronic deception' means the deliberate radiation, re-radiation, alteration, suppression, absorption, denial, enhancement, or reflection of electromagnetic energy in a manner intended to convey misleading information and to deny valid information to an enemy or his electronics-dependent weapons. In the current scenario, this would include Cyber Deception. Among the types of electronic deception are:

- Manipulative electronic deception – actions to eliminate revealing or convey misleading, tell-tale indicators that may be used by hostile forces;
- Simulative electronic deception – actions to represent friendly notional or actual capabilities to mislead hostile forces;
- Imitative electronic deception – introduction of electro– magnetic energy into enemy systems that imitates enemy emissions;
- Electronic attack deception.

There are many more types but the aim here is to highlight this strategic gap and to stress the absolute necessity of capacity building in this critical area through a dedicated organisation, technology, platforms, training and highly skilled human resource. For true and secure net-centricity, operationalisation of National Policy on Electronics, 2012, and establishment of viable Defence Industrial Base are strategic imperatives and pre-requisites.

Survivability

With the battlefield transparency as high as 90 per cent, the warfare will have to be conducted in an entirely different manner. Survivability of own assets would be critical requirement and must be factored separately in our war-fighting doctrine. While camouflage and concealment will always be important, greater emphasis will be on deception, dispersal, mobility and organisation transformation. Decision making will have to be very quick in an environment of greater ambiguity, uncertainty and information overload.

Deception would include electronic, optical, physical and cyber deception. Perception management plans by skilled exploitation of intelligence, communication assets, and social, electronic and print media must be integrated and executed as part of the overall deception to ensure greater survivability. Deception plan for each phase must be integrated with the operational plan, rehearsed and have viable alternatives to cater for contingencies. There is a definite requirement of dedicated organisation for carrying out deception. Innovative ideas like 'crowd sourcing' must be tried out to generate resources and increased involvement at the national level. Human resource will have to be highly skilled, and trained to ensure flawless execution. The impression one gets is that probably the criticality of this area in the conduct of 21st century warfare is not understood and if otherwise, it is not receiving the importance that it deserves.

We must design and produce requisite dummies, platforms and associated equipment and content for deception indigenously. One, however, does not see much action in this critical area.

Information Warfare

IW is both an asset and a challenge to net centricity as it deals with protection, interference and destruction of information and the information assets/systems including the human resource.

Information Assurance concerns protecting own information in all its stages of capture, storage, processing and dissemination. The challenge is the design, production and fielding of cryptographic systems and their integration within the Services and other organs of decision making in the country. The networks and other communication assets will have to be secured through different levels of secrecy and protected from cyber-attacks and cyber espionage. Concurrently, counter-intelligence and crypto-analysis capabilities will have to be enhanced substantially.

Information Dominance demands availability of potent electronic and optical warfare and intelligence systems in all dimensions of a digital battlefield. Development of capabilities to launch cyber-attacks including use of cyber weapons for creating physical disruptions will have to be a part of our national security doctrine and the implementation of net centricity.

Perception management will start well before the commencement of the conflict and last much after its termination. Development of capability to launch 'Social Engineering' Attacks in concert with deception and kinetic energy operations must be part of our capacity build-up for net-centricity.

Information Management

Net centricity is all about information sharing to create synergies. Yet, very surprisingly, one has not come across any information management strategy enunciated by any headquarters. The commanders and staff want right information at the right place and at the right time. We also say that they should not be subjected to information overload. So who is responsible for these? One would like to believe that creation of an Integrated Information Management Eco-System within the Defence Forces should be the responsibility of the Headquarters Integrated Defence Staff. Within the Army, this would be an appropriate responsibility of the Directorate General of Information Systems.

Information management is an umbrella term that encompasses all the systems and processes within an organisation for the creation and use of information. Effective information management is not easy. There are many systems to integrate, a huge range of operational needs to meet, and complex organisational and cultural issues to address. Information Management is a subject by itself. It is complex but not 'technical'. The aim in this article is to flag the issue and hope that this critical area gets due attention. It is a glaring strategic gap, a massive task and we need to start right away.

Digital Imagery

Inherent to a digital battlefield is an efficient Geographical Information System (GIS), high-resolution digital imagery from multiple sources and the ability to manipulate, model and combine the images. This mandates the availability of digital maps, overlays, sophisticated hardware and software and very well trained human resource in the forms of image analysts and interpreters. With rapid advancement in the sensor's capabilities and the availability of different sensors, the capability of fusing images from visible light to radar images to images transmitted by multi-spectral satellites is an operational imperative. Acquisition of this capability is a challenge as indeed is the development and manufacturing of sensors indigenously. This would form an important component of information management along with digital asset management.

Data Management

The sensors at the tactical, operational and strategic levels, as indeed other intelligence sources, create a very large amount of data running into tens of terabytes. This data has to be stored, processed, analysed and transmitted in a fully secure manner to all concerned ensuring its integrity and timeliness. The real challenge is synthesising and analysing the data collected, convert the same to usable information, and to quickly disseminate the results, in the desired format, to all those who need it in an extremely hostile electronic and physical environment. It requires modern data storage and retrieval systems, highly qualified human resource and very robust and resilient data networks supporting bandwidth on demand. Related challenges are the standardisation of formats amongst the Services, digitisation of the existing information and its integration and indigenous development/absorption of technologies like the Big Data and Analytics.

Indigenous Position Locating System

Indian Regional Navigation System (IRNS) is likely to be available by mid-2016. This would meet the strategic requirements of the pointing, navigation and target detection of indirect fire weapon systems, radars, intelligence systems, communications, combat aviation, special operations, maneuver, own and enemy force tracking and forward observers. The IRNS will have to be integrated with our digital maps, weapons and systems and be able to function in an extremely hostile physical and electronic environment. Also, we would need ruggedised GPS hand-held terminals.

Internet Protocol (IP) Addresses

In a digital battlefield, all resources at land, sea, air and space are integrated through complex communication and data networks. These networks are likely to be working on IP. This would necessitate that every soldier, weapon and support system has an IP address. This is a huge challenge both from the allocation and communication security points of view and a great vulnerability to be managed. We need to have a dedicated organisation at the National level for this as also to decide on the standards to be incorporated. Purely from security and survivability points of view, it may be desirable to have an alternate to IP addresses or perhaps have a dedicated internet.

Training

This is an area in which we are lagging seriously and have not made the requisite investment. Our training setup requires major re-orientation. It is surprising that in spite of full-fledged Training Commands, we do not have training institutions and infrastructure for IW, outer space operations, Electronic Combat, asymmetric warfare, special forces operations and so on. There is a great deficiency of language experts. There is an urgent need to have joint training establishments in these areas and hasten the establishment of the Indian Defence University.

Net-centricity capability demands highly qualified and skilled human resource. Their induction, training, periodic upgradation and retention would be major challenges as is the creation and availability of the related training infrastructure. More important is the training and orientation of the Commanders and Leaders to absorb and exploit this capability and integrate the same in our war-fighting concepts.

Conclusion

India has serious strategic gaps in her orientation and capacity building for the 21st century warfare. This is of grave concern particularly with reference to her Eastern neighbour which has undergone almost four decades of modernisation and major organisational transformation backed by a strong defence industrial base and a state-of-the-art training infrastructure. There is an immediate need to adopt a 'systems approach' and leapfrog the capability building through exploitation of dual technologies, national information infrastructure and involvement of private sector, Indian diaspora and Academia. This requires organisational, cultural and attitudinal transformation to bring in synergy, mutual trust and transparency. While one can see a few green shoots in the policies and decisions of the present Government, it will have to display greater political will and urgency in capacity building through incorporation of advanced net centricity in our Armed Forces.

*

November, 2017

26

Changing Contours of Air Threat and Its Implications in our Scenario

Lieutenant General (Dr) V K Saxena, PVSM, AVSM, VSM

"*Air power may either end war or end civilisation.*"[1]

– **Winston Churchill, House of Commons, 1933**

Air Defence

Since the *raison d'etre* for the existence of air defence, be it on land, sea or in the air, is to counter the air threat from the adversary, its assessment in terms of quality and quantum must, therefore, become the source of all deliberations concerning the air defence.

The Cause-Effect Relationship

The term 'air threat' essentially implies the cumulative potential danger which the adversary holds as his capability to cause damage and destruction to our vulnerabilities through the use of aerial threat vehicles and munitions in furtherance of, or in support of his war effort on land and sea. This danger is basically assessed in two dimensions. First is the qualitative dimension which includes the lethality, severity and technological advancement of the adversary's air threat vehicles, whereas the second is the quantitative dimension that relates to the numbers which constitute the air threat punch. Accordingly, the defender aims to put together such resources on land, sea and air that can counter the threat defined as above. Thus, the air threat on one side and the air defence means on the other are tied to each other in an eternal cause-effect relationship.

Two Verticals of Metamorphosis

The multi-dimensional growth of the air threat over time has mainly taken place along two major verticals. The first of these is the multiplicity of air threat vehicles. In that, the erstwhile duo of aircrafts and helicopters as main threat vehicles are today joined by a multidimensional strike punch consisting of attack helicopters (AHs), unmanned aerial systems/vehicles (UAS/UAVs), Tactical Ballistic Missiles, Cruise Missiles, Precision Guided Munitions (PGMs), Anti-Radiation Missiles (ARMs) and the now emerging soft-kill offensive weapons. The other vertical is the spatial growth of the threat in all its three dimensions of range, reach (implying altitude) and hours of applicability. Starting from early 1970s, when the air threat was prosecuted mainly in the visual domain of the defenders using mostly short range guns and a small arsenal of unguided rockets and missiles, today the capability is to strike deep with precision and accuracy from long ranges standing off hundreds of miles away from the defenders visual domain, and also to strike with multiple vehicles any time of the day or night, remain nearly invisible to defenders' radars, employ the unmanned with its multiple combat virtues and hit both with hard and soft kill munitions.

Manifestation of Metamorphosis over Threat Vehicles

The revamping-transformation of the air threat over time as stated above is spread over the multiple threat vehicles, most prominently on today's aircrafts. These 4th and 5th generation war machines are truly multi-role, structurally lighter, detection resistant, carry an array of on board sensors with a packaged electronic warfare (EW) suit for survivability and sustainability, and are armed to the teeth with smart and intelligent munitions including the PGMs. The AHs have become all weather with avionics providing the technological muscle for nap-of-the-earth operations. The unmanned revolution has taken over with its unmatched capability of all-weather, all-terrain operations with incredible endurance and no crew fatigue. Multiplicative affects are being achieved by manned and unmanned teaming (MUMT) and the missiles, both in the surface-to-surface (SSM) and Air-to-Surface (ASM) modes, are scaling new dimensions in range, reach and kill probabilities. The soft kill weapons are emerging in three domains, namely, laser, charged particle beams (CPBs) and high power microwaves (HPM).

A brief analysis of air threat from Pakistan and China follows.

Pakistan

The mission of Pakistan Air Force (PAF) is to provide in synergy with the other Services the most efficient, assured and cost-effective aerial defence of Pakistan.[2]

PAF has an inventory of some 450 combat aircrafts organised into 20 front line squadrons. It operates four main types of combat aircrafts, namely, the French Mirage V attack aircrafts (90), Mirage III interceptors (90), the Chinese J-7 fighters (39), JF 17 multirole aircrafts (86) and the US F-16 multirole strike aircrafts (76). It is reported that by 2025, PAF will only operate two multirole aircrafts namely F-16 and JF-17.[3] Over a period of time, the old and obsolete aircrafts (A5, F6, Super F7, FT7P) have been phased out. The F-16s have undergone major upgrades to include NATO compatible Link 16 communications, GPS/INS flying, weapon upgrades to include high-speed ARMs, PGMs, Stand Off weapons and wind corrected munitions dispensers. JF-17 has been operationalised with high-grade weaponry, night flying capability and electronic warfare package. Similarly, Mirages have been put through systems and weapon pack upgrades.

Talking of AHs, PAF has a fleet of AH 1F Huey Cobras (2 squadrons), 32 helicopters and the Chinese K-8 (one squadron 28 numbers). AH IFs have seen upgrades involving Forward Looking Infra-Red (FLIR) night sights and TOW missiles. Besides AHs, PAF operates a small fleet of UAS to include ASN 105, 106 from China, Snipe and Streak from UK and Luna from Germany. In September 2015, Pakistan became the ninth nation in the world to develop and use an armed UAS named *Burraq*. It is armed with *Barq,* an ASM with pin-point precision.

Under the Armed Forces Development Programme (AFFDP 2006-2019), the PAF, besides procuring some modern combat aircraft from the US and China, has also acquired several cutting edge systems. These include PGMs for J-17 aircraft (LS-6 and LS-6P and SD-10A Beyond Visual Range Missiles). Other known PGMs and ASMs with PAF are Shrike Anti-Radiation Missiles (ARM), laser guided bombs (LGBs), Maverick missile and AS 30 ASM useable with Mirages (III&V) and F 16 aircrafts. As regards the cruise missile, Nasr (HATF IX) is a solid fueled tactical ballistic missile developed as short-range (60 km), high-accuracy, low-yield battle field deterrent. On 19 Sep 2017, PAF announced that it will acquire three new Saab 2000 Erieye Airborne Early Warning and Control (AEW&C) aircrafts. This will join the three existing Erieye and four Y-8600 based ZDK-03 AEW&Cs, taking a total of such aircraft to 10 by the end of the decade.[4] The first of these aircrafts is likely to be delivered by December 2017 and the balance two by December 2018. This will provide a tangible enhancement in the airborne surveillance and targeting capability of PAF. It has also been reported that Pakistan is in talks with China to acquire 30-40 J F31 stealth fighters. This will add a totally new qualitative dimension to its strike capability.

In the unmanned category, while the Burrack represents the front edge, UAVs from China (ASN 105A, ASN 206, B2B,) UK (snipe Mk II), Germany (Luna), Italy (Falcon), South Africa (Seeker) besides the indigenous (Bravo, Ababeel, Baaz, AWC Mk I & II, Vision I, Shaper, Vector, Huma 1 and Thunder) constitute the unmanned fleet .

Some implications from the PAF capability, which need be factored into our quality and quantum calculation of air defence resources on a tri-service format, are covered below:

- 20 combat squadrons of PAF comprising of 17 strikes, four multi-role and three air defence aircraft squadrons.
- There has been a continuous qualitative upgradation wherein the dead weight of old and vintage aircrafts are being done away with sharp focusing the fleet to four major front line strike aircraft types (F-16 series, Mirage III/V, J7/JF17).
- There has been a continuous attempt to re-vamp the threat beyond aircraft in terms of AH, Cruise Missiles, ARMs, SSMs, UAS, and PGMs.
- A limited night/all-weather attack capability and a tangible mix of EW capability stands inducted in front line aircrafts.
- Limited induction of AWACs and missile warning capability provide the force multiplier effect.
- The front edge of the strike force now features the stealth threat which needs to be addressed by the defenders.
- The known radii-of-action of the front line combat aircrafts provide the capability to PAF to strike up to India's hinterland making our rear areas strategic assets vulnerable.

China

In keeping with China's high growth trajectory, the People's Liberation Army Air Force (PLAAF) has followed an impressive growth profile. From a near antiquated status in around 1990-91, PLAAF is more operationally able today than any time in its past. As a part a major revamp of its air power, its earlier inventory of some 5000 plus aircrafts that included some 2000 obsolete aircrafts stands right-sized to about 3000 aircrafts (2755-3010),[5] in which the combat edge is held by J-7 (fighter – 388), JH-7 (fighter bomber – 70), H6 (strategic bomber – 120), Su 30 (air superiority fighter – 76), J-8 (Interceptor 96), J-10 (multi role fighter – 237), J-11 (air superiority fighter – 196), Q5 (strike aircraft – 118) aircrafts.

Taking pride in flying the first prototype of its latest Stealth Fighter (J-20) in

January 2011, ostentatiously at a time when the US Secretary of Defence, Mr Robert Gates was in Beijing, the PLAAF is steadily modernising. Predictions on future PLAAF fleet indicate that it will consist of large quantities of Chengdu J-10 and Shenyang J-11 as mainstay platforms and JH-7A as the PLAAF's backbone precision strike fighter. J-20 is likely to enter PLAAF around 2018.[6,7]

The mainframe of future transport fleet is likely to be anchored around Y-9 medium-range transport aircraft duly supported by the IL fleet. The AH inventory is likely to be populated by WZ-10, WZ-9 and Z-11. The AWACS fleet is likely to have refined variants of KJ-2000 and KJ-200 and a reported (50, unconfirmed) numbers of similar platforms are likely to be imported from Russia. Aviation Industry Corporation of China (AVIC) is reported to be working on six developmental combat aircraft programmes. These include the significantly enhanced Chengdu J-10B multirole fighter, Shenyang J-11B5 heavyweight strike fighter, Shenyang J-15 carrier-borne fighter and Chengdu J-20 fifth-generation fighter demonstrator. There is at least one more fifth-generation fighter project yet to be publically reported. Besides this, continuing enhancement of current frontline types such as the JH 7A and H-6 bomber family is in progress.[8]

PLAAF has a very strong muscle in UAVs. Besides the existing inventory of UAVs (Xianglong, WZ-9, Yi Long, CH-3, Anjian, etc.), some additional inputs are as under:

- Chinese UAV experiments have shown impressive levels of innovation by building and flying unmanned vehicles of every conceivable design and genre. These include stealthy UAVs, morphing UAVs, annular wing Vertical Take-off and Landing (VTOL) UAVs, micro-UAVs, unmanned airships, flying wings, modified light aircraft and sailplanes, UFO-style flying discs and even ornithopters (utilising flapping wings). Innovators, both professionals and greenhorns/debutants, have been allowed to run free and explore almost every UAV configuration.
- Two other features are very visible in Chinese UAV development, namely, arming of the UAVs and equipping them with enabling sensor payloads. China has followed a logical process in arming its UAVs by first adapting existing air-to-surface weapons and then developing purpose-built small light weight munitions. In each case, the weapons involved are relatively new. Weapon-vehicle matching has been thoughtful. Some examples are Wing-Loong and CASIC UAV.

Besides the conventional payloads, the PLAAF is emphatically present in the field of smart, intelligent and precision ammunition with surgical strike capability. Way back in 2007, China developed a powered smart bomb (KD-88) having an IR TV guidance system. The estimated range is about 110 km with a capability to hit small targets.[9] The other state-of-the art arsenal in use are the supersonic Russian and Chinese made ARMs (KH 31P, YJ-91) for operational use with SU-30, JH 7A and J-11; LASER-guided and satellite-guided bombs (on board Q-5 aircraft).[10] It is now estimated that almost all the modern aircrafts of PLAAF today are capable of carrying the PGMs.[11]

Chinese Build-up in Western Theatre Command

In February 2016, the erstwhile seven Military Regions (MRs) of China have been reorganised into theatre Commands (Eastern, Southern, Western, Northern and Central). Western Theatre Command (WTC) is opposite India. This Command has been created by merging the erstwhile Chengdu and Lanzhou MRs. In WTC, what is of special significance is the build-up in the Tibet Autonomous Region (TAR) that directly adjoins India. Tibet Military Command (TMC) under WTC is responsible for operations in India.[12] As regards PLAAF, there are three Fighter Divisions (6, 33 and 37), one Bomber Division (36) and one Transport Division (4) in the WTC.

Apart from a nuclear missile base in the Quinghai Province which clearly targets India, China has built five fully operational air bases (Gongar, Pangta, Linchi, Hoping and Gar Gunsa) and an exclusive rail network and over 58,000 km of roads in TAR.[13] In 2015, another full-fledged air base at Kashgar located 600 Km north of Srinagar was operationalised. Open source reported in April 2017 about the construction of Nyingti airport close to borders of India and Myanmar. This civilian airfield is reported to be capable of dual use. Construction of new airfields and upgradation of Advance Landing Ground (ALG) is a continuous process in TAR.[14] The limitations of high-altitude operations with combat aircrafts of yesteryears stand diluted to a large extent with the induction of modern aircrafts of the likes of SU-27 and J-10. To add to this, are the other 'enablers' like air-to-air refuelers, AEW aircrafts and a strong ground-based air defence/Ballistic Missile Defence (BMD) cover centred around S-300/400 and a hierarchy of air defence missiles.

While weapon-by-weapon analysis of the Chinese air threat across the entire spectrum is beyond the scope of this chapter, *what needs to be done by the defenders in countering the said threat* is covered below:

- Capability to carry out effective surveillance of the TAR region with sensor efforts integrated across ground/shore/space mediums resulting in a comprehensive air situation picture.
- A seamless Air defence Battle Management System anchored on auto/ real-time data transmission on satellite media with due redundancy.
- Wherewithal and capability to carry out all weather Counter Air Operations (CAO), interdiction and Counter Surface Force Operations (CSFO) operations across the border both in pro-active/pre-emptive, as well as, retaliatory mode.
- Building a degree of survivability in air defence command, control and communication centres both electronically, as well as, through equipment redundancy.
- Building an integrated family of ground-, air- and shore-based Air Defence Weapon Systems to ensure continuous and successive punishment to the air threat right through its ingress into own territory.

For ground-based air defence, the above capability must result in the following:

- Modernised and technologically enabled gun-missile deployments to cover the entire range-height spectrum from long range to terminal weapons along with their sensors and associated support systems.
- Capability to take on contemporary, as well as, futuristic threat from PLAAF in including stand-off threat and the threat of a slew of smart/ intelligent weapons and PGMs.
- Futuristic kill capability in the form of directed energy (laser, CPB, HPM) weapons and fielding a counter for stealth aircrafts, ARMs and cruise missiles, and building BMD capabilities at the national level to take on the threat of SSMs.

NOTES

1. https://www.skygod.com>quotes>airpower. Accessed on 22 Aug 17.
2. Pakistan Air Force – Official Website at https://www.paf.gov.pk[3]. Accessed on 30 Aug 17.
3. Pakistan Air Force Squadrons at https://wwwGlobalsecurity.org[4]. Accessed on 31 Aug 17.
4. Pakistan will acquire three new Saab Erieye AEWC&S at https://www[5]. quwa.org>2017/ 05/21. Accessed on 19 Sep 17.
5. Peoples Liberation Army Airforce at https://www[5].en.m.wikipedia.org. Accessed on 10 Oct 17.
6. http://en.m.wikipedia.org[6] Chengdu J 20.
7. http://www.popsci.com[7]; "Stealthier stealth? Seventh upgraded Chinese stealth fighter".
8. IHS Janes' International Defence Review, Vol. 45, Feb 2012, p. 45.
9. www.strategy[8] page.com/htmw/ht air w/20070516.aspx.

10. Roger Cliff, John Fei, Jeff Hagen, “Shaking the Heaven and Splitting the Earth”, Chinese Air Force.
11. Indian Defence Review Vol 30.4 (Oct-Dec 15).
12. https:// Western Theatre Command at https://www.global[9] security.com. Accessed on 13 Oct 17.
13. https://www.times[10] of India.indiatimes.com/2011-03-08/india/28668105.
14. China's Infrastructure development in Tibet evaluating trend lines at https://wwwclaws.in/images/publication.pdf/1317312941MP%2032%20inside.pdf[11].

*

August, 2018

27

Making Sense of Missile Shield

Lieutenant General (Dr) V K Saxena (Retd), PVSM, AVSM, VSM

The media picks up the tag line, "India puts up a missile shield" every time there is news related, one way or the other, to the plan to acquire a surface-to-air-missile (SAM) system. The so called "missile shield" filled the media space when there was a talk of S-400 system. The same was all over again, when the Defence Acquisition Council (DAC) accorded the acceptance of necessity (AoN) for the procurement of national advanced surface-to-air (SAM) missile system II (NASAMS II) from USA.

Media plays up the hype of "Missile Shield"

This article tries to make sense of the oft quoted term "missile shield" by presenting to a discerning reader, the various dimensions related to the issue.

The Eternal Cause Effect Relationship

The SAMs, or for that matter, the entire family of air defence weapons on land sea and air exist for the sole purpose of countering the air threat by the adversary. The term 'air threat' essentially implies the cumulative potential danger which our adversary holds, as his capability to cause damage and destruction to our vulnerabilities through the use of aerial threat vehicles and munitions in furtherance of, or in support of his war effort. This danger is basically assessed in two dimensions. First is the qualitative dimension, which includes the lethality, severity and technological advancement of the adversary's air threat vehicles, while the second, is the quantitative dimension that relates to the numbers which constitute the air threat punch. Accordingly, the defender aims to put together such resources on land, sea and air that can counter the threat as defined above. Thus the air threat on one side and the air defence means on the other are tied to each other in an eternal cause-effect relationship.

How Air Threat got Revamped Over Time

The multi-dimensional growth of the air threat over time has mainly taken place along two major verticals. The first of these is the "multiplicity of air threat vehicles". In that, the erstwhile duo of aircrafts and helicopters as main threat vehicles, are today joined by a multi-dimensional strike punch consisting of attack helicopters, unmanned aerial systems/vehicles (UAS/UAVs), tactical ballistic missiles, cruise missiles, precision guided munitions (PGMs), anti-radiation missiles (ARMs) and the now emerging soft-kill offensive weapons.

The second vertical is the 'spatial growth of the threat' in all its three dimensions of range, reach (implying altitude) and hours of applicability. Starting from, say, early seventies when the air threat was prosecuted mainly in the visual domain of the defenders by using mostly short range guns and a small arsenal of unguided rockets and missiles, today, the capability is to strike deep with precision and accuracy from long ranges standing off hundreds of miles away from the defenders' visual domain. Also to strike with multiple threat vehicles at any time of the day or night, remain nearly invisible to defenders' radars, employ the UAS with its multiple combat virtues and to hit both with hard and soft-kill munitions are other signature features of the air threat of today.

Prosecution of the Threat

The prosecution of the air threat as stated above is spread over the entire spectrum of multiple threat vehicles. Today, the 4th and 5th generation war machines are truly multi-role, structurally lighter, detection resistant, carry an array of on-board sensors with a packaged electronic warfare (EW) suit for survivability and sustainability and are armed to the teeth with smart and intelligent munitions including the PGMs. The attack helicopters have become all weather with avionics providing the technological muscle for nap-of-earth operations. The unmanned revolution has taken over with its unmatched capability of all weather, all terrain operations with incredible endurance and no crew fatigue and multiplicative affects are being achieved by manned and unmanned teaming. The missiles, both in the surface-to-surface (SSM) and air-to-surface (ASM) modes are scaling new dimensions in range, reach and kill probabilities and the soft-kill weapons are emerging in three domains, namely, laser, charged particle beams and high power microwaves. That briefly is a glimpse of the challenge that the air defence weapons have to face today and in which, the term missile shield must find its place.

Much like the prosecutors of the air threat, the story in the defenders camp has also evolved over decades in keeping up the spirit 'for every sword a shield'. This is how it has unrolled. In early days with only aircrafts and helicopters to guard against and that also in fair-weather and only against such munitions as front guns and unguided bombs and rockets, the air defence challenge was not as grave. Also, the Vulnerable Areas/Points (VAs/VPs) to be protected by air defence weapons were limited and essentially required fair weather weapons.

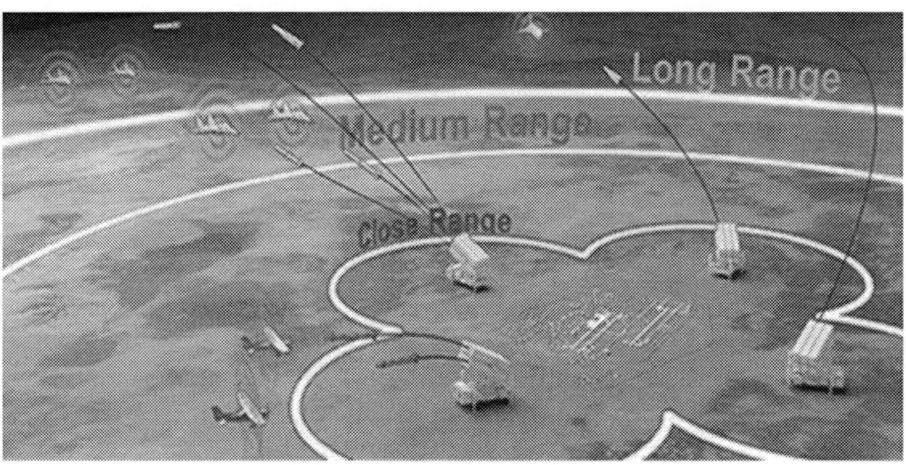

A conceptual depiction of layered-and-tiered defence

It was thus considered appropriate to deploy multiple rings of terminal air defence guns around the vulnerabilities to be protected in the 'point defence' mode or go for 'carpet layouts' (increasing densities of guns) where the VA/VP was that critical. Such a scalar defence is totally dysfunctional in the current threat environment. Today, since the multiple threat vehicles can strike our vulnerabilities from very long ranges right up to the terminal end, the basic requirement is to inflict 'continuous punishment' to the attacker as it transits from long ranges to the end-game. This punishment has to be all weather, seamless and must switch from weapon-to-weapon (long to medium to short to very short range) cutting across Service boundaries. For meeting the above requirement, a need was felt to deploy a series of SAMs from long to medium to short range patching up on the erstwhile point defence weapons at terminal end (called very short range air defence systems, or VSHORADS).

The SAM, by virtue of their ranges and altitudes, covered various layers. Such a deployment was therefore called layered-and-tiered defence. Taken together with their associated sensors and battle management command and control (BMC2) systems, it was called the Integrated Air Defence System, or IADS for short.

The IADS Today

Today, the IADS anchored on the trio of 'sensors', 'shooters' and 'BMC2 systems' creates an area air defence capability on a theatre grid. The sensors span the entire spectrum of frequency bands to optimise their multiple functions of early warning, target designation, missile guidance, fire control of guns etc., besides packing such capabilities as to detect stealthy targets and survive in a hostile electronic warfare environment.

The shooters comprise the entire pack of aircrafts and missiles. The IADS as a whole is capable of providing area air defence to large swaths of areas in which the individual weapons provide air defence in their effective range and reach envelopes as a part of layered-and-tiered defence. The BMC2 system features the best in communication and data transfer technology providing for the complex interrelated functions of detection of targets, fusing of inputs of multiple sensors to cut out duplication, recognition of detected targets as friendly or hostile (identification friend or foe or IFF), creation of recognised air situation picture (RASP), prioritisation of the threat as to its immediacy and lethality, selection of weapons for punishment, designation of targets to the selected weapons, seamless switching of fire from weapon-to-weapon and exercising minute-to-minute control over air defence battle.

Besides this, the system also addresses a huge vertical of air space control wherein, finite resource of air space is allowed to be used by its multifarious users with minimum restrictions and maximum freedom of action and avoiding fratricide at all costs. Keeping the current realities in mind where multiple systems of different makes and genres populate the battle space at the same time, another capability of the BMC2 system is to knit dissimilar systems in one seamless voice and data loop through Common Data Links, or CDL.

Missile Shield

It is against the above backdrop, that the so called 'missile shield' has to find its place. Basically, whenever a SAM system is on a line of planning for procurement or actually gets inducted, it will fit itself in the hierarchy of SAMs which taken as a whole, is loosely referred to as missile shield. There is also another misnomer of portraying every SAM as capable of taking on enemy's SAMs and making such claims as 'the so-called missile shield will not let any adversary's SAM enter into our air space (impregnable)'.

Firstly, it is to be understood that our own SAMs do not defeat adversary's SAMs; it is our Ballistic Missile Defence System (BMD) that will defeat enemy's SAMs, and secondly, it is stated that no shield is impregnable. A determined attacker pressing his attack in quality (avoiding radar detection) and quantum (overwhelming the IADS's target handling capability) will be able to penetrate this shield, hopefully to be attacked by the next layer. A constant battle thus rages between the prosecutors of the air threat and the valiant *vayu rakshaks.*

Specifics of the Missile Shield

Besides the terminal end VSHORADS (provided by towed and self-propelled guns and a series of very short range missiles) extending to 6-10 km, the balance of the missiles, namely the short-range SAMs (20-30 km), medium-range SAMs (70-100 km) and long-range SAM (more than 100 km), constitute the current missile shield complete in three components of sensors, shooters and BMC2 system.

Besides this, the current BMD capability is promised to be provided by the Defence Research and Development Organisation (DRDO) via its BMD programme, codenamed 'Programme AD'. This Programme is in two phases. Phase 1 is to provide a capability of taking on enemy's ballistic missiles up to a range of 2000 km, while Phase II is to enable the defenders in taking on the ballistic missiles up to ranges of 5000 km. The projected date of completion of phase 1 was 2012 and phase II by 2016. It is reported that while both the phases stand realised, it will take a few more years for phase II to be operationalised.

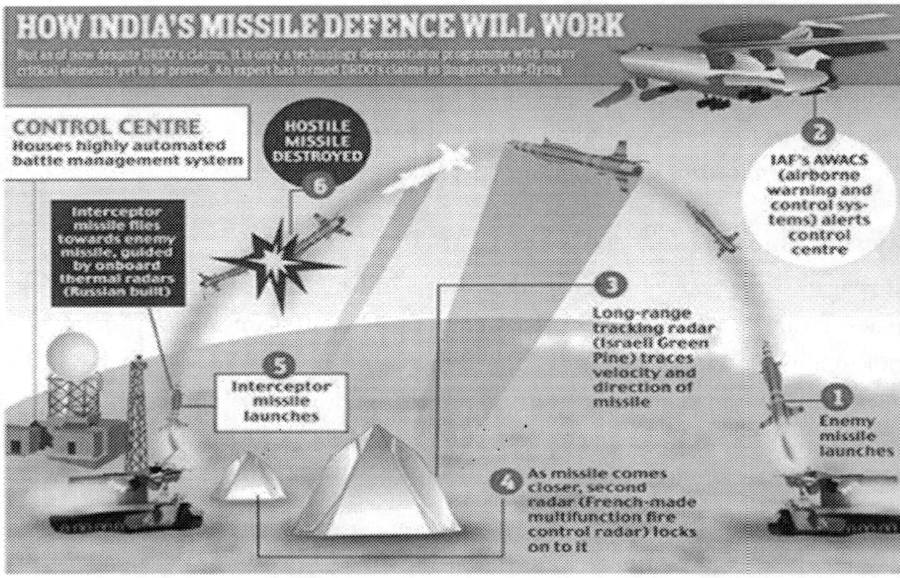

A conceptual depiction of Programme AD system

It is in this regime of IADS and BMD the S-400 will get into. Following points are notable:

- It is reported that the plan is to procure of five Regiments of S-400 at a likely cost of $ 4.5 billion.
- S-400 has four interceptors with ranges from 40-400 km. This is a way higher capability from the existing range and reaches capability of IADS, as explained above.
- The system can cover huge swaths of area providing a degree of air defence cover to all the vulnerabilities located therein.
- S-400 is not only an air defence system, but is also an anti-missile system capable of providing effective defence against adversary's ballistic missiles. In this role, it will complement the indigenous BMD system as mentioned above. In that, the fire units of S-400 and Programme AD can be deployed in a complementary manner.

Another addition to the so-called missile shield is the reported NASAM II which, as stated, has been granted AoN by the DAC lately. The NASAM has interceptors with ranges from 55 to 180 km. With these ranges, the weapon system will bring considerable increment in the range and reach envelope of the current IADS. Though the open sources do not describe NASAMs II as an anti-missile system, should the system possess limited BMD capability, it could augment the Programme AD capability.

Reality Check

Having stated the facts, some points of reality check are relevant.

Immediate Step

In their euphoria and rat race for breaking news and TRP, there is a tendency by the media to actually misinform people. In that, they project that the systems being talked about (S-400, NASAMS II etc.) have arrived yesterday and being deployed today! With the contract for S-400 yet to be signed and NASAMs only at the AoN stage, it must be appreciated that the weapon systems are far into the future.

Suffice to say that even after all clear is given, the mere induction of the weapon as full-fledged fire units would take 2-4 years. Prior to this, there is a haul of several years (minimum 3-4) for the long-drawn procurement procedures, off-sets, Transfer of Technology (ToT) issues, selection of Indian public and private partners in joint ventures, etc. This is the reality of time which must not be sold as 'immediate'.

On Integration

Systems like S-400, NASAMs II etc. are strategic systems. Integrating them properly in the eco-system of the existing IADS is a huge challenge. Their sensor systems need to get looped in our grid of early warning and tactical control, systems and thereby provide to it a huge qualitative jump in surveillance and target handing capability. Their interceptors have to seamlessly merge into our layered-and-tiered defence systems taking the ceiling of air defence and anti-missile cover many notches up. Most importantly, their BMC2 systems have to have a 'one-on-one' and 'one-on-many' connect with our existing BMC2 system.

In this context, it is also pertinent to mention that the weapon systems like NASAMs II are totally dissimilar to the Russian systems, about 76 percent of which populate our air defence weapon inventory. In fact, these belong to a totally dissimilar NATO weapon philosophy. Integrating it with Russian dominant eco-system, it will be a huge issue.

Even for the Russian block S-400, while our existing BMC2 infrastructure belongs to one generation, S-400 will bring in a totally different generation. A mention has been made earlier of the common data links. These will have to be played up in a very big way to really absorb and amalgamate these systems as capability enhancers and not as stand-alone verticals. Even in the BMD domain, the linkages of S-400 and NASAMs will have to be established with Programme AD system.

Associated Structures

It is not the weapon alone that matters; the associated capabilities and infrastructures to realise the Indian portion of the responsibility in the work share, missile testing and storage sheds, repair and overhaul facilities, simulators, spare support for the life cycle of the weapon system and more, also have to be ensured.

Acquisition and Operation

While we are far away from the actual terms of contract which will decide how the weapon systems will actually materialise and what will be the Indian responsibility, a word of caution here is important, while deciding the Indian work share/responsibility and load in case of joint venture with ToT etc., it must be ensured that the finite capability of manufacturing of our public sector players or the technological threshold of the private industry must not get overwhelmed or overloaded. If this happens, the end result will have time and cost overruns at the expense of the user.

Finally, strategic systems like S-400 and NASAMs II should be under the domain of the Strategic Forces Command (SFC), like Programme AD is.

*

November, 2018

28

Relevance of India's Nuclear Triad

Ajit Kumar

It may be recalled that India's 1999 Draft Nuclear Doctrine had stated that its nuclear forces would be based on a triad of aircraft, mobile land-based missiles and sea-based assets. The summary of the official Nuclear Doctrine of 2003 also mentioned about maintaining a credible minimum deterrence, a posture of 'No First Use' and that any nuclear retaliation would be massive. With the successful deterrence patrol of INS Arihant, India has operationalised its nuclear triad by filling the missing link with this capability to launch nuclear capable missile from a potent maritime platform.

Prime Minister Modi has termed this achievement as historic. This has led to significant enhancement of India's nuclear position and needs. It also means that the 2003 Nuclear Doctrine of a credible minimum deterrence with a posture of 'No First Use' has been made really credible. By strengthening the second strike capability, it also shows that with the completion of India's nuclear triad, massive retaliation to inflict unacceptable damage in event of a nuclear attack is now real.

Earlier, India was vulnerable as land and air delivery platforms for nuclear weapons could be easily identified with satellites and other means. With a Ship Submersible Ballistic Nuclear (SSBN) in place, it means that a fully functional ballistic missile becomes a strategic weapon which can fire missiles from ocean at very long ranges. Its advantage over land and air missile delivery platforms is that it can remain undetected for a long time. SSBN can strike a deadly blow to an adversary, firing ballistic missiles deep into his territory from afar.

INS Arihant is India's first indigenously built nuclear submarine. With it,

India has taken a giant leap forward in technological sophistication. While India had mastered the nuclear fuel cycle, placing a smaller reactor in Arihant, leading to it becoming critical in 2013 was a complex process. Having secured a holy grail to build and operate strategic strike nuclear submarine, India became the sixth country to join the exclusive league of Non-Proliferation Treaty (NPT) recognised fully fledged nuclear triad powers, i.e. USA, Russia, France, UK and China.

Completion of India's nuclear triad is a tribute to its long-term defence strategy as the Advanced Technology Project (ATV) was started in the 1980s. India is the youngest of the operational nuclear triad powers. INS Arihant has started with 12 nuclear capable missiles with range of 750 km, and will later carry missiles with the range of 3,500 km. The planned induction of the next nuclear submarine – Arighat in 2020 and its later and bigger versions which will carry longer range Agni Missiles shows that the nuclear triad development is in right direction to ensure India's strategic independence.

Another notable feature of development of India's nuclear triad is the thriving public-private partnership. Some major Indian companies have collaborated in making of INS Arihant. This is consistent with 'Make in India' policy and the policy to encourage participation of more private players in the defence sector. After all, in some major nuclear powers like USA, it is the private companies who conclude the major defence contracts. Russia, a long-time friend of India, has provided valuable technical assistance for INS Arihant.

15 years after declaration of its nuclear doctrine, India has taken a major step towards a survivable nuclear triad. While this is a cause for national satisfaction and a tribute to our hardworking scientists and naval personnel, much more complex work lies ahead for the reported five more submarine projects and creation of a robust command and control system. To place the longer range missiles in SSBNs would require much more efficiency, hard work and rigorous trials. If India has to acquire a true status of a nuclear weapon State, it needs more SSBNs to counter China as several Chinese submarines are patrolling in the Indian Ocean Region. China is believed to have SSBNs in double figures and has vastly increased its naval strength so as to flex its muscles in the South China Sea. Besides, it is acquiring ports in Pakistan, Sri Lanka and Myanmar.

India's experience of the negotiations over the Non-Proliferation Treaty (NPT) and Comprehensive Test Ban Treaty (CTBT) shows that the idea of nuclear disarmament was a mirage and the nuclear weapon states only paid lip service to it. The lesson learnt was that India had to be self-sufficient for its nuclear defence in a challenging neighbourhood. This also resulted in Pokhran nuclear tests in 1998 and led to the announcement of a nuclear triad in the Draft Nuclear Doctrine, 1999. It is only with the completion of the nuclear triad that India has walked the talk.

Pakistan's response about INS Arihant raising concerns among the Indian Ocean littoral states and the international community and over India's membership of Missile Technology Control Regime (MTCR) reveals its own vulnerability. Pakistan could be well advised to manage its own economy as any attempt to match India's nuclear tried would lead to its complete bankruptcy – as it is already going to Saudi Arabia, China and IMF with a begging bowl. Cost of a maritime nuclear platform runs into hundreds of millions of dollars, which Pakistan can ill afford due to its precarious economic situation. Trying to match India's nuclear triad would lead to its collapse like Soviet Union – one of the reasons for that collapse was its costly arms race with the USA. More bellicose statements on nuclear weapons have emanated from Pakistan and PM Modi's statement on nuclear blackmail was a fitting response.

Successful completion of the nuclear triad has enhanced India's strategic position. In its quest to become a full-fledged nuclear triad power, India will have to be more diligent and efficient to master complex technological advancements needed to construct bigger SSBNs with longer range missiles. Secondly, it has to strengthen its command and control system, duly supported with continuous budgetary allocations. Thirdly, India should try to shorten the timelines wherever possible, including retaining the key personnel having the requisite expertise. It can also learn from the experience of some of the fully operational nuclear triad powers. Fourthly, the public-private partnership should continue and private companies should be encouraged to join in this nuclear project. Lastly, it can learn from its own mistakes during the making of Arihant.

Operationalisation of the nuclear triad with induction of INS Arihant is a first major step forward. The road ahead will be more challenging to make India's nuclear deterrent even more stronger and credible.

*

January, 2019

29

Is Artificial Intelligence (AI) Changing the Nature of War?

Major General P K Mallick, VSM

Introduction

The professional military body differentiates between an objective nature and a subjective character of war by drawing upon Clausewitz. Nature of war describes what war is and character of war describes how it is actually fought. Nature of war is violent, interactive between opposing wills and fundamentally political. War's character is influenced by technology, law, ethics, culture, methods of social, political, and military organisation and other factors that change across time and place. Character of warfare changes in concert with the tools that become available and how they influence the ways militaries organise themselves to fight wars.

In his book *On War*, Carl von Clausewitz highlighted how failing to understand the character of war leads to disaster. He chastised Prussian generals for using the old tactics of Frederick the Great against a Napoleonic army waging a new type of warfare. They had not appreciated the changes in how war was being fought or in the character of war. Future development and deployment of human-machine teams and autonomous weapons systems represents such a shift in the character of war.[1]

In near future, we will see significant advances in autonomy and machine learning, to include the emergence of robots working together in groups and as swarms. New and powerful robotic systems will be used to perform complex actions, make autonomous decisions, deliver lethal force, provide intelligence, surveillance, and reconnaissance, coverage and speed response times over wider areas of the globe. Military organisations must plan now for this new era of warfare. Governments must be prepared for the political, strategic and ethical dimensions of this shift in the character of war.[2]

Major technological breakthroughs that could occur in robotics as well as information, cognitive, and material sciences are, by themselves, truly revolutionary. Military applications of Artificial Intelligence (AI) have the potential to change the very nature of war. At the strategic level, this could affect how the armed forces organise ground forces, how it fights and what types of major weapon systems it will need. At the operational and tactical levels, enemy's AI capabilities could dictate specific weapon systems design, the development of new types of units to address his AI capabilities and how brigade- to squad-level units conduct tactical operations.[3]

Today, we are at a major inflection point, one in which technology is reshaping the way wars are fought. The future of warfare will be shaped by the role of smaller drones, robots on the battlefield, offensive cyberwar capabilities, extraordinary surveillance capabilities both on the battlefield and of particular individuals, greater reliance on special operations forces operating in non-conventional conflicts and militarisation of the space.

There is an argument that AI has the potential to go beyond shaping the character of war and change the nature of war itself because wars will be fought by robotic systems, not people. AI has the potential to engage in planning and decision making that were previously human endeavours. U.S. Defense Secretary James Mattis speculated in February 2018 that AI was "fundamentally different" in ways that raise questions about the nature of war. The character of warfare will clearly change, and these changes could significantly influence the Clausewitzan elements that frame our understanding of war's nature. No one is arguing that warfare is not changing. Where people disagree is whether the nature of warfare, the character of warfare, or both are changing. An analysis of whether AI will change the nature and character of warfare is discussed here.

AI and the Character of War

The character of warfare changes in concert with the tools that become available and how they influence the ways militaries organise themselves to fight wars. AI systems have the potential to increase the speed with which countries can fight. Even if humans are still making final decisions about the use of lethal force, fighting at machine speed can dramatically increase the pace of operations. There are several military applications of AI currently in development or are at early stages. The neural networks can utilise imagery databases and classify particular scenes (such as a mountain), that allow for a more accurate assessment of specific locations. The processing power that is possible with narrow AI systems has the potential to increase the speed of data analysis. Image recognition can achieve faster, more accurate results than humans can achieve today.

Gen. Mark Milley, Chief of Staff for the U.S. Army, says the character of war is changing in real time and the US Army is trying to keep up with it. Milley said, "The character of war, though, gets to how you fight, with what weapons you fight, what terrain you fight on, the doctrine you fight with, how you do leader development, how you organise yourselves to fight. The character of war is changing very significantly." AI and machine learning can also help in that information gathering and decision-making process. The private sector is just now beginning to explore what its capabilities are and the military is watching closely. "How fast artificial intelligence comes upon us as a society across the world, and how that gets adapted to use in military operations, I think, will have a fundamental impact. It's too early to tell right this minute, but it's fast approaching", Milley said. He said experts are torn on just how fast. Some say it's 5-10 years out, some say 50, and still others say it's more than a century away. It doesn't matter how far out it is; what matters is that it's coming, and it benefits us to get there first.

Successful implementation of AI might lead to new concepts of operation that could influence force structure and force employment, or how militaries organise themselves and plan operations. One possibility is the use of large numbers of smaller platforms, known as swarms, for military operations. Algorithms and control systems designed to enable 'swarming' already exist in the private sector and in academia. Expensive, high-quality platforms could become vulnerable to swarms of sensors and lower-cost weapons platforms that are effectively networked together. AI could thus help bring quantity back into the equation in the form of large numbers of robotic systems.

Another potential application for AI that could shape the character of war is coordination through layers of algorithms that work together to help manage complex operations like expert systems. AI could accelerate trends that challenge these long-running force structure imperatives, such as the need to defeat adversaries with advanced anti access, area denial (A2/AD) networks with tolerable costs.

Two Schools of Thought

There are two schools of thought. One feels that nature of war is not changing. The other finds that with the rapid development of AI, the nature and character of warfare are definitely changing. Among the former, there are the opinions:

> "The nature of war is immutable." – Lt Gen Van Riper;
>
> "The essential nature of war has not changed, is not changing, and will never change...." – Lt Gen Dubik;
>
> "The nature of warfare and conflict between nations and states is fundamentally unchanging.... However, the character of warfare is changing just as societies, political entities and technologies change." – Vice Admiral Cebrowski.

Military professionals swear by the one of today's most sacred mantras by the Prussian Clausewitz: *The character of war is changing, but the nature of war is not.* Pro-Clausewitzans believe war, by its nature, is violent, chaotic and prone to escalation. This has always been and will always be the case. Colin Gray has written, "Many people confuse the nature of war with its character. The former is universal and eternal and does not alter, whereas the latter is always in flux." But does it mean that nature of war is eternal and unchanging? Clausewitz himself seemed less sure about this than many of his followers". He further writes, "Clausewitz, for once, is less than crystal clear. The great Prussian wrote, confusingly, that 'the nature of war is complex and changeable."[4]

People from this school of thought remain extremely skeptical that war's objective nature can be modified. Traditionalists say, war has always been violent, chaotic, destructive, and murderous – and will thus always be so. They contend war is inherently human, a clash of wills, politically driven. Technology cannot mitigate its essence or shed reliable insights to remove its uncertainty. Historian Williamson Murray is skeptical the Information Age can dissipate war's nature, especially battlefield uncertainty. He contends that war's nature includes the fog and the friction of war, and that the arguments contending its nature can be altered are false.[5] Murray argues, "No amount of computing power can anticipate the varied moves and the implications of an enemy's capacity to adapt in unexpected ways."[6]

The claim that has been made many times in the past is that AI and other technologies will enable military commanders to have "a qualitatively unsurpassed level of situational awareness and understanding heretofore unavailable to strategic commanders". This has not happened. The chaos of war, its fog, friction, and chance will likely never be deciphered, regardless of what technology is thrown at it. As long as humans are responsible for directing war, for writing code, and for fielding and maintaining machines, warfare will remain an instrument of policy to be made by warriors. How can AI, deep learning, autonomous systems work with or without humans to achieve the military objectives that create the conditions ultimately required for a political resolution of conflict? Those warriors may have machine augmentation, delegate decisions to cyber assistants and operate more remotely; but they will be directing the fight. While AI-enabled technologies will be able to gather, assess and deliver heretofore unimaginable amounts of data, these technologies will remain vulnerable to age-old practices of denial, deception and camouflage.

Brad D. Williams, in an introduction to an interview he conducted with Amir Husain asserts, "Generals and military theorists have sought to characterise the nature of war for millennia, and for long periods of time, warfare doesn't dramatically change. But, occasionally, new methods for conducting war cause a fundamental reconsideration of its very nature and implications." Williams then cites "cavalry, the rifled musket and Blitzkrieg as three historical examples."[7] Franz-Stefan Gady argues that in today's tech-crazed world, where many of us see technological solutions as a panacea to just about anything, defense analysts have a tendency to overestimate the impact of technological changes and new innovations on warfare.[8] Regardless of the tools of warfare, they remain tools. While they will be the primary tools of the warfighter, the decision to enable the warfighter to employ those tools will come from political leaders bent on achieving a certain goal with military force. The violence of warfare will never change.[9]

All the modern armed forces face the same challenge. In spite of spending billions in upgrading existing capabilities, very few of these platforms were designed to seamlessly integrate AI or partner with autonomous robotic systems. This means retro-fitting is required, making emergent technology an integration problem. Culturally, it is also likely to take significant time and effort for the armed forces to adapt entrenched command and control approaches to absorb the shock generated by the introduction of AI and autonomous systems.[10] Advanced militaries have to be careful to avoid a situation where military technical determinism guides strategic thinking. Technological superiority does not guarantee military success. Sun Tzu warned, "tactics without strategy is the noise before defeat." Technology without integration, or a conceptual underpinning, is the hype before the letdown. Technology enables tactical actions to advance a strategy – but technology cannot replace tactics. Artificially intelligent, autonomous machines are almost certain to create new integration challenges. AI is likely to be among the greatest military integration challenges due to the additional complexities it creates for network architectures.

Despite some rapid advances in AI development, it is estimated that it could take until 2060-2070 for it to reach the level of maturity required to satisfy many imagined military purposes. While this should not prevent militaries from taking heed of AI's potential applications, it also should not distract from resolving urgent force modernisation challenges like network capacity and combat system integration.[11]

The Other Opinion: Nature of War is Changing

The most significant elements of war, violence, human factors, fog and friction and chance, will always remain. War's essence as politically directed violence will remain its most enduring aspect, even if more machines are involved at every level. As technology advances at rapid pace, the nature and character of war will be changed. In the upcoming military revolution of autonomy, we will have to consider new sources of combat power and assess how they impact each level of war.[12]

Autonomy will change the nature of war in several ways. These are:

- It could weaken the role of political direction by forcing response delegation to lower echelons for faster forms of attack.
- Autonomy can lessen the ability of governments to gain the support and legitimacy of their populations, while making it easier for foreign governments to manipulate their adversary's populations.
- Deep learning forms of AI will augment the intuition and judgment of experienced commanders.
- Automated technologies could reduce popular support for professional military institutions, which paradoxically could free governments to employ force more readily since the political consequences are reduced.
- As with the earlier ages, friction and uncertainty will endure.
- The age of autonomy can introduce new forms of friction while reducing human factors in tactical contexts.[13]

The nature of war has definitely changed since the Cold War; globalisation, violent non-state actors, identity wars, non-trinitarian (irregular) wars, and Information Technology (IT) have fundamentally altered nature of war. Anti-Clausewizians believe that Clausewitz's theories are passé, not having kept up with revolutionary technological and social changes. The new thinkers argue that capabilities in robotics, AI, and human-machine teaming will change more than just the way warfare is waged. As US Deputy Secretary of Defense, Bob Work identified AI and human performance enhancements as potential breakthroughs in defense technology, "We believe we are at an inflection point at artificial intelligence and autonomy." He later told an AI conference, "I am starting to believe very, very deeply that it is also going to change the nature of war."[14]

Technology has started changing lot of fundamentals of warfare. The lethality of modern weapons has emptied out the battlefield. What can be 'seen' by sensors of diverse types can be targeted by increasingly precise direct and indirect fires. AI has the potential to sharply enhance defense, continuing to empty out the battlefield and turning it into a no-man's zone where automated systems and semi-autonomous devices wage attrition warfare. The Russo-Ukraine war in the Donbas hints that in future wars between State-based military forces, tactical units will need to remain unseen to survive and that they will now 'occupy' territory principally through long-range firepower. If both sides have intelligent machines, war may become simply a case of machines being violent to other machines.

Drone crews firing missiles at insurgents from 3,000 miles away or navies blockading countries and starving their people into submission do not experience war the same as those infantry soldiers did years ago. The experience of violence in some wars has become one sided, while wars are now increasingly waged against civilians well behind any defensive front lines. If a nation's borders cannot be penetrated and its critical centers of gravity attacked using kinetic means, perhaps non-kinetic means are the offensive style of the future. In that case, war's changing nature comes into play.

Application of information warfare by strategic competitors against the US political system hints at new cyber techniques that AI may greatly enhance. Instead of destroying another's capabilities and national infrastructures, they might be exploited and used as bearers to spread confusion and dissent amongst the populace. In this century, starvation may not be necessary to collapse a nation; AI may offer more effective methods. War may no longer be violent and murderous but it may still be, as Clausewitz wrote, a "true political instrument."[15]

Over the years, Ex-US Secretary of Defense Jim Mattis, an avid reader of military history and theory, has cultivated a reputation for deep thinking about the nature of warfare. He came to a few conclusions about what he calls the 'fundamental' nature of combat. He said, "It's equipment, technology, courage, competence, integration of capabilities, fear, cowardice – all these things mixed together into a very fundamentally unpredictable fundamental nature of war. The fundamental nature of war is almost like H20, ok? You know what it is." However, his opinion about change in nature of war has changed. He said, "I'm certainly questioning my original premise that the fundamental nature of war will not change. You've got to question that now. I just don't have the answers yet". Mattis further said, "The character of war changes all the time. An old dead German [Carl von Clausewitz] called it a 'chameleon.' It changes to adapt to its time, to the technology, to the terrain, all these things". As Mattis put it, "If we ever get to the point where it's completely on automatic pilot and we're all spectators, then it's no longer serving a political purpose. And conflict is a social problem that needs social solutions."[16]

But should the technology develop the way it is expected to, removing a man from the loop could allow machine warfare to be fully unleashed. Mattis and his successors will have to grapple with the question of whether AI so radically changes everything that war itself may not resemble what it has been for the entirety of human history.

Present Status

At the present state of development AI technologies are immature. Modern unmanned aircraft in service can operate autonomously, but cannot yet execute the sorts of complex missions that manned equivalents can achieve. Land robots are clumsy on uneven terrain. Concepts fail to deliver significant breakthroughs in autonomous decision making. There is considerable wariness that the hype and publicity surrounding deep learning will not pan out as dramatic breakthroughs.

The present developments of AI technologies in military domain have not reached the level when it can be said that it would change the nature of war. In fact, it is in a nascent state of development. However, the scenario is changing fast. Despite best efforts, no nation-state can ever be fully prepared for the character of the next war. As such, potential military applications of emergent technology should not be viewed as a panacea for the chaos, friction, and chance that will continue to define war in the future. Regardless of the possibilities offered by technological advances, success in the next conflict is likely to be just as reliant on human genius.[17]

NOTES

1. From a Clausewitzan perspective, that war is human fundamentally defines its nature. Carl von Clausewitz, *On War*, trans. Michael Howard and Peter Paret (Princeton, NJ: Princeton University Press, 1989).
2. Joint Force Development, Joint Operating Environment JOE 2035: The Joint Force in a Contested and Disordered World (Suffolk, VA: Joint Chiefs of Staff, 2016).
3. See CRS Report R45178, Artificial Intelligence and National Security, by Daniel S. Hoadley and Nathan J. Lucas and Peter Singer; "Getting to Grips with Military Robots," *The Economist*, January 25, 2018; and Aaron Mehta, "AI Makes Mattis Question Fundamental Beliefs About War," C4ISRnet.com, February 17, 2018.
4. Colin Gray, Modern Strategy (New York: Oxford University Press, 1999).
5. Admiral William A. Owens (with Edward Offley), *Lifting the Fog of War* (New York: Farrar, Straus, and Giroux, 2000).
6. Williamson Murray, *America and the Future of War: The Past as Prologue* (Stanford, CA: Hoover Institution Press, 2017).
7. John Allen, Amir Husain, "On Hyper-War," Fortuna's Corner, July 10, 2017.
8. Franz-Stefan Gady, 'The Fog of Peace': Why We Are Not Able to Predict Military Power February 04, 2015, available at: https://thediplomat.com/2015/02/the-fog-of-peace-why-we-are-not-able-to-predict-military-power/
9. https://fortunascorner.com/2017/07/10/on-hyper-war-by-gen-ret-john-allenusmc-mirhussain/ General John R. Allen, US Marine Corps (Retired) and Amir Husain, On Hyperwar, available at: https://www.usni.org/magazines/proceedings/2017-07/hyperwar
10. F. G. Hoffman, Will War's Nature Change in the Seventh Military Revolution?, Parameters 47(4) Winter 2017–18.
11. Mark Gilchrist, Emergent Technology, Military Advantage, and the Character of Future War, July 26, 2018, available at: https://www.realcleardefense.com/articles/2018/07/26/emergent_technology_military_advantage_and_the_character_of_future_war_113655.html
12. Hoffman, op. cit.
13. Kareem Ayoub and Kenneth Payne, "Strategy in the Age of Artificial Intelligence," Journal of Strategic Studies 39, 5-6(2016): 793-819, https://doi.org/10.1080/01402390.2015.1088838
14. Sydney J. Freedberg Jr., "War without Fear: DepSecDef Work on How AI Changes Conflict," Breaking Defense, May 31, 2017.
15. "The Tenth Man" – War's Changing Nature in an AI World, October 15, 2018, available at: http://madsciblog.tradoc.army.mil/90-the-tenth-man-wars-changing-nature-in-an-ai-world/
16. Aaron Mehta, AI makes Mattis question 'fundamental' beliefs about war, February 17, 2018, available at: https://www.c4isrnet.com/intel-geoint/2018/02/17/ai-makes-mattis-question-fundamental-beliefs-about-war/
17. Maj Gen PK Mallick, VSM, Artificial Intelligence in Armed Forces: An Analysis, *CLAWS Journal*, Winter 2018.

*

September, 2019

30

Chief of Defence Staff: A Far-reaching Decision

Lieutenant General Gautam Banerjee, PVSM, AVSM, YSM

"*The best time to plant a tree was 20 years ago. The second best time is now*"
– **Chinese proverb**

A Need Unattended

Though it is known that the recommendation to have an institution of the Chief of Defence Staff (CDS) in the nation's defence establishment was made in Year 2000 by the 'Kargil Committee', actually the need had been felt some years before that. That was the time in the early 1990s, when the defence budget was so squeezed that the war-worthiness of the armed forces fell well below the level as mandated in the Government's directive.[1] The case, however, received more serious attention, when post-nuclearisation, an architecture for national command authority had to be devised.

A decade down the line, the need remains unattended yet. This inertia is particularly jarring when compared to the great restructuring that proceeds briskly in the rest of India's state-apparatus. In contrast, the military institution, the entire defence sector in fact, continues to wallow in a system long rendered obsolete, much to the detriment of national interest. The matter therefore calls for serious attention.

This paper argues that the necessity of the institution of CDS goes deeper than nuclear weaponisation or lessons of Kargil War. It suggests that an institution of *CDS is needed to foster that level of operational efficiency in the Indian armed forces which would allow the nation to reap full benefits of its investments in military security within the its technological, industrial and economic capacity.*

The Proposition

The proposition of the Kargil Committee was straight forward for the nation's policy-making body to understand its limited familiarity with the complexities of management of the military institution notwithstanding. Briefly put, the case was built around the argument that it was necessary to have a professional body of highest standing to render single point advice on matters of the nation's military security to the Raksha Mantri (RM) and the Cabinet Committee on Security (CCS), including the articulation of nuclear weapons and its conventional imperatives. Factual no doubt, yet this line of argument was open to dilution from many angles of contrived validity. Without going into the merits of such repudiations, it may be appropriate to touch upon these just to build up the discussion.

One, it was pointed out that the existing system of advisory confabulations among the political leadership and the three service chiefs could not be stated to have failed. Therefore, it really did not matter whether the advice came from single point or three points; difference of opinion among one or more of the individual services could be managed either way, as indeed it has been the case so far. *Two*, the Government having made it clear that it factored its nuclear assets as an answer to intimidation from neighbouring adversaries rather than as weapons of war, the necessity of installing a CDS was not found so overwhelming; a collegium of National Security Advisor, service chiefs and the Strategic Forces Commander could be marshalled to perform that role.

Of course, the whole issue remains mired by that eternal fear among the power-wielders, that of being marginalised on the high table, besides of course the innate wariness of unfamiliar ventures. Thus, the three service chiefs in various permutations, aided by subtle endorsement from the bureaucracy – who as arbitrators of inter-service matters assume the role of *de facto* CDS – have put paid to that proposition for more than a decade. More disconcertingly, the political leadership, inert as ever in acquiring the art of political management of military power, has adopted the expediency of 'measured inaction'. They have thus let the military institution stagnate against mounting challenges of national security.

As opposed to the afore-stated position, the obligation of creating an institution of CDS is best justified by what may be termed as the phenomenon of *'strategising'* for a robust and cost-efficient national *'defence policy'*. It is this phenomenon that must be the fundamental motive for installing a CDS; the other oft cited reasons – coordination of joint-services operations, theatre, strategic, special forces, and cyber commands, defence procurement etc. – are but the natural fallouts of that obligation.

This would need some elaboration.

The Universal Philosophy of Military '*Strategising*'

Flanked by two innately hostile, naturally militarist and collusive neighbours, the criticality of strategising for India's military security continues to gain salience. That salience is further enhanced by the range and pace of geo-political churnings of the region. Conversely, the Indian state-craft stands dictated by societal, political and economic imperatives that pose contradictory priorities. The severest contradiction is that in the coming years there would remain a void between technological, industrial and fiscal resources on the one hand, and the assumption of that desired level of modern military capability which would offer guaranteed achievement of all our security goals on the other. Thus is necessitated a foresighted political, industrial, economic and military balancing act to reconcile objectives enticing with those unsavoury. Indeed, even powerful countries are obliged to limit their politico-military goals to fit within the resources that they find feasible to commit to their military build-up.[2]

No doubt, it is the burden of India's political and the military leadership to address the disconnect between political mandate, techno-industrial capacity, fiscal affordability and military capability. Further, intrinsic to that burden is the challenge which compels military strategists to devise unique means of multiplying the possessed military power in achievement of the national security objectives. This is what the philosophy of '*military strategising*' entails.

Examples of Strategising

The concept of military strategising has ever been an obligatory part of the state's articulation of political power by military means. In recent times, repowering of the American military forces in the post-Vietnam War and post-Cold War periods, military restructuring in Britain, France, Germany and Russia and 'informationisation' of China's People's Liberation Army are some examples of the afore-stated strategising. To illustrate, when debilitated by war-weariness in the government after the Vietnam War, and its reflection in drastic budget cuts, the US military leadership rose to the occasion. They propagated a war doctrine which was built around just five affordable weapon systems and a compatible force-structure. That helped America when she reverted to her political preference for military solutions.[3] More relevant illustrations of military strategising under situations somewhat akin to India, however, come from Vietnam and China.

A weaker power, Vietnam, when attacked by China in 1979, refused to commit its regular military formations till the Chinese had advanced across the mountainous border belt, choosing instead to contest that belt with irregular mode of warfare. Thus confronted with the prospect of having to fight across the wrong end of a difficult terrain and a tenuous logistic chain, China had to find a face-saving exit – with a bloody nose. In a similar vein, to prevent Taiwan's assumption of sovereignty, China propounds a strategy that is commensurate to her limited military capability as compared to the adversary, the US. Rather than risking the massive US military might, they propose to make it prohibitively costly for the US forces to dominate the China Sea – Taiwan Strait. This is a recourse to be met within their indigenous missile-information war capability, limited as it might be, but nevertheless, effective enough within that localised theatre to make the US military wary.

Military strategising therefore is a phenomenon that harnesses military genius in multiplying force-capabilities to secure success against odds posed by resource limitations. It is a joint political and military responsibility, with bureaucracy and defence industry facilitating the endeavour.

Prevalent Norms of Strategising for National Defence Policy

Political wisdom rules that the nation's security objective must be backed up with commensurate military power, and yet, that power must be structured in conformity with the nation's economic and industrial capacity. Herein lie the complexities:

(a) *One*, there is no use of setting political goals which cannot be backed up with military power;

(b) *Two*, it is wasteful to raise a military force that cannot be optimally equipped and trained within an affordable budget;

(c) *Three*, when sovereignty lies with people deprived, socio-economic charter assumes salience over military expenditure;

(d) *Four*, military power remains the most robust recourse in preserving the nation's core interests, including economics.

In other words, the military structure must be truly in sync with the political, techno-industrial and economical endeavours. We may term this imperative as optimum *force-structuring*.

Next, the objective of optimum force-structuring is sustained by long term budgetary provisions to support force-modernisation. Further, the parameters of modernisation is influenced by the nation's techno-industrial capacity. Notably therefore, structuring military power in consonance with political objectives, harnessing techno-industrial capacity and regulating flow of funds have, in modern times, become intrinsic to military strategic decision making. This is the imperative of optimum *force-modernisation*.

The process of national defence policy-making is set in motion when the concepts of force-structuring and force-modernisation, within the nation's resource affordability, are co-opted into the philosophy of *military strategising*. There is, however, a caveat. Tri-service joint operations being an imperative for success in modern warfare, there is a role to be played by a 'high arbitrator' in devising an appropriate *joint-strategy* of force-application. In terms of military preparedness, this joint-strategy dictates optimal tri-service force-structuring, and as a corollary, the scope of overall force-modernisation. Thus emerges a 'defence policy' to dictate the harnessing of techno-industrial and economic capacities and fine-tuning the phases and time-lines of military modernisation schemes under a dispensation of *jointness*.

Within the ambit of defence policy, the joint-strategy must find reflection in appropriately tuned joint-training, apportioning of budgetary provisions and management of military schemes to control duplications, deviations, and mid-course corrections. Simply put:

(a) In fulfilment of the political mandate, there is a need to *synergise the three services to propagate one military strategy*, and back it up by tri-service force-structuring and joint-training.

(b) Equally important would be a *rational prioritisation of defence research, development, production and procurement – and of course, fund-allocation*.

Obviously, this role cannot be shouldered by the three chiefs, committed as they must be to primacy of their own service, not the least by the defence bureaucracy, scientists and industrialists who cannot have the requisite military insight. Only a professional body, possessing the requisite authority, foresight and the ability to rise above all considerations but the national cause, can articulate that role.

Finally, in the context of harnessing 'dual-use' resources, shaping up the nation's the war effort must transcend the orthodox civil-military barrier. Indeed, civilian sectors such as law-and-order, transportation, supply chain, industry, communications, cyber activity etc. have more prominent roles to play in military strategy today than ever before. Many aspects of policy-making at the apex level therefore need to be tempered with military wisdom to reap the benefits of:

(a) Firstly, highlight of military implications of civil endeavours, and
(b) Secondly, dove-tailing dual-use resources into military endeavours.

Obviously, an authoritative body of dedicated military professionals, assisted by civilian experts as necessary, is needed to nurture that kind of inter-dependency which would promote the phenomenon of 'military strategising.'[4]

It needs to be noted that to fulfil the roles discussed above, the aforementioned body of military professionals must be competent in command as well as advisory roles – both being integral to military command functions. Half-measures would not do.

The Indian Scene

At the receiving end of a vicious geo-political gangsterism, India is obliged to maintain one of the world's largest armed forces – even as her millions struggle to live under abject conditions. The situation is exacerbated by her near-total dependence on war-material imported at excruciating costs. Truly therefore, it is obligatory of the nation's governing establishment to shape her military institution in a manner that not only secures her national interests, but, in so doing, also makes every penny of her defence investments count. Disconcertingly, however, the situation is quite the opposite. Let us see as to why it is so.

One, the defence sector in India depicts characteristics long irrelevant, wherein each of its components functions in cocoons of their comfort environment, meeting up only when it just cannot be avoided. To illustrate, each of the three services are committed to their own brand of war-doctrine, data networks, information warfare architecture, logistics – nearly every aspect in fact, even the staff duties. Going further, each service is smug in propagating its primacy in national defence, the other two being assigned to peripheral roles! No doubt, in the era of joint warfare, this is an absurd disconnect. Besides being a burden on the exchequer, this affliction retards the application of true 'Revolution in Military Affairs' (RMA). Happily, there is rising appreciation of this concern and many steps are underway to address it.

Two, outside the Services, the instinct of indulgence envelops the entire realm of the Defence Ministry. Thus, even if they exist to attend to the military's requirements, defence research, industry, estates etc. are run according to charters that might not be in consonance with what the armed forces seek. Contrarily, in many instances, these venture managers land up undermining the armed forces' cause in favour of their own turf consolidation! Very well known, this aspects needs no elaboration.

Three, in the comfort era of post-1971 War, the nation's infrastructural ventures seem to be in oblivion of their mandated strategic responsibilities. Thus many times, the practice of incorporating military considerations is overlooked while planning major civil projects of permanent nature like irrigation, highways, railways and power projects. This is a lapse that the nation can ill afford.[5]

Four, the attention being drawn by glamorous range of weapons, equipment and drills, the intellectual aspect of *strategising* is discussed but rarely. Even when discussed within the incumbent hierarchy, it remains shrouded under a cloak of phoney 'confidentiality'. Contrast this with the volume of discussion, debate and experimentation that modern militaries carry out – with active participation of professionals past and present. Obviously, therefore, introspective and perspective joint strategising cannot be expected from the hierarchies who prefer to remain ensconced in their protected cocoon.

These are debilitating and costly infirmities in our national defence planning. An apex body is therefore needed to assist the Government in streamlining the defence strategy and to apportion appropriate tasks and resources to each of its Service components. Next, it is also needed to guide the Government in allocating corresponding targets for defence research, production, procurement etc.

Charter for India's CDS

Having established that a purposefully mandated institution of CDS is obligatory to *tune in the Indian military structure according to the national objectives within an affordable techno-industrial and fiscal regime*, we may now venture to consider the major aspects of its charter:

(a) The foremost charter would be the advisory role in the Government's formulation of the 'National Security Strategy', the current 'Raksha Mantri's Directive' having become irrelevant in the contemporary context.

(b) Advice, training and force-structuring are the inseparable ingredients of military command function. Overall command and inter-services management functions would therefore be intrinsic to the above role;

(c) Next, it would be to involve in inter-departmental guidance and integration of defence-oriented public and private ventures in implementation of the defence policy.

As already discussed, the CDS would be the prime mover of strategising for joint warfare, formulation of joint war-fighting doctrine, tri-service force-structuring, joint-training and overall force-modernisation. The practice of inter-service cooperation not being enough in contemporary warfare, the CDS would need to foster true '*jointmanship*' in the nation's armed forces, cutting down on redundancies and fostering a regime of inter-dependency and interoperability among the three Services. It is so that, more than just the limited responsibilities of nuclearisation and tri-service organisations, there are wider responsibilities that the CDS would need to undertake.

Today, in the absence of that institution, these crucial responsibilities lie unattended, much to the detriment of the nation's military security.

Affliction of Half-measures

We have seen that defence planning is shaped by complex and incongruous factors, and that requires an apex body of military professionals to perform the role of interface between the abstract theology of military strategy and the nation's politico-economic-technological-industrial compulsions. Truly, that body has to perform beyond prejudice to conceptualise, guide, monitor and control the nation's military institution as an integral component of the Government's policy-making establishment. These are the ordinations which impart salience to the case for creation of an establishment of the CDS in India.

On the Government's past attempts to fulfil the need, confabulations had veered around many options. Needless to state, these proposals were in contravention to the fundamental idea, motivated by partisan inter-service, intra-ministerial turf-protection agenda, and duly iced over with wariness of disturbing the comfort of an entrenched, if anarchical, system. One suggestion was to appoint a 'Permanent Chairman of the Chiefs of Staff Committee', who behind a facade of equal status but little authority was expected to remain chair-bound in a toothless committee. Another idea was to occupy the CDS with some pretentious charter of control over such diffused organisations as the strategic forces, the Andaman & Nicobar Command, special forces, cyber security, defence procurements etc., and little else.

Indeed, besides violating the hoary 'Principles of War', these are options contrived to undermine the institution of CDS as it had been done earlier to the now defunct Defence Planning Staff and the presently asphyxiated Integrated Defence Staff, the purpose being to deflect the proposition from challenging the licence enjoyed by the military as well as civilian defence bureaucracy. Diversionary urge was also manifested when the issue was mired by the supposed likelihood of:

(a) *One*, the CDS assuming partisan tendencies to override the system; and
(b) *Two*, linking it with establishment of integrated theatre commands to the ostensible detriment of 'single-service autonomy'.

No doubt, these protestations are unfounded. If Finance Commission, NITI Aayog and various other regulatory bodies have not gone off the tangent, there is no scope for the CDS to do so. Further, the Service Chiefs would remain as celebrated as before, may be more, the sole difference being that the CDS would fill up the void of an ombudsman or moderator of national defence matters.

Pandering to group afflictions over national interests thus, our nonplussed political leadership had found it convenient to freeze the proposition.

Time to Act

It will take years to streamline the archaic system of higher defence management in India. Meanwhile, trapped in the complexities of the geo-political adversities, India's compulsion of fostering cost-efficient security is rising by the day. However, in a trend converse, so far our political leadership have not even attempted, let alone succeed, in marshalling the military institution to the requisite level of efficiency. Further, it has been unable to make the fiscal allocations count, adopting instead a simplistic expediency of imposing *ad hoc* budgetary constraints which further exacerbate imbalance in force-modernisation. To top it all, it had chained defence research and military industry from breaking free into the realm of innovations and modernity. In the context of national security, that had been a road to disaster.

Institution of a body of military professionals to participate in defence policy-making at the apex level, duly empowered in highest level of command, management as well as advisory roles, is a call of strategic wisdom. This call must be attended to with alacrity, institution of a *fully empowered CDS* being the inaugural step towards that end.

With the Prime Minister's announcement on the Independence Day 2019, the Government has just done that.

NOTES

1. At that time the services had been forced to accede to what they all knew to be true but were chary of admitting under the influence of the notion of 'service interests'. The fiscal clampdown

had led to the realisation that the CDS would be effective in rendering the military force-structure more cost-effective while discarding its redundant elements, and thereby optimising the nation's military security within an affordable defence budget.

2. Major powers, who have accepted that end are Britain (adoption of supporting role to US, UN and NATO objectives to downsize military assets), France and Germany (scaling down level of preparedness in favour of long mobilisation time) and China (freezing attempts to 'liberate' Taiwan by force).
3. Truly, that is a saga of dedicated professionalism. It saw a 'hollow' US Army resuscitated to strategise a new doctrine. It focussed on affordable upgrades – mechanised forces, weaponised helicopters and air defence while correspondingly revamping training, personnel management and logistics. All this was achieved by single-minded pursuit of a succession of military leaders who rose above the earthy instincts. Similar exercise, albeit to a smaller extent, was undertaken after the Gulf War I when special operations came to prominence.
4. Progress on strategic roads, rail alignments and sidings has been languishing over the years, the priority being routinely ignored. Similar fate has befallen the military-sponsored oil pipeline extension and data highway projects.
5. There are many instances when canals and roads have been constructed and aerial mapping carried out in border areas without military clearance.

*

INDEX